Provided By
Governor's Reading Initiative
Governor Zell Miller
Georgia General Assembly
1998

RAIDERS OF THE REICH

AIR BATTLE WESTERN EUROPE: 1942-45

MARTIN BOWMAN AND THEO BOITEN

992744

Motorbooks International
Publishers & Wholesalers ®

This edition first published in 1996 by Motorbooks International Publishers & Wholesalers,729 Prospect Avenue, PO Box 1, Osceola, WI 54020 USA

© 1996 Martin W. Bowman and Theo Boiten

Previously published by Airlife Publishing Ltd, Shrewsbury, England.

Library of Congress Cataloging-in-Publication Data Available.

ISBN 0-7603-0391-6

Printed and bound in Great Britain.

CONTENTS

ACKNOWLEDGEMENTS

The authors would like to thank veteran aircrews, friends and fellow researchers in Britain, Belgium, France, Holland and Germany, whose welcome encouragement, research and photographs, all of which were given unreservedly, have made this book possible: Steve Adams; John Archer; Frans Auwerda; Mike Bailey; Bart Beckers; Charles L Brown; Don Bruce; Len Collins; Bob Collis; Jim Coman; Coen Cornelissen; Leslie Cromarty DFM; the late Charles E Cupp; Tom Cushing; Barney D'Ath Weston; Cynrik de Decker; Ken Dix; Rob de Visser; Bill Donald; Ken Dunn; Hans-Dieter Eitle; Patricia Everson; Robert E Foose; John Foreman; Ken Gaulton; Earl Gillespie; Klaus Hahn; Charles Hall; Andy Height; Neville Hockaday; Hans Höhler; Marcel Hoogenhuis; Ab A Jansen; Karl-Heinz Jeismann; Eric 'Syd' Johnstone; Friedrich J Kowalke; Emil Lechner; George Luke; Dr Fritz Marktscheffel; Alan McSweyn; Eric Mombeek; Jim Moore; Jan Mulder; Richard Osborn DFC; Simon Parry, Air Research Publications; David Penman; John Price; Ron Pütz; Bill Rae; Barry Randall; Dan Raymond; Connie and Gordon Richards; Adrie M Roding; Dieter Schmidt-Barbo; Josef Scholten; Robert W Seelos; Robert H Sherwood; Jonathan Smith; Steve Smith; Otto Stammberger; John W Stanford; Alec Taylor; Fritz Ungar; John Vasco; Hille van Dieren; Barbara Adams Westbrook; Hans Wijers; Werner Zell.

CHAPTER 1

THE DEFENCE OF THE REICH 1942

On 22 February 1942, having been recalled from the USA where he was head of the RAF Delegation, Air Chief Marshal Arthur T Harris arrived at High Wycombe, Buckinghamshire, to take over as Commander-in-Chief of RAF Bomber Command from AV-M J E A Baldwin, who since 8 January had been standing in for Sir Richard Peirse, who had been posted to India. Harris was directed by Marshal of the RAF Sir Charles Portal, Chief of the Air Staff, to break the German spirit by the use of night area rather than precision bombing and the targets would be civilian, not just military. The famous 'area bombing' directive, which had gained support from the Air Ministry and Prime Minister Winston Churchill, had been sent to Bomber Command on 14 February, eight days before Harris assumed command.

Bombing German cities to destruction was not an entirely new concept. Ever since October 1940 crews had been instructed to drop their bombs on German cities, though only if their primary targets were ruled out because of bad weather. During 1941 more and more bombs began falling on built-up areas, mainly because pin-point bombing of industrial targets was rendered impractical by the lack of navigational and bombing aids. Up until May 1940 the night air defence of the Reich was almost entirely the province of the flak arm of the Luftwaffe. The small force of night fighters at the time consisted of a handful of single-engined Bf 109s, flown by pilots who relied heavily on searchlights in the target area and moonlight to illuminate their prey for them. The subject of night fighting was raised at a conference of German service chiefs just before the war and, according to Oberst Josef Kammhuber who was present at the conference, it was dismissed out of hand with the words, 'Night fighting! It will never come to that!'

In July 1940, German night fighting resources consisted entirely of one flak searchlight regiment and one night fighter Gruppe, of which two Staffeln were equipped with Bf 110s and one with Do 17Zs. Up to

9

this time about ten RAF night bombers had been shot down, chance victories mainly by night fighters working in collaboration with searchlights. On 17 July Reichsmarschall Hermann Göring, Commander-in-Chief of the Luftwaffe, entrusted Oberst Josef Kammhuber with the setting up of the first night fighter division. By the end of 1940 there existed three night fighter Gruppen and three searchlight battalions. Up to 31 December 1940, only forty-two bombers had been shot down by German night fighters, mainly in illuminated night fighting with the aid of searchlights (Helle Nachtjagd) as against about thirty brought down by flak. On 24 March 1941, by command of the Oberbefehlshaber der Luftwaffe, the staff of the Luftwaffen-befehlshaber Mitte (Luftflotte Reich or German Air Force Command Centre) was set up and in April the night fighter division under Generalmajor Kammhuber was placed under its command.

In July 1941 the night fighter division was remodelled into Fliegerkorps XII and Kammhuber, now Generalleutnant, was given the further office of General der Nachtjagd (General of Night Fighters). Kammhuber's conception of the basic principles of night fighter defence found final expression in the 'Kammhuber line', a continuous belt of combined searchlight and radar positions stretching from the Schleswig area over Kiel, Hamburg, Bremen, Ruhrgebiet, Arnhem and Venlo to the Liège area and further to the south, with a second belt for the protection of Berlin covering the Gustrow–Stendal area and extending in the direction of Gardelegen. These areas were clear of the German cities and therefore away from the flak areas.

In spite of the increasing success against the RAF bomber formations using Helle Nachtjagd, however, Kammhuber fully appreciated the limitations of the searchlight technique which was entirely dependent on weather conditions. With 10/10ths cloud they were entirely ineffective and even at 6–10/10ths the cloud created difficulties. In Holland and the Ruhr 6–10/10ths cloud was quite usual and Kammhuber therefore concentrated his energies on the development of an efficient ground-controlled interception (GCI) technique ('Dunkelnachtjagd'), later called Himmelbett (literally translated, 'bed of heavenly bliss' or 'four-poster bed'). Kammhuber arranged his GCI positions in front of the searchlight zones and encouraged crews to attempt interception first under ground control, and if that failed the searchlights were then at their disposal.

By the winter of 1941–42 the Kammhuber line was complete. The night fighter Geschwader, equipped almost entirely with Bf 110s, were stationed almost exclusively in Holland, Belgium and north-western Germany. The completion of night fighter bases for controlled Himmelbett night fighting, with two giant Würzburgs and one Freya, progressed well and was planned to cover firstly the north German coastal area and Holland, and later Belgium. Heavy flak batteries were brought into operation in Luftgau VI (about 200 batteries in the Ruhr) and Luftgau XI (about 100 batteries in the coastal cities of the North Sea and the Baltic). In addition, Politz, Leuna, Berlin and Frankfurt am Main were strongly protected. A considerable increase in protection for Berlin was planned and for the larger cities of central and southern Germany and the Saar regions. The searchlight batteries, which up until now had been stationed in the Helle Nachtjagd belt on the western boundary of Germany, were, in accordance with the increasing completion of night fighter radar sites, withdrawn to protect targets in Germany proper, chiefly the Ruhr, Berlin, central Germany, Hamburg and Bremen. The light batteries were consolidated almost exclusively in the larger cities and industrial areas of western Germany, but had no operational experience. Approximately thirty per cent of heavy flak batteries were without ranging apparatus (for box barrages), and only about the same proportion of the guns had their own radar.

Such was the effectiveness of fully radar-controlled Himmelbett night fighting that by the spring of 1942 successes obtained through the searchlight and GCI techniques were about equal. At this stage Hitler decreed that all searchlight regiments, except one, should be given up to the flak for the protection of special targets. Kammhuber contested the decision strongly at the time though he later decided that the step proved beneficial to the development of the Himmelbett system. The one remaining searchlight regiment was kept in action in the Venlo area for experimental purposes against the possible resumption of the searchlight techniques at some later date.

The GCI technique was so far developed by the beginning of 1942 that all that was necessary to make good the loss of searchlights was the further extension of the existing radar positions. To achieve the greatest density of interception, Kammhuber retained these positions intact, though for more coverage he might have spread them more widely apart. Further positions were equipped, first covering the entire foresector up to the coast, then gradually taking in the main target areas in the rear. His double aim was to leave no gap through which attacking aircraft might penetrate undetected and to be in a position to attack raiders continuously along the penetration and return flights. The old

'Grossraum' was combined with new positions to form the new 'Nachtjagdgrossraum', under the command of a Nachtjagdführer. Night fighter divisions eventually consisted of four to six of these night fighting areas. Individual Himmelbett positions were equipped with a Freya AN, two Würzburg Giants, a Seeburg plotting table, a ground-air transmitter, one to two light radio beacons and a visual beacon. Positions near the coast were equipped with a Wassermann or Mammut long-range search installation in addition to these.

From early 1942 individual aircraft were equipped with the first operational German AI radar, the Lichtenstein BC. Procedure was for one night fighter to be taken under GCI control in each Himmelbett box affected by the raid, while one or two other night fighters orbited the radio beacon at different heights in the waiting area. The first night fighter was vectored towards an individual bomber picked up by the ground radar in the bomber box until such time as it picked up the enemy visually or on its Lichtenstein BC, whereupon it was released from control and the remaining aircraft were called up and sent into action one by one. Night fighters were at first restricted to activity within the area of their boxes.

This, therefore, was the defence set-up which confronted Harris's crews in Bomber Command in 1942. Harris saw the need to deprive the German factories of its workers and therefore its ability to manufacture weapons for war. From 1942 onwards mass raids would be the order of the day, or rather the night, with little attention paid to precision raids on military targets. F/Lt John Price, a wireless operator on 150 Squadron Wellingtons, recalls: 'There have been many arguments for and against the indiscriminate bombing of civilian targets. For what it is worth, I have reason to believe that the High Command on either side knew that this course of events was inevitable even before the war started. Germany commenced this "terror" tactic as long ago as 1936 with the wholesale bombing of civilians in the Spanish Civil War against Guernica. Both the Luftwaffe and the RAF avoided this during the early war years. In my year of bombing (1941) we were briefed in the Ops room to hit military targets only. In 1942 no army was ready to invade the continent, the Royal Navy dare not put to sea in view of the *Scharnhorst, Gneisenau, Graf Spee* and *Tirpitz* etc., being more concerned with the protection of convoys with food and ammunition from America. Therefore, in logical terms, the only weapon we had to retaliate with was our own Bomber Command. In other words, the Germans were hitting us badly with their raids so we had no recourse except to fight with the only weapon we had – the bomber.'

However, 'Bomber' Harris did not possess the numbers of aircraft necessary for immediate mass raids. On taking up his position he found that only 380 aircraft were serviceable. More importantly, only sixty-eight of these were heavy bombers while 257 were medium bombers. Undaunted, Harris selected the Renault factory at Billancourt near Paris, which had been earmarked for attack for some time, as his first target. A full moon was predicted for the night of 3/4 March so Harris decided to send a mixed force of some 235 aircraft, led by the most experienced crews in Bomber Command, to bomb the French factory. It was calculated that approximately 121 aircraft an hour had been concentrated over the factory, which was devastated, and all except twelve aircraft claimed to have bombed.

During March the first Gee navigational and target identification sets were installed in operational bombers and these greatly assisted bombers in finding their targets on the nights of 8/9 and 9/10 March in attacks on Essen. On the latter, 187 bombers, including 136 Wellingtons, bombed the city. On 28/29 March 234 bombers, mostly carrying incendiaries, went to Lübeck, an historic German town on the Baltic, with thousands of half-timbered houses making it an ideal target for a mass raid by RAF bombers carrying incendiary bombs. Twelve bombers were lost but 191 aircraft claimed to have hit the target. A photo-reconnaissance a few days later revealed that one-third of the city, some 190 acres, had been obliterated.

On the night of 6/7 April 157 bombers went to Essen, but the crews encountered severe storms and icing and there was complete cloud cover at the target; only forty-nine aircraft claimed to have reached the target area and there was virtually no damage to the city. Five aircraft were lost, two of them Hampdens, a Manchester, one Stirling and a Wellington. A 149 Squadron Wellington crew had a narrow escape. Sgt Jim Coman, the WOP/AG in P/O Mike Evans' crew recalls a dog fight with a Bf 110 night fighter over the Friesian Islands: 'We were returning from Essen in N3726 OJ-G when we were attacked by a Messerschmitt 110 over the Dutch coast just south of the Friesian Islands at about 18,000ft. The 110 hit us in our port wing, holing one petrol tank and causing us to lose about 400 gallons of fuel. The gunners returned fire and it broke off the attack and dived back through the clouds trailing smoke. Before landing at base we lowered the under-carriage to examine the port wheel for damage but nothing appeared amiss. However, the pilot decided to keep the weight off the wheel for as long as possible and landed port wing up, but on reaching stalling speed and the wheel touching the ground, it collapsed. The wing hit the ground and swung us round 180 degrees and the wing broke across one of the fuel tanks. We all evacuated the aircraft quickly as we could hear the engine sizzling in the petrol spillage. Fortunately, it did not catch fire.'

For four consecutive nights, beginning on the night of 23/24 April, it was the turn of Rostock to feel the weight of incendiary bombs. By the end only forty per cent of the city was left standing. The raids on Lübeck and Rostock prompted the Luftwaffe into reprisal, or Baedeker raids after the German guidebook to English cities such as Canterbury, Exeter, Norwich and York.

Meanwhile, top-level consultations between Harris and his subordinate commanders had revealed that the raids on Rostock had achieved total disruption. Whole areas of the city had been wiped out and 100,000 people had been forced to evacuate the city. The capacity of its workers to produce war materials had therefore been severely diminished. Harris had for some time nurtured the desire to send 1,000 bombers to a German city and reproduce the same results with incendiaries. Although RAF losses would be on a large scale, Churchill approved the plan. Harris (now Sir Arthur) gave the order Operation Plan 'Cologne' to his Group Commanders just after midday on 30 May so that 1,000 bombers would be unleashed on the 770,000 inhabitants.

All bomber bases throughout England were at a high state of readiness to get all available aircraft airborne for the momentous raid; 12 Squadron at Binbrook, for instance, managed to put a record twenty-eight Wellington IIs into the air. To accomplish this task, however, all aircraft had to fly without second pilots and this placed an added strain on the crews. Many aircraft came from OTUs and were flown by instructors. F/Lt John Price recalls: 'The target area was the centre of Cologne and the map clearly showed the red crosses of every hospital in the city. I would have nightmares after the war thinking about all the women and babies we had killed that night. It is now obvious to me that we in England were determined to save our land at whatever the cost, and killing the enemy, of whatever gender, was the only answer.' A quarter of the 1,046 aircraft despatched came from 3 Group which operated in a fire-raising capacity, carrying loads of 4lb incendiary canisters. Some 599 Wellingtons, including four belonging to Flying Training Command, made up the bulk of the attacking force, which also included eighty-eight Stirlings, 131 Halifaxes and seventy-three Lancasters. The rest of the force was made up of Whitleys, Hampdens and Manchesters. One of the chief hazards for each crew was the risk of mid-air collision in the highly congested target area. For ninety-eight minutes a procession of bombers passed over Cologne. Stick after stick of incendiaries rained down from the bomb bays of the 3 Group Wellingtons, adding to the conflagration. F/Lt Pattison, who piloted a 419 Squadron Wellington, wrote: 'When I bombed there was a huge fire on the east bank of the Rhine and another just starting on the west bank. When I left the target area both sides were getting it thick and fast and, eventually, large concentrations of fires were spread practically across the length and breadth of the entire built-up area.'

Some German night fighters were encountered and forty bombers failed to return, twenty-three were claimed by night fighters. In all, 898 crews claimed to have hit their targets. Post-bombing reconnaissance photos certainly showed that more than 600 acres of Cologne had been razed to the ground. The fires burned for days and almost 60,000 people had been made homeless. Squadrons repaired and patched up their damaged bombers and within forty-eight hours they were preparing for a second 'Thousand-Bomber Raid', this time against Essen. On the night of 1/2 June a force of some 956 bombers was ready. F/Lt John Price was at this time instructing at 10 OTU:

> We only had 700 first-line bombers. To make up the difference, the other 300 were drawn from the OTUs. I was doing my usual so-called 'rest' period of six months between Ops, the idea being to give seasoned aircrew a brief respite from real operations, and also to teach others. I found it ironic that so many of us got killed on these OTUs. Pilot error (the pupil was flying), navigational errors, bad weather over England in wintertime – the losses were horrendous.
>
> To return to the thousand-bomber raid on Essen, at briefing we were told our part in the operation was to kill as many of the workers as possible. Other bombers would go for the Krupps factory itself. Real bombs were not used on an OTU station, so I was a bit shaken to see them come rolling on to our airfield at Harwell. We had Whitley aircraft, unbelievably slow: we climbed at about 125mph with a full bomb load. The same turrets as the Wellington – no protection for the poor old air gunners front and rear, just Perspex. I felt very sad that day. As an instructor, I had been ordered to go, but as there were not enough instructors to fill the aircraft, pupil pilots were called upon, ditto navigators and air gunners. I was besieged by my pupils, pleading with me to let them go. I knew that half of them would not

come back, but I chose my dozen or so, then prayed for their safety. None came back – eighteen-year-old boys!

In all, thirty-one bombers were lost out of the 956 that reached the target, at least five destroyed by night fighters. One of them, Hampden AT191 EQ-A of 408 Squadron, was damaged by Lt Voellkopf and Uffz Heinz Huhn of II./NJG2 at 0006 hours north of Texel. The aircraft crashed into the Zuider Zee. The pilot, P/O W Charlton, and his three crew were killed and were later interred in Holland. Again, as in the Cologne raid, some bombers returned early with mechanical and engine problems. Although seemingly lacking the concentration of the earlier raid on Cologne the bombing was nevertheless effective enough to saturate the defences. One skipper went as far as to say that the fires were more impressive than those of Cologne. A belt of fires extended across the city's entire length from the western edge to the eastern suburbs. Many fires were also spread over other parts of the Ruhr.

This time Harris could not immediately mount another thousand-bomber raid but had to be content with smaller formations, as on the night of 3/4 June, when 170 bombers were despatched on the first large raid to Bremen since October 1941. Eleven aircraft were lost; they included Stirling Mk I W7474 HA-K of 218 Squadron, flown by twenty-nine-year-old P/O James Garscadden and nineteen-year-old P/O John Richard Webber, which was shot down by Uffz Heinz Vinke of II./NJG1 just south of Den Helder at 0032 hours. All the crew of seven were killed. (Vinke was killed on 26 February 1944 having shot down fifty-four aircraft.) Another aircraft lost was a Manchester of 50 Squadron, flown by F/O J Heaton, which fell to Oblt Viktor Bauer of III/NJG1 and crashed near Apeldoorn. Sgt Ken Gaulton, the wireless operator, recalls:

Our aircraft took off from Swinderby at about 2200 hours on 3 June. We flew across Northern Holland and dropped our bomb load on Bremen. I switched to the aircraft inter-communication system to advise the pilot that we were cleared to return to our base, this information having been received on the 0230 hours' broadcast from Group HQ.

On our return flight we were attacked by a Messerschmitt 110. The starboard wing of our aircraft was burning, and the pilot advised that he was going to dive in an attempt to 'blow out' the fire. This did not succeed. The German aircraft did a victory roll near the tail of our aircraft and Sgt P Buttigieg, our tail gunner, shot him down. I was amazed to hear the yelling from the tail gunner who was engaging the Me 110 with his guns.

After diving for some thousands of feet, I requested the pilot's permission to have the tail gunner and mid-upper gunner join me to prepare the rear escape hatch for evacuation. This was done and we jumped in turn; firstly the tail gunner (the only married man in the crew) then the mid-upper gunner, and then came my turn. The aircraft kept on diving and crashed, killing Heaton, P/O J Steen, the co-pilot, P/O A Sheen, the navigator, and Sgt S Thomas, the front gunner, all of whom were in the front of the aircraft. I left the aircraft when it was slightly under 1,000ft, quickly pulled the rip cord, and was promptly knocked out by the chest parachute striking me under the jaw. I landed in the Zuider Zee on an ebbing tide and speared up to my chest in mud. An Alsatian dog woke me by licking my face, and its owner took me to a medical doctor at about 5.30 a.m. I was unable to walk. The doctor quickly established that the man was a collaborator and was therefore unable to hide me. I was transported by car to Arnhem where I was interrogated by the Gestapo, and then by train to Amsterdam, where I was jailed in the Amsterdam watchtower for four days. While I was there a German captain from the fighter squadron visited me about 6 June and advised me that our aircraft had crashed on to a hunting lodge near Apeldoorn (a lodge owned by the Dutch Royal family). He told me that we had shot down one of his aircraft, killing two airmen. He claimed the Germans were two up as four of our crew had been killed.

Another two 50 Squadron Manchesters were lost on the night of 6/7 June. Sgt Leonard Thomas Baker's aircraft was shot down by Ludwig Becker at 0044 hours and crashed into the North Sea off Ameland. (Hptm Becker was killed a year later, on 26 February 1943, having destroyed forty-four aircraft.) P/O A D 'Don' Beatty and his all-RAAF crew ditched their Manchester off the coast of the Dutch Friesians after their Manchester developed engine problems. Altogether, nine aircraft – three Manchesters, three Wellingtons, two Stirlings and one Halifax – were lost from the 233 aircraft despatched. Both Stirlings were shot down by German night fighters: W7471 of 7 Squadron was downed by Oblt Ludwig Becker of 6/NJG2 between Blija and Holwerd and N3761 BU-E of 214 Squadron, flown by F/Lt R W A Turtle DFC, whose crew were on only their second operation, crashed in the North Sea off Terschelling, the victim of Oblt Prinz zur Lippe Weissenfeld of II./NJG2. All the crew were killed.

On 22/23 June, 227 aircraft comprising 144 Wellingtons, thirty-eight Stirlings, twenty-six Halifaxes, eleven Lancasters and eight Hampdens attacked Emden. Some 196 crews claimed good bombing results but

17

decoy fires are believed to have diverted many bombs from the intended target. Six aircraft – four Wellingtons, one Lancaster and a Stirling – were lost while Emden reported that fifty houses were destroyed, a hundred damaged and some damage caused to the harbour. Six civilians were killed and forty were injured.

The third and final thousand-bomber raid took place on 25/26 June when 1,006 aircraft, including 102 Hudsons and Wellingtons of Coastal Command, went to Bremen. P/O Earl Gillespie, an observer in 407 Squadron at Bircham Newton in P/O Arnett's crew, remembers the problems of mixing in Coastal Command aircraft: 'The raid was directed by Bomber Command who at briefing told us to fly at 12,000ft at an indicated airspeed of 130. The first leg of the flight was from Bircham Newton to the mouth of the Elbe, then south to the Weser River, then follow this river to Bremen, bomb the docks and then turn north-west and reach the North Sea south of Wilhelmshaven and so home. The first error was our airspeed – had we followed orders we would never have reached home as our fuel would have gone. Our [Coastal Command] aircraft flew in knots and our airspeed indicators were calibrated in knots, which is about fifteen per cent faster than mph which Bomber Command used!'

Once again instructors and OTU crews were pressed into the night action, as S/L David Penman, an instructor at Waddington, recalls:

On 25 June the operations board showed a 'maximum effort' and much to my surprise my name was down to take Lancaster R5631 with F/Sgt Tetley, my student, as second pilot and five crew members I had never seen before. At briefing it was explained that this was to be a 1,000-bomber raid, needing all fit aircrew to get all the serviceable aircraft in the air for an attack on Bremen. With a number of different types taking part I was glad to be in a Lancaster.

Briefing completed with six 1,000lb bombs aboard as well as three SBCs. The take-off was on time and we climbed and eventually levelled out at 16,000ft with patchy cloud above and enough gaps below to see the target area. There was considerable flak and soon the evidence of night fighters in the area as aircraft caught fire and blew up. Forty-eight aircraft went down this night and I saw most of them. I was certainly glad to be in a Lancaster but sad to see so many aircraft on fire and exploding at lower levels. We were lucky with a suitable break in the cloud to enable the bomb aimer to drop on target. With aircraft going down all round, we were glad to get clear of Bremen without being hit, and with all the weight gone made a very fast run back to Waddington. Total flying time, four hours twenty minutes. My visit to Bremen in a Hampden on 1 January 1941 had taken six hours ten minutes carrying only 2,500lb of bombs! This time the weight of bombs, and with the whole area on fire, the damage must have been dreadful. We lost a lot of aircraft and crews but the losses on the ground must have been very much greater. I felt sorry for the people on the ground who were being killed and injured and having their houses destroyed. Unfortunately it appeared to be the only way to bring the war to a close more quickly. It was a relief to transfer later in the war to Transport Command and do something constructive rather than destructive.

P/O Arnett's crew, meanwhile, had headed for Bremen. Earl Gillespie continues: 'It was a lovely night with the moon shining on white scattered cumulus clouds at about 7,000ft. We bombed the city and then decided to return to the sea on the same route as we used coming by going north to the mouth of the Elbe and then home. There was little flak on this route. It seemed to be just coming up and not really directed at us as we were used to. We could see others getting a good deal of flak on the planned route. We of course started to meet incoming aircraft by the dozen. No one told us it was a 1,000-plane raid! The pilot realised what was up so we lost height quickly and crossed the coast at about 500ft. Once we were over the sea it felt like home.'

Crews were given the opportunity of either bombing the red glow of the fires, using Gee as a check, or proceeding to a secondary target in the vicinity of Bremen. The cloud conditions prevailed at many of the targets of opportunity and many crews, unable to bomb, brought their lethal cargoes home. The risk of collision and enemy fighter activity proved a constant threat and crews had to be ever watchful. S/L Wolfe's Wellington from 419 Squadron was involved in an engagement with a Bf 110 night fighter north of Borkum at 4,200ft over the North Sea. Sergeant D R Morrison opened fire and the enemy fighter's port engine was seen to burst into flames, which almost at once engulfed the entire wing. It dived into the sea, leaving a large circle of fire around the point of impact.

Other bombers were not as fortunate in their encounters and the forty-eight aircraft lost (including five Coastal Command aircraft) was the highest casualty rate so far, the bomber OTUs of 91 Group suffering particularly heavily, losing twenty-three of their 198 Whitleys and Wellingtons. No. 24 OTU sent out sixteen aircraft this night and four failed to return: Whitley Z9441, flown by P/O J A Preston, was shot

19

down at 0254 hours by Major Kurt Holler of II./NJG2 north of Vlieland in the North Sea, all five crew killed (Holler himself was killed on 22 June 1943; he had nineteen victories); Wellington T2773 of 20 OTU, from Lossiemouth, flown by Sgt N W Levasseur was shot down in an encounter with Oblt Egmont Prinz zur Lippe Weissenfeld of II./NJG2, who shot the Wimpy into the sea off Terschelling, all six crew killed; and Whitley Mk V BD379, piloted by twenty-one-year-old F/O James Brian Monro RNZAF was hit by flak from 5/Marine Flak Battery 246 and crashed into the sea off Terschelling at 0418 hours, all six crew (a 'screened' crew and all OTU instructors) killed. Three members of the crew were removed from this wrecked aircraft on 26 June and buried the following day while P/O Ian Patterson Clark, the WOP/AG, was washed ashore on 27 June and buried on 29 June. A third Whitley of 24 OTU which failed to return was BD266 of 'B' Flight, which was shot down by Lt Löwa of II./NJG2 and crashed in the North Sea just eight minutes after BD379, at 0426 hours. Lt Lothar Linke, Lt Denzel, and Lt Boetel, also of II./NJG2, each claimed a Wellington apiece. (Denzel was killed on 26 June 1943 having destroyed nine aircraft.)

Night fighters of II./NJG2 might also have been responsible for bringing down two Hudsons off Holland this night. Hudson Mk V AM762 VX-M of 206 Squadron crashed into the sea north-west of the Friesian Islands and F/Sgt Kenneth Douglas Wright, the twenty-two-year-old pilot, his WOP/AG and an air gunner were killed, while the other two men aboard were made PoW. Twenty-nine-year-old S/L Cyril Norman Crook DFC's Hudson V AM606 VX-S, also of 206 Squadron, crashed into the sea off the Friesians. None of the crew survived. A third Hudson, flown by F/L Derek Hodgkinson of 220 Squadron, was shot down by a Bf 110 over the Dutch coast. Hodgkinson ditched the aircraft and at dawn on 26 June he and his navigator walked ashore at Ameland and were taken prisoner.

Bremen was the third and final thousand-bomber raid in the series of major saturation attacks on German cities. Although the raid was not as successful as the first thousand-bomber raid on Cologne, large parts of Bremen, especially in the south and east districts, were destroyed; the price paid was high. The German High Command was shaken but at Leeuwarden, at least, morale soared: II./NJG2 had claimed seventeen of the forty-eight bombers shot down this night. June 1942 proved to be the 'harvesting' month for the night fighters based at Leeuwarden: no less than sixty-two RAF bombers were claimed shot down by the crews of II./NJG2.

20

II./NJG2 were again in the thick of the action on the night of 29/30 June when Bomber Command returned to Bremen. Sgt Neville Hockaday, pilot of a 75 (RNZAF) Wellington, was flying his first trip with his new crew, but after having flown as a second 'dickie' on the Essen raid, 5 June 1942, he was aware of the dangers: 'I am not ashamed to admit that after briefing for my first trip I had to wash my underpants. That evening I knew the real meaning of fear, but after the trip it was no longer the fear of the unknown. Once the veil over the unknown is drawn to one side and its true nature revealed you become aware of what it is you have to combat and you can set about preparing yourself to cope with it. The night we flew to Bremen, of the five of us in the aircraft, I was the only one who knew what we had to fear. I was conscious of the route across Holland which would place us near the night fighter bases at Schiphol and Leeuwarden.'

W/O Len Collins, a Stirling WOP/AG in 149 Squadron at Lakenheath, was on his thirty-third trip. He recalls:

Having completed my tour I had been posted to an EFTS to train as a pilot. I volunteered to stand in for the mid-upper gunner on F/L Bill Barnes DFC's crew, who was ill. Other than the second pilot, W/C Alexander, on his first trip to gain experience, the remainder of the crew were on their thirtieth. All were RAF. I was the only Aussie.

As we assembled outside the canteen, waiting for the flight bus to take us to our aircraft at the dispersal bay, we noticed several black limousines heading towards the Squadron aircraft. On take-off, we were told that an adjustment had been made to each aircraft's IFF. This modification, after ten seconds' warming-up, was designed to make German radar feed inaccurate readings to its flak batteries.

The trip to Bremen was uneventful. Conversing with the Wing Commander, I found he was most interested with the pyrotechnic display from the flak and the colours of the searchlights as we crossed the enemy coast. I predicted we were in for trouble when a blue one slid off our wing tip. However, either our doctored IFF did not work or the Germans were given a tip-off. Over Bremen we received a direct hit from flak on our inner starboard engine, killing W/C Alexander and P/O C W Dellow, the observer, and injuring the WOP D S Hickley. The bombs were dropped live, a photo taken, and we headed for home on three engines.

Over the Zuider Zee a night fighter appeared [Bf 110 flown by Lt Bethel of II./NJG2]. I can still recall the flash of his windscreen in the darkness as he opened fire. As I was speaking to the rear gunner, Sgt R Gallagher, he was blown out of his turret. I was ringed with cannon shells and injured in the leg by shrapnel. Owing to the electrical cut-out which protected the tail of the aircraft from the mid-upper guns, I was unable to fire on the fighter attacking us. Fortunately, the turret became jammed in the rear position, allowing me to vacate it. Forward, the aircraft was burning like a torch. I could not contact any crew member. The position was hopeless. I felt I had no option but to leave the aircraft. My parachute was not in its storage holder. I found it under the legs of the mid-upper turret with a cannon shell burn in it. I removed the rear escape hatch, clipped on the parachute and sat on the edge of the hatch. I pulled the rip cord and tumbled out. The parachute, having several holes from the shell burn, 'candlesticked' [twirled] as I descended and I landed in a canal.

The Stirling was shot down at 0204 hours and crashed in the Ijsselmeer near Wons just south of Harlingen. Collins was apprehended the following day and he was taken to Leeuwarden airfield for interrogation: 'Here I met the pilot of the Messerschmitt 110 who claimed to have shot us down. I abused him in good Australian. He understood, having spent three years at Oxford University.'

Sgt Neville Hockaday of 75 (RNZAF) had set course at 2340 in his Wellington.

I scanned the sky and saw aircraft lights from Lakenheath, Mildenhall and Honington. After crossing the coast guns were tested cruising at 165mph at 8,000ft, where it was moonlight. Just before one a.m. we saw the first bursts of flak from at least half a dozen gun sites dead ahead. I saw no activity a little to the right between Ijmuiden and Haarlem, which could have been a trap containing night fighters. I decided to head for Haarlem and turn into the gap at the last moment. We crossed the coast about ten miles south of the planned track.

'Skipper,' an urgent and tense call from Mike Hughes, my WOP/AG: 'Fighter on your port bow. Ju 88, I think.' We all saw it but apparently it had not seen us and it disappeared from sight. There was plenty of evidence of both night fighter and flak activity all around us against other unseen aircraft however. Just as we were turning on to the final course over the Dummer Lake Bruce Philip, the rear gunner, called, 'There's something behind us.'

'I see him,' said Mike. 'Ju 88, 2,000 yards, slightly below, starboard quarter.'

'He's seen us and he's starting to turn,' said Bruce.

22

I started a 'weave' and for nearly a minute there was absolute silence. Then Mike began the commentary from the astrodome. 'He's coming fast, prepare to dive to port.'

I put the mixture to 'rich' and the propellers to fully fine pitch. Then there was a three-second burst from the rear turret. 'Closing fast, 200 yards. Hold her steady, 170 yards.'

Suddenly, tracer bullets shot past the port wingtip and I weaved to starboard. More tracer shot past, this time to starboard and closer: '150 yards, 120 yards, 100 yards, diving turn to port – GO!'

Pushing the nose down I stood on the left rudder pedal as more tracer shot past us followed by cannon shells while we plummeted down in a steep diving spiral. As we went there was a ten-second burst of firing from the rear turret, a brief silence followed by another short burst. 'You've hit him Bruce,' shouted Mike excitedly. 'You've hit him. Well done. His port engine's on fire.'

I recovered from the dive and started the climb back to 8,500ft having lost some 6,000ft in that manoeuvre. 'Nice work, Bruce.'

'Thanks. He's just hit the ground and exploded.'

'Nice going, Mike.'

'Thanks skipper.'

Sgt Alfie Drew, my New Zealander navigator, logged the time and position for our claim on return to Feltwell.

A few minutes later we saw the flashes of ack-ack guns ahead and the sky filled with the beams of searchlights. Explosions on the ground told us that the first aircraft had arrived on the target, nearly half an hour late. I wondered why and realised that this would lead to congestion over the target. I continued the climb to bomb from 10,000ft.

By now the sky was full of searchlight beams and bursting shells adding to the illumination of the Northern Lights and the nearly full moon – too much like daylight for comfort! Directed by the bomb aimer, I flew as accurately as I could on instruments alone, hearing the crump of bursting shells and smelling cordite filling the cockpit. I had been advised not to worry about that – you only smelled the ones that had missed you!

'Steady, steady, right a bit, steady. Hold it there. Steady, steady, bomb gone!' He didn't have to tell me; with the release of the 4,000lb cookie the aircraft seemed to lift a hundred feet into the air and immediately became easier to handle.

I went into a steep diving turn to port, and only just in time as a blue master searchlight probed close to us as we had been on a steady course long enough for the predictors to line up on us. Speed built up to 230mph as we lost height and I wondered idly at what speed the wings of a Wimpy fall off. Suddenly it was dark and quiet around us and I levelled off at 7,000ft.

We soon came back to our cloud cover and flew just above the tops. We could see aircraft all around us heading homewards and I appreciated the 'safety in numbers' that this conferred. Every now and then tracer could be seen flying both ways, but there were no casualties to either side.

It was far too soon to relax. 'Water ahead,' said Bill as we came up to the Friesians and I reminded the crew of the fighter bases on either side.

'Skipper, there's a fighter coming up on starboard.'

I dived into cloud and turned towards him, holding the course for nearly five minutes and, turning back on course, eased out of the cloud.

'I see him, skipper, he's about two miles to starboard, going away. You've given him the slip.'

We enjoyed hot coffee crossing the sea. Mike loaded the Very pistol with the colours of the day, only just in time as a convoy appeared. We landed at 0520 on the grass airfield. We owed our lives to the dedication to their jobs of Bruce and Mike.

Sgt W Ken Dunn and his crew of a 115 Squadron Wellington, on their thirty-first operation, also encountered enemy fighters. Dunn recalls:

We had been routed to the target along the coast and advised to return the same way but as we turned for home I saw two aircraft shot down within a minute and I decided to take a more direct route some forty miles inland, hoping to avoid the fighters. We set course for Texel, the most western island of the Friesians, at 10,000ft. Visibility was good. There was low stratus at 2,000ft and some medium at 12,000ft.

We were flying on a course of 335 degrees just west of Groningen when the attack came as a complete surprise. Normally one of the crew, usually the rear gunner, saw or 'sensed' the approach of a fighter and so warned the pilot but on this occasion the first intimation I had was the sight of tracer shells and bullets shooting past me on both sides of the cabin and the noise of explosions as some of them hit parts of the aircraft. The enemy aircraft was first observed by the rear gunner diving out of a patch of cloud on to our stern, but before he had a chance to report the enemy aircraft opened fire. The rear gunner returned fire and registered hits on the fighter's port wing. I was skidding and sideslipping the aircraft to present as difficult a target as possible.

The enemy aircraft, identified as a Me 110, then dived away to port and the front gunner gave it a short burst, with no visible result. The wireless operator, now in the astrodome, reported that the Messerschmitt had worked its way round to the port quarter and lined up for a second attack, but before he could get within range we had turned on him and he skimmed over the top.

Again he came round on the port quarter and again we turned. He stayed with us for quite a time and followed us as we spiralled to practically ground level and making for the stratus cloud at 2,000ft where we eventually lost him. In his subsequent attacks I don't think he hit us again, but his first attack was so successful – from his point of view – that he probably registered us as a 'highly probable?'

We flew back to Holland very low and I remember seeing the lights of houses, which should have been blacked out, I suppose. The cloud cleared as we crossed the coast at about 1,000ft. Just west of the Friesians we flew over a convoy which sent up red and green tracer. Over the North Sea we climbed up to 7,000ft, with some difficulty, and began to check. We had sustained considerable damage. The flying instrument panel was unserviceable. The trailing aerial fairway had been shot away. Petrol seemed all right at first sight but the hydraulic oil tank was empty. There was a large hole in the fabric by the wireless operator's cabin and a strip nearly three feet wide had been torn off to the tail. I put in the automatic pilot and went down the catwalk and there was the North Sea clearly visible through the geodetic construction.

It soon became clear that the port petrol tank had been hit and was leaking. We switched the balance cock to use up what remained before running both engines off the starboard tank. Although the hydraulic system was not working the turrets could be operated manually. The undercarriage had fallen but did not lock. However, we managed to lock it later by using the emergency hand pump.

It was not possible to use any flap on landing. As we landed at base the port main wheel burst. As we lost flying speed on landing the port wing sagged when gravity took over – a cannon shell had struck the main spar. The nacelle tanks had been holed by bullets and the reserve petrol had leaked away. When the engineering officer came over to inspect the aircraft he declared it was a 'write off'. Obviously, the officer's opinion on the state of the aircraft was revised on closer inspection; the badly shot-up Wimpy was repaired and flew on Ops again a few months later.

P/O Alan McSweyn, the pilot of another Wellington, R1509 'P' of 115 Squadron, also encountered a night fighter. He recalls:

Our first enemy action was heavy flak as we were en route for Bremen. Apparently, although we were not aware of it at the time, we had been hit, because some ten minutes before reaching the target the port engine over-heated, the oil pressure dropped and I had to cut the engine just as we reached the target area. We went ahead and bombed the target, dropping from about 13,000ft to some 11,000ft after the engine failure and there having difficulty in maintaining height on one engine after leaving the target.

As usual we experienced searchlights and flak after leaving Bremen and I had to decide whether to try to stay at 9,000ft, where we seemed able to maintain height, but would have to run the gauntlet of both light and heavy flak, or whether to take violent evasive action, losing even more height in the process, or dive for the ground to get out of danger at roof-top level. The latter two choices lessened the chance of getting home on one engine, so I elected to stay at 9,000ft, warning the crew to watch for night fighters.

Sure enough, the flak ceased while we were still coned by searchlights and then without warning I saw tracer fire passing us and felt the shudder of our rear guns firing. Some days later we were told by other crew members that Jimmy Gill, my rear gunner, had shot down a single-engined fighter, probably a Me 109. Almost simultaneously there was another burst of cannon and machine-gun fire which came straight up the fuselage from rear to front, swathed the right side instrument panel, knocked off the navigator's left earpiece as Wilf Hetherington stood in the cockpit beside me, hit Bill Wilde, the co-pilot, in the thigh as he stood looking out of the astrodome, and seriously wounded Jimmy Gill in the shoulder and chest. Immediately the starboard motor caught fire, and ahead and climbing right in front of us I saw the Me 110 which had caused the damage, but which could not be seen by Ted 'Laddy' Gibbs, the front gunner. Within seconds the whole starboard wing and fuselage was alight; the fire extinguishers were ineffectual and I found the aircraft virtually uncontrollable, so I gave the order to bale out.

Wilf Hetherington crawled forward to the front turret to release Teddy Gibbs, while Bill Wilde, though wounded, crawled to the rear escape hatch to warn Jimmy Gill to leave and bale out from there. I saw Laddy Gibbs, Wilf Hetherington and Frank Davidson, the WOP, leave by the forward hatch and, looking back, I could see that Bill Wilde had gone out the rear hatch and Jimmy Gill had gone from the rear turret.

By now the starboard wing had disintegrated and the aircraft was spin-ning down out of control. With some difficulty I was able to reach the forward hatch and after some effort got it open and baled out. My parachute descent was unsensational, although my flying boots blew off as I left the aircraft and landed in the rear of a farmyard in fairly long grass, landing so quietly among an unconcerned herd of thirty or so cows that I remained on my feet and didn't roll over. I was surprised by the quietness. I had no idea where my aircraft or crew had landed and realised that surrounding wooded areas probably concealed both. I was able to grab a bicycle from the farmhouse nearby and began riding and walking in a vain hope to reach Holland and perhaps help.

Alan McSweyn reached a military aerodrome and managed to get in the cockpit of a Bf 110 but was apprehended while trying to start the engines. Apparently, he motioned from the cockpit to a Luftwaffe ground crewman to assist him with starting the engines. The German fell for it but when McSweyn pressed the starter button the prop nearly took the German's head off. He then spotted McSweyn's dark blue Australian uniform and the game was up! McSweyn concludes: 'The rest of the crew all landed in the same area. Jimmy Gill, apparently dazed but not fatally injured, landed in a tree, did not realise how high he was, released his parachute harness and dropped about forty feet to the ground, badly hurting his back. Bill Wilde, meanwhile, could not walk, so rather than leave the two wounded men, the other three alerted some Germans and asked for medical help. Although the wounded were given the best possible medical treatment in hospital, Jimmy Gill died, mainly from a broken back. Wilde fully recovered and the doctors told him that while they regretted being unable to save Gill, his death was really a blessing because had he lived he would have been a paraplegic for life.' (Although the surviving crew members were all confined to PoW camps, P/O Alan McSweyn soon successfully made his escape, though his fellow escapee died from exposure while they were crossing the Pyrenees. Alan was back in England by Christmas 1942, nearly six months after he was shot down. Awarded the Military Cross, he then served with Transport Command until returning to his native Australia in January 1946.)

As can be seen, Bomber Command suffered heavy casualties this night and many of them, like the forementioned, were victims of NJG2 over Holland. Halifax II W1113 LQ-G of 405 (RCAF) Squadron, piloted by P/O Echin, was shot down at 0148 hours by Oblt Rudolf Sigmund of II./NJG2 and crashed between Wolvega and Noordwolde; all the crew were killed. (Hptm Sigmund himself was killed on 3 October 1943 after having destroyed twenty-eight aircraft.) Another 405 Squadron Halifax

II, W7714 LQ-K, flown by W/O Sidney, was shot down at 0214 hours by Major Helm of II./NJG2 and crashed at Sybrandaburen; all the crew were killed. A third 405 Squadron Halifax II, W7715 LQ-H, crashed at Bimolten seven kilometres north-north-west of Nordhorn, Germany; F/Lt Liversidge and crew were killed. Stirling I N6082 OJ-Q of 149 Squadron was shot down at 0204 hours by Lt Bethel of II./NJG2. It crashed in the Ijsselmeer near Wons, just south of Harlingen; the mid-upper gunner was made PoW, the rest were killed. Another 7 Squadron Stirling I, N3706 MG-S, was probably shot down at 0233 hours by Lt Löwa, pilot, and Fw Moeller, radar operator, of 5./NJG2 in Bf 110 Wkr Nr 2669 R4+JN. The bomber crashed in the North Sea thirty-five kilo-metres north-west of Vlieland. The pilot, mid-upper gunner and rear gunner were made PoW. Löwa probably collided with the bomber and crashed in the sea near his final victim; both men were killed. A third Stirling I, BF310 OJ-H of 149 Squadron, was shot down at 0302 hours by Oblt Leopold Fellerer of II./NJG2. It also crashed in the Ijsselmeer off Schellingwoude. P/O Simmons and crew were killed and were buried in Amsterdam. Wellington III X3539 of 75 (RNZAF) Squadron was shot down at 0308 hours by Oblt Prinz zur Lippe Weissenfeld of II./NJG2 and crashed in the Waddenzee south of Ameland. P/O W J Monk RNZAF and crew were killed. A Wellington III of 57 Squadron, which returned to Methwold, carried P/O Buston, rear gunner, killed in a night fighter attack.

On 26/27 July 1942, 403 bombers went to Hamburg in a maximum effort. Twin-engined types like the Wellington and, to a lesser extent, the Hampden, still formed the backbone of Bomber Command, but Air Chief Marshal Harris was gradually building up his numbers of four-engined types, and the 181 Wellingtons and thirty-three Hampdens were joined on the raid by seventy-seven Lancasters, seventy-three Halifaxes and thirty-nine Stirlings. They caused severe and widespread damage to Hamburg, mostly in the housing and semi-commercial districts, but, because of the clear moonlight conditions along most of the route, night fighters were active and over the target flak was accurate. Some twenty-nine bombers (7.2% of the total force despatched) – fifteen Wellingtons, eight Halifaxes, two Hampdens of 420 Squadron, two Lancasters and four Stirlings – were shot down and two aircraft crashed on return. Ten of the bombers were shot down over northern Holland and in the area of the Friesians, eight by night fighters of II./NJG2 based at Leeuwarden, and two by I./NJG2 at Venlo. Oblt Lothar Linke of II./NJG1 shot down Lancaster R5748 of 106 Squadron at 0205 hours and it crashed at

Rottevalle in Friesland. (Oblt Linke was killed on 14 May 1943 having recorded twenty-seven victories.) Thirty minutes later Hptm Helmut Lent brought down a Halifax, probably W1142 of 102 Squadron, at 0235 hours. His victim crashed in the North Sea off the German coast. Four minutes later, at 0239 hours, Lent destroyed Wellington Mk III BJ615 'G' of 115 Squadron, off the north-west German coast. (Oberst Lent was killed on 7 October 1944 after having shot down 110 aircraft.) A Halifax of 158 Squadron piloted by P/O F S White was shot down by a night fighter and ditched in the sea off Borkum or Schiermonnikoog with both starboard engines on fire. P/O Eric 'Syd' Johnstone, the navigator, recalls:

> We successfully bombed the docks area of the city but in taking evasive action from all the flak being fired at us, we lost height and found ourselves in the defensive balloon barrage. This was a pretty hair-raising experience, but after much difficulty we got clear of the barrage and course was set for the North Sea. This was cleared, but while gaining height a couple of night fighters had a go at us and in three firing passes set fire to both engines on the port wing. There was no chance of getting home after this, but the skipper called to say he was going to try and put it down in the sea and he ordered us to take up ditching positions.
>
> I made my way towards the rear of the aircraft and got down behind the main spar, where I was soon joined by both gunners. A few minutes later we hit the sea. The impact was pretty severe and there was a tremendous crack and the rear fuselage just broke away from the rest of the kite. Although we had all been bounced about, we managed to get out and cling on to a piece of the wing, which had broken off in the crash and was still afloat. There was no sign of the rest of the aircraft, which must have gone straight to the bottom.

The four crew in the cockpit area of the Halifax were killed. The three survivors held on to the floating parts of the wreckage and sixteen hours later were spotted by a German seaplane. It landed near the airmen, picked them up and flew them to Nordeney.

Three Wellingtons of 115 Squadron which were damaged by flak at the target all ditched in the North Sea. This night A Flight of 115 Squadron lost four Wimpys, or half its strength that set out from Marham. Two other aircraft, probably Wellingtons, were shot down by Lt Wilheim Beier and Oblt Siegfried Wandam, both of I./NJG1. (Oblt Beier finished the war with thirty-six confirmed victories; Wandam was killed on 4 July 1944 having shot down ten aircraft confirmed.) Another Wellington pilot, S/L Richard Osborn DFC, 'A' Flight Commander of 460 (RAAF) Squadron, witnessed the shooting down of a Wimpy on this night:

> So as not to go near the heavily defended areas of Heligoland and Cuxhaven we were routed to fly first to some point off the south end of the North Friesian Islands, off the Danish coast, and from there to turn south and fly directly down to our target. We were to use the same track out for our return flight. Hamburg was as hot a target as ever this night, but we dropped our load of incendiaries and got a fairly good photo in the process.
>
> But now we were back out over the North Sea, probably a bit west of Heligoland and cruising happily homewards. It was around full-moon time and, being near to midnight, the moon was to the south so that the sea below us on our port side was a vast sheet of silvery light. Suddenly, I noticed the unmistakable shape of another Wimpy silhouetted against the silvery sheet. It was slightly below us and not more than a couple of hundred yards away. I let our plane sink down closer to his level, perhaps for a bit of company.
>
> But by sinking that little bit lower, that shifted the Wimpy up higher in my field of vision with the result that I could now see more of the silvery space down below him. At once I saw the shape of another plane that was not far below him – not a Wimpy this time, but a silhouette that I didn't immediately recognise. I noticed that its tail shape was somewhat similar to that of a Blenheim but I couldn't quite recognise what it was. Even as I studied this new plane the gap below the Wimpy began to close. At the very moment that I managed to identify the plane, it reared up on its tail and blasted away with its guns. Too late had I realised that it was a Ju 88! Bursting into flames, the Wimpy fell sideways and spiralled down, crashing into the sea. The Ju 88 immediately disappeared. I felt sick from realising that I had sat and watched all this happen as if I had been in the front row of the stalls at the theatre – I hadn't given my comrade the slightest warning of his danger, nor had we tried to attack the Ju 88. We probably could have shot that Hun down as easily as he had just shot that Wimpy down!

Normally, death was not seen at such close quarters. Sgt Bill Rae, rear gunner of a 142 Squadron Wellington, who was made PoW on 16 November 1942, recalls: 'It is held now in some quarters that saturation bombing of German cities with large-scale civilian casualties should not have been carried out, but few of us at that time felt any remorse. It was all too impersonal for that. Germany was simply a large blacked-out area which had to be crossed to find the target, to avoid flak, searchlights and night fighters, to release the bombs and get away as soon as possible. We had no thoughts of people being killed or cities being devastated. The only Germans we thought about were night fighter pilots, flak gunners and searchlight operators. They were our contacts, often with unfortunate results to ourselves. It is difficult to describe but for five or six hours you entered a different world in which you were completely cut off from your normal life. On landing back at base you suddenly switched back to real life – the next op.'

Even back at base there was death and destruction, as F/Lt John Price remembers:

> One of my friends' aircraft crashed and caught fire when returning from Germany one night, with some bombs on board. We all rushed to help, but the heat from the fire drove us back. I could only stand and watch my friend turn black as he burned to a cinder. We turned and ran just before the bombs exploded.
>
> Of course we pretended not to be afraid. In order to keep up the pretence we cracked jokes and sang dirty songs. Morale and discipline were every-thing. If you refused to go on a particularly dangerous operation, or cracked up on an operation, the RAF were much harsher than their American coun-terparts. USAAF combatants were told by their doctors they were suffering from 'battle fatigue', given rest, leave with their loved ones in the USA and eventually returned to duty after psychiatric help. In the RAF all aircrew [NCOs] were stripped of their rank and became an ordinary airman, and whatever RAF station you were posted to you had to produce your flying logbook with the dreaded words stamped in black letters: 'Lack of Moral Fibre'. Naturally through the Orderly Room word spread throughout your new station: 'He's a coward' – it must have been hell on earth for some of these once brave aircrew whose nerves were stretched to breaking point. Thereafter, they peeled potatoes in the kitchen or were forced to perform menial tasks.

F/O Barney D'Ath Weston, an air gunner on 115 Squadron Wellingtons, who was shot down and made PoW on 26/27 July 1942, adds: 'At this stage of the war the average life expectancy of bomber crews was eight operations – a quarter of a tour. No. 75 Squadron at Feltwell had seventy crews shot down before one crew completed a tour in mid-1942. I remember admiring aircrew because I never knew of anyone breaking down or showing a lack of morale. The fear of being tagged LMF was ever-present to some. I did speak to a sergeant on a squadron who said that when he had requested a break the Squadron medical officer had replied. "What's wrong with you is that you're yellow." The lad had been the only survivor in a crash after an operation. He was killed a few nights later. I believe he was a genuine case of severe stress and had reached his breaking point.' F/Lt Alec Taylor, second pilot on 218 Squadron Stirlings, concludes: 'Stress of operational flying over Germany? Nil. It was down to training. Any training is a form of "brain washing". A good example is the USAAF. It was being rather badly hit on daylight raids so some aircrew were sent to RAF squadrons to fly at night for a few trips to acclimatise them to night flying. One I knew did one trip and decided he was not going to fly at night when he could not see anything outside the plane. The opposite of course with us; no way would we have liked to fly in daylight when we could easily be seen by fighters etc.; all part of the initial training. Also, it was the natural feeling it would always be some other crew shot down. If we saw one plane hit it was, "Poor devils, hope they get out", and you did not consider it could be you, until it happened. The training again took over, the boring parachute drops from the plane escape hatches, while the plane was on the ground, on to thick mats paid off in automatically doing the correct thing. The psychology of flying was basic; young men eager to fly trained (brain-washed) into accepting the best time to fly was night time (RAF) and daylight (USAAF).'

By the summer of 1942 the few American heavy bomber groups of the 8th Air Force in England were just getting into their stride, and in August they put their daylight precision bombing campaign to the real test, over the Greater Reich.

CHAPTER 2

BATTLES OF THE BOMB GROUPS

In the USAAF in 1942 there were thousands of young men eager to fly and they were trained into accepting that daylight was the best time to fight the aerial war in Europe. This was mainly because the American High Command believed in their own mistaken prophecy that their bombers, heavily armed so as not to need escort fighters, could, during daylight hours, penetrate even the strongest defences and achieve 'pickle barrel' bombing accuracy that bombardiers had performed in the clear skies of Texas and the southern states. Drawing upon their own bitter experience of the disastrous daylight bombing campaign of 1939–40, few in the RAF believed that the 8th Air Force in England could succeed where they, and the Luftwaffe during the Battle of Britain, had failed. Eventually, the British, notably Winston Churchill, came to accept the American method of bombing and it would grow into a formidable 'round the clock' bombing strategy that would contribute decisively to the defeat of Germany.

In August 1942 though, General Eaker, Commander of VIIIth Bomber Command in Britain, could call upon only a few B-17 Flying Fortress and B-24D Liberator bomb groups when the USAAF fully entered the fray in Europe. It had an immediate effect on the Luftwaffe however. German day fighters now had to drive the heavily armed and armoured American bombers from the skies by co-ordination of fighter formations and closed formation attacks, particularly since the standard 8.8cm flak promised no great results at altitudes above 8,000 metres. By early August 1942 three B-17 bomb groups, the 92nd, 97th and 301st, had arrived in England. The 97th BG had the honour of flying the first heavy bomber mission, when it attacked Lille on 17 August.

On 19 August the 97th BG despatched twenty-four of its B-17Es in support of the Allied landings at Dieppe. Their target was the airfield at Abbeville–Drucat in northern France, home of the infamous II./JG26, or 'Abbeville Kids', whose yellow-nosed Fw 190 pilots were among the Luftwaffe élite. JG26 and the American bombers would meet on many occasions in the coming months. Two of the B-17s aborted because of mechanical failures but the rest of the Group plastered the airfield, destroying a hangar and severely cratering or 'potholing' the runways. Fortunately, the Luftwaffe was heavily engaged over the Dieppe area and did not show. British High Command reported that sixteen fighters were either destroyed or damaged as a result of the bombing strike and the airfield itself was put out of action for a vital two hours. In addition, the controllers of the whole of the fighter area remained out of action until that evening. Air Marshal Sir Trafford Leigh-Mallory, Chief of RAF Fighter Command, added his congratulations: 'The raid on Abbeville undoubtedly struck a heavy blow at the German fighter organisation at a very critical moment during the operations . . .' RAF fighter pilots reported the following day that the main area of the Drucat aerodrome appeared to have been 'completely demolished'. Yet despite these successes, JG26 was in action over Dieppe all day. The three Gruppen of JG26 flew no less than 377 sorties, both against the Allied aircraft and against sea and ground targets. For six Fw 190s lost, the Geschwader claimed thirty-eight aircraft shot down, plus another eleven probables.

On 21 August the 97th BG came under attack from JG26 again when a dozen B-17s ventured to the Wilton shipyards at Rotterdam. None of the Fortresses was lost and the US press praised the American bombers' ability to 'destroy' six of the twenty-five attacking fighters. On 24 August the 97th BG again escaped without loss when they hit the shipyards at Le Trait. All nine Fortresses returned safely from the raid on the Wilton shipyards on 27 August and there were no losses on 29 August when the 97th bombed the German fighter base at Courtrai–Wevelghem in Belgium. Results appeared good and even the British press, which had at first been cautious of American claims, now openly praised them. On 5 September the 97th BG were joined by the 301st BG in a raid on the marshalling yards at Rouen and all thirty-seven B-17s returned safely. Although aircrew had been badly wounded during the first nine Fortress missions, not one B-17 had been lost. It could not last.

On 6 September Eaker mounted his largest bombing mission so far, to the Avions Potez factory at Meaulte using the 92nd BG for the first time. The 92nd scraped together fourteen B-17Es and crews, filling in with ground personnel, some of them privates. They joined with twenty-two B-17Fs of the 97th in the main strike while the 301st BG flew a diversionary raid on St Omer–Longuenesse airfield. Thirty Fortresses crossed Meaulte but only six in the 92nd BG attacked the target.

Focke Wulf 190s of II./JG26 were encountered continuously from the

French coast to the target and the escorting four squadrons of Spitfire IXs failed to rendezvous with the bombers. JG26 intercepted the Spitfires and shot down three. The Fortresses were bounced by about fifty Fw 190s and a handful of Bf 109s. Lt Clarence C Lipsky's B-17 in the 97th BG was attacked by Hptm Conny Meyer, CO of II./JG26, and it went down north-west of Amiens at 1855 hours. It was the Luftwaffe's first American heavy bomber victory of the war. Four parachutes were seen to open. (The Red Cross reported on 17 October 1942 that Lipsky and five of the crew were PoWs.) The second B-17 lost on the mission belonged to Lt Leigh E Stewart of the 92nd BG, who was pursued by at least five Fw 190s. Ofw Roth of 4./JG26 finally shot it down at 1906 hours and Stewart crashed into the sea north-west of Le Treport. RAF Air-Sea Rescue launches searched the area but without success. Over Cayeaux, Capt Frank G Ward of the 92nd BG was attacked by six Fw 190s and one fired into the tail, killing Cpl John E Bungard, the tail gunner, mortally wounding Cpl Hubert W Crowell and severely wounding Sgt Robert C Smith. John F Segrest, the navigator, was slightly wounded. One 97th BG gunner, Sgt Julius L Kleiman, was killed and three others wounded. One died of his wounds three days later in hospital.

On 9 October, 108 B-17s and, for the first time, B-24s of the 93rd BG were despatched to the vast steel and locomotive works at the Compagnie de Fives, Lille. Also flying their first mission this day were the 306th BG from Thurleigh, Bedfordshire. At between 0800 and 0830 hours Col Charles 'Chip' Overacker Jr, the CO, led twenty-three crews off from Thurleigh in a 369th Squadron Fortress with Capt James A Johnston and his crew. Each plane had a crew of nine, a second waist gunner not thought necessary. As the B-17s circled the airfield, 2/Lt Albert W La Chasse, the bombardier in *Snoozy II* in the 367th Squadron, flown by Capt John Olsen, waved goodbye to his buddy, 'Butterball' Jones. 'His aircraft was grounded because we were using some of their parts to fly the mission. I never saw him again. He fell out of his ship's bomb bay on a mission to the sub-pens in France after his ship was forced into the water by enemy fighters.'

The large formation of B-17Fs of the 306th and B-17Es of the 92nd, 97th and 301st Bomb Groups, with the B-24Ds of the 93rd BG falling in behind the Fortresses, began crossing the coast of England at Felixstowe at 0912. At about the same time III./JG26 Kommandeur, Hptm 'Pips' Priller, was leading his pilots off from their airfield at Wevelghem. They headed north to intercept the bombers. Two of the

306th BG B-17s aborted the mission before reaching the enemy coast. Nearing the target flak enveloped the formation and in the 306th, Col Overacker's Fortress was hit in the No. 2 engine and he was forced to relinquish the lead. Al La Chasse recalls: 'Some smoke and dust covered the target area. As we continued the run a line of B-24s out of position were coming across the target area from the east, heading towards England. Flak hit our right inboard engine and set it on fire. Norman Gates, the co-pilot, somehow extinguished it. Flak increased. I was surprised it came in so many colours. On the bomb run Capt Olsen trimmed the ship before turning the control over to me. I released the bomb load not knowing there would be several malfunctions causing bomb rack problems. The plane lifted, lightened by the bomb drop. The B-24s were now behind us. It was 0942, time over the target as per mission plan. For *Snoozy II* the war was about to begin, and end. With only three engines pulling we began a silly 360° turn into enemy territory. Where were the P-38s? None!'

As the Thurleigh Group came off the target about fifty of the 'Abbeville Kids' attacked from the rear and head-on. La Chasse continues:

At about 1,000 yards at three o'clock there immediately appeared, in line astern, a gaggle of Me 109s stalking us with four years' war experience. 'Ass-end Charlie' was about to become a 'sitting duck'! The interphone came alive with voices.

'Top turret: Jerries climbing into the sun behind me.'

'Red lights flashing on the instrument panel; four bombs hung!'

I couldn't bring the doors up with the armed bolts still there. One stray armour-piercing bullet in the right place and boom, no anything!

Bandits were everywhere. Where are those Goddamn P-38s? Sounds like typing on loose paper indicated enemy shells were ripping into the ship's skin surfaces. *Snoozy II* began to lag behind the rest of the formation. 'Honest John' McKee's ship tried lagging back with us. Good old 'Honest John'. He tried.

Tracers were coming and going in all directions. 'How can I toggle armed bombs in a canted ship?' I thought. They hadn't taught me that in cadet training. I thought, 'Salvo! that's it: dump the whole damn load, bombs, shackles and all.'

Now we were headed west, towards the white cliffs of Dover. Then suddenly, S/Sgt Bert E Kaylor, the tail gunner, screamed, 'Jerries at six o'clock!'

I thought, 'Boy that's right up our butts.' Out of the sun the bastards came. I could feel each gunner's position as they fired. Tail, ball and waist gunners each took turns. Again, where are those —— P-38s?

Now only Truman C Wilder, the ball turret gunner, was still firing. Oh, oh, a belly attack was coming. All at once a German fighter flew right by our nose with a dirty yellow belly and nose with a white prop' spinner and black-painted corkscrew lines like a top. I tried to contact anyone on intercom but there was no sound.

'Pips' Priller had singled out *Snoozy II* (he identified it as a Liberator!) and he pumped cannon and machine-gun fire into the B-17 leaving Olsen and Gates dead in their blood-spattered cockpit. T/Sgt Erwin Wissenbeck, who was knocked out of his top turret, came to and found Olsen was leaning far out of his seat, bleeding profusely, and Joseph N Gates was slumped over his wheel. Also dead were T/Sgt Thomas W Dynan, the radio man, S/Sgt Bruce Nicholson, waist gunner, Wilder and Kaylor. La Chasse wrote later: 'From behind came a hell of a thumping noise. We had taken a full burst of 20mm cannon into the flight deck. Shortly thereafter the sun went by the nose as the ship went into a flat spin. We were lucky: it could have been in a tight vertical spin. Bill Gise, our navigator, got caught in the centrifugal force of the spin. Everything loose flew through the air and plastered on the side of the ship. We finally made it back to the escape hatch to bale out into the "wild blue yonder". I followed Gise out after some trouble with the hatch. God must have opened it. The ride down was just like the book on parachutes said it would be: scary but nice. I was alive.' La Chasse, Gise and Wissenbeck were the only three to bale out.

Three other bombers were lost. Two of them fell to JG26. III./JG26 engaged the four-engined American bombers in combat for the first time on this day. From the recollections of Oblt Otto Stammberger, leading the 9th Staffel, it becomes clear that for both sides it was quite a novel experience:

On 9 October the Staffel had just landed under my command at Wevelghem, when around 0830 hours we were scrambled. We should climb into the direction of St Omer. However, we didn't gather systematically as when we were flying at a height of 3,500 to 4,000 metres, we already spotted a quite large pile of formidable fat bluebottles, which were approaching from the direction of St Omer. They were American bombers of the Boeing B-17 type. They were not flying in a tight formation, as they flew in three rows and all 'vics' obviously flew higgledy-piggledy. Up to a height of 6,000 metres, vics of Viermots were cruising along and above these I saw the vapour trails of fighter aircraft. In the meantime, the bombers had flown just past the west of Lille. Until we arrived at the bombers, the stream had turned tightly to the left and to the south of Lille, and at last I got into a firing position.

We charged into the single vics with our fighters attacking in pairs. We came in from behind, throttled back and fired our guns. The things grew bigger and bigger and all our attacks were commenced and broken off much too early, as we were afraid of flying into the 'barn doors'. I was wondering why I didn't register any hits, until I thought about the size of the lumps: a wing span of forty metres! Therefore, charge in at much closer range and so fast that nothing would happen to us anyway. Then commence firing, starting with the engines in the left wing. At my third pass, both engines were on fire, and I succeeded in hitting the right outer engine as well, which belched forth smoke, and the 'Kahn' [Luftwaffe slang for 'ship'] plunged down to the left and towards the ground in wide spirals. At a height of some 2,000 metres, four or five men baled out and to the east of Vendeville and the 'Kasten' [slang for very large aircraft] crashed. I watched this from above and then I decided to go after the others. Yet miraculously, the sky was empty! Anyway, I was out of ammo for my cannons so I backed out towards home.

Hptm Klaus Mietusch, meanwhile, led his 7th Staffel in an attack on the Liberators, which he mistook for British Stirling bombers. He despatched *Big Eagle* of the 93rd BG near Lille (a second 93rd BG B-24 crash-landed at Northolt). Then Mietusch pursued a B-17. Return fire downed his wingman, Uffz Viktor Hager, who baled out badly wounded, but he could not open his parachute and he fell to his death. Mietusch made a second pass and damaged the B-17. It got as far as the Channel. 1/Lt James M Stewart's *Man O'War* lost the No. 2 engine, then both outboard engines began to overheat and lose power. Stewart nursed the ailing ship to the Channel and was prepared to ditch until a lone Spitfire flown by F/Lt A J Andrews of 91 Squadron turned up and guided him safely to Manston. Capt Alexander Simpson's B-24 in the 93rd Bomb Group was also missing in action.

Only sixty-nine bombers hit their primary targets and many of the bombs failed to explode. The inexperienced 93rd and 306th had placed many of their bombs outside the target area, killing a number of French civilians. Traffic control was bad and some of the bombardiers never got the target in their bombsights. During the post-mission interrogations crews revealed that they had made 242 encounters with Luftwaffe fighters and put in fighter claims for forty-eight destroyed, eighteen probably destroyed and four damaged. With so many gunners firing at the same targets it was inevitable that 'scores' would be duplicated. When the heat of the Lille battle had died away the American gunners' scores were whittled down to 25–38–44 and, finally, 21–21–15 (the Germans lost only one fighter). At the time the figures did much to compensate for the largely inaccurate bombing.

On 20 October 1942 Brigadier-General Asa N Duncan, Chief of the Air Staff, issued a revised set of objectives to be carried out by VIIIth Bomber Command. In part it stated, '. . . Until further orders, every effort of the VIIIth Bomber Command will be directed to obtaining the maximum destruction of the submarine bases in the Bay of Biscay . . .' On 21 October some sixty-six B-17s from the 97th, 301st and 306th BGs, and twenty-four B-24s, were despatched to Keroman, about eleven miles from Lorient. The two forces flew a long over-water flight in the Bay of Biscay to reduce the threat of Luftwaffe interception. However, thick cloud at their prescribed bombing altitude of 22,000ft forced all except the fifteen Fortresses of the 97th BG to return to England. The 97th BG bombed the target but just after re-crossing the French coast they were bounced by a swarm of yellow-nosed Fw 190s. The attacks were ferocious and incessant and centred upon the rear of the formation. Three B-17s were shot down and six were badly damaged. The 97th now had the highest losses of any group to date.

On 1 November the 91st BG made its inaugural mission when VIIIth Bomber Command went to Brest and came through without loss. On 7 November the VIIIth returned to Brest. Heavy cloud ruled out accurate bombing and while in the target area the 306th BG were jumped by about twenty enemy fighters but they failed to down any of the B-17s. Lt Julian A Harvey, pilot of *Hellsadroppin'* in the 93rd BG, crashed at Exeter after sustaining battle damage to his Liberator. Next day thirty Fw 190s made at least 200 attacks on the five B-17s of the 369th Squadron, which chose to make a second run on their target at Lille. Capt Richard D Adams' B-17 was downed by flak. Bombing altitudes were getting lower and lower and next day, 9 November, when forty-seven B-17s and B-24s ventured to St Nazaire, three Fortresses in the 306th BG were shot down in rapid succession by flak.

On 17 November the 303rd BG flew their maiden mission, when the VIIIth went to St Nazaire. Twenty miles north-west of the target the

306th BG, bringing up the rear of the formation, were hit by fifteen Fw 190s. The Luftwaffe fighters caused mayhem and casualties. Capt Robert C Williams in *Chennault's Pappy* was badly shot up and force-landed at Exeter. It never flew again. Next day *Floozy* was shot down by a combination of flak and fighters over St Nazaire and it crashed in the Bay of Biscay. Later, the German fighter pilots who had shot them down visited the survivors in hospital. *Katy Bug* from the 93rd Bomb Group crashed at Alconbury killing four of the crew.

On 23 November Col Curtis E LeMay's 305th BG was blooded. Some fifty-eight Fortresses set out from their advance base at Davidstowe Moor for a raid on St Nazaire. Bad weather and mechanical problems forced thirteen B-17s to abort, leaving forty-four B-17s in formation. On previous missions the B-17s had been intercepted from the rear where enough guns could be brought to bear on enemy fighters. However, Luftwaffe experiments had now proved that the frontal area of a B-17 offered very little in defensive firepower and despite the dangers of very high closing speeds this was now considered the best method of shooting them down. Obstlt Egon Mayer, commander of III./JG2, who led the attacking fighters this day, is credited with developing the head-on attack. Fw Fritz Ungar, fighter pilot with JG54 and JG26 between August 1943 and May 1945 (scored three confirmed kills), tells of the head-on tactics: 'During an attack from behind, we were under defensive fire from the bombers too long, and at least three machine-gun positions fired at us from each aircraft. In addition, the escorting fighters had the task of keeping us away from the bombers. So, we had no option left but to attack from head-on. Everything went very quick in this tactic, every second brought us 220 metres closer together! And of course, we didn't want to collide, but pull away over the bomber. For this pulling up and over the bomber, one needed almost the whole last two seconds [= 400 metres]. Our guns were adjusted to 400 metres. Therefore, we had two options: to fire too early, already at a distance of 600 or 500 metres, or to pull up half a second later. A very dangerous business. We didn't have one second to fire our guns. It is incredible, when one thinks of all the efforts we had to make for just one second. One thing was absolutely necessary: aim very precisely for this short moment.'

The new tactic worked well. The 91st lost two bombers to head-on attacks and the commanders of the 322nd and 323rd Squadrons, the group navigator, bombardier and gunnery officers, were among the casualties. Two other B-17s were badly hit, one of which crashed near

Leavesden, Hertfordshire while trying to make it home to Bassingbourn and three of the crew were killed. *Quitchurbitchin'* was the only 91st B-17 to return. *Lady Fairweather* from the 303rd BG was shot down in flames near the target and 1/Lt Clay Isbell's B-17 in the 306th BG was shot down on the bomb run. Isbell and six of his crew were trapped when the Fortress exploded.

Pin-prick raids continued to be made on the U-boat pens. Eaker was not helped by the decision to send three squadrons (twenty-four Liberators) of the 93rd BG to North Africa on 6 December but this was offset to a degree by the 67th Bomb Squadron in the 44th BG at last receiving its full quota of B-24Ds. It enabled the Eightballs to fly its first full Group mission the same day. Some nineteen B-24Ds took off from Shipdham and flew a diversionary mission to the JG26 base at Abbeville–Drucat airfield, while thirty-six B-17s attacked the Atelier d'Hellemmes locomotive works at Lille. The attacking formations were covered by sixteen squadrons of RAF Spitfires but it did not deter the Luftwaffe, which attacked in some strength. In one of the fighter attacks a 305th BG B-17 flown by William A Prentice, 422nd Squadron, went down in flames ten minutes from the target, possibly by Uffz Schnell of 3./JG26, who shot down a bomber west of Etaples. All the crew were killed.

Near the French coast an abort signal was radioed to the 44th after British radar tracked oncoming enemy aircraft. Unfortunately, only the 66th and 67th Squadrons received the signal, leaving six B-24s of the 68th Squadron to continue to the target alone. No. 6 Staffel of JG1 came to the rescue of the Abbeville Kids and Ofw Hans Ehlers and Uffz Wloschinski each claimed a bomber (it was Ehler's seventeenth confirmed kill, Wloschinski's first). The 44th BG lost one B-24D, a 68th Squadron Liberator captained by 1/Lt James D Dubard Jr. Their bomber was attacked by upwards of thirty fighters in waves of two or three from twelve o'clock high, and very early in the battle Dubard lost his No. 4 engine and had the No. 3 damaged. Dubard and his co-pilot, 2/Lt Henry B Kaitala, fought valiantly to keep in formation but they could not maintain speed on the remaining engines and were picked off by the fighters. Although they must have known that they were doomed to a watery grave, none of the crew baled out, choosing instead to keep firing and take as many fighters with them as possible. For their bravery and gallant action each man was awarded a posthumous Silver Star.

It was not a completely one-sided affair, however, on 6 December. 1./JG26 lost one of its most promising pilots in the air combats near

41

Etaples when Lt Graf Uiberacker did not return from his 169th 'Feindflug'. Two days previously he had claimed his seventh victim in air combat.

The Eightballs were out again on 20 December when the bombers raided the airfield at Romilly-sur-Seine, 150 miles south-east of Paris. Capt Howard F Adams, pilot of *Maisie* in the 66th Squadron, recorded in his diary:

> I was leading the second element of four planes while Col Taylor and 'Wild Bill' McCoy led the first element of the 66th. It was bitter cold – way below zero – but in a few minutes, we all forgot about that as we were attacked by some Fw 190s. I closed in behind the first element until we almost touched wingtips, but all of a sudden a Fw 190 came down in a screaming dive shooting at Major Key's ship just ahead of me and passing between him and my ship. This was my first sight of a German plane despite the fact that I have been in England almost three months now! He was so close that I could easily see the pilot and the beautiful yellow and silver markings of the plane. I watched him until he disappeared some five or six thousand feet below us but it didn't take long as he was going close to 600mph. I was too busy to be scared but managed to call the crew on the interphone and told them to keep their eyes peeled for more fighters.
>
> My navigator had fired a quick burst on his .50 calibre nose gun at the first Fw 190 to no avail. It took all my time and energy to keep in tight formation and so I did not see Paris as we passed almost over it. The Germans kept buzzing around us but I didn't see them. One of them dived on Major Key's ship just to my front and fired his 20mm which hit one of the gunners square in the head and that was the end of him. Now and again I would hear a short burst from one of our guns and would look over at my tiny co-pilot, 2/Lt Stanley M McLeod, huddled underneath his steel helmet. I returned his weak smile and went back to flying which was real work now as my fingers were like ice and my oxygen mask was full of water and ice. Every once in a while my plane would rock viciously, and I knew that the flak was getting uncomfortably close. Being faster than the B-17s we flew back and forth over the top of them, finally working our way up so we were in the middle of the formation, which was lucky as the Fw 190s were concentrating on the front and rear. We continued our running dogfight and after a wee bit, I saw Paris spread out beneath us. The Eiffel Tower stood out like a sore thumb even from our altitude.
>
> It was not long before I saw several squadrons of RAF Spitfires cutting capers high above us. The white vapour trails against the blue sky was a

beautiful and comfortable sight. *Maisie* roared along as faithful as ever, but I thought I never would reach the English Channel. We soon passed up the B-17s and headed for home feeling very happy and gay about our good luck. We chattered over the interphone like silly schoolboys though when our radio operator told us that there was a wounded man on Major Key's ship we sobered up some. I peeled off and landed very cold and tired. Food and sleep were all we could think about after our five-hour ordeal. So ended our first real raid!

On 13 January 1943, when seventy-two B-17s went to Fives–Lille, the fighters struck again, even though the 44th went on a diversionary raid over to the Dutch coast in an attempt to draw them away from the real raid. Howard Adams brought up the rear of the seventeen-ship formation. He wrote: 'As the sun streamed into the cockpit a feeling of peace and serenity settled over me as I lazily shifted back and forth behind our leader, "Wild Bill" McCoy. The German fighters and the bark of their guns were remote from my thoughts though the ever-present sense of danger kept us all on our toes.' For the B-17s, the contrast could not have been more different. Singled out for attack this time were the leading 305th BG which were forced to defend themselves against upwards of twenty-five Fw 190s from I and II./JG26. They attacked in line astern, making their attacks from head-on at the same altitude as the Fortresses. They downed the B-17 flown by Conrad J Hilbinger's crew, and damaged another ten. Major T H Taylor, 364th Squadron CO, who was flying with Brigadier-General Hansell, CO 1st Bomb Wing, in *Dry Martini II*, was killed by a cannon shell in the chest during one of the attacks.

The Luftwaffe revised its tactics deciding that simultaneous attacks would produce more casualties than attacking in trail. The new tactics were tried on 23 January when the Americans attacked Lorient, and five bombers were shot down. Four days later, on 27 January, VIIIth Bomber Command attacked Germany for the first time. Some sixty-four B-17s and Liberators started the mission, to the naval base at Wilhelmshaven on the north-west German coast, but by the time the target was reached only fifty-five Fortresses remained. The 306th BG led the mission with Col Frank A Armstrong, the CO, in the lead ship. Crews reported being attacked by about fifty fighters, including some twin-engined types. Jagdgeschwader 1 lost seven fighters and four pilots killed. Nine bombers were claimed shot down. Oblt Hugo Frey, Lt Dieter Gerhard and Uffzs Herbert Hänel and Löhr, the last two sharing the spoils were the claimants. (Hänel was killed just three days later, while shooting down an RAF Wellington, thirty-five kilometres north-west of Terschelling on 30 January. His Fw 190A-4 was hit by debris and plunged into the North Sea.) In actuality, the Americans lost three ships, one of them a 305th BG B-17 piloted by Lt Vance W Beckham. Only five men survived.

Howard Adams, who had to abort the mission at 17,000ft with a clogged line to the supercharger on No. 3 engine, went down to watch the others return to Shipdham after dinner and noticed that two Liberators were missing. He wrote:

Later I found out that they were my friend and West Point classmate, 1/Lt Maxwell W Sullivan [flying *Spirit of 76*], and a Lt [Nolan B] Cargile, both of the 68th. On talking with the others, I learned what had happened. As they neared the German border around thirty enemy fighters came up to meet them – mostly Fw 190s and Me 109s. For around half an hour they were under attack and not being able to find their target, they dropped their bombs on a [Dutch] coastal town [at Lemmer]. During one of the numerous frontal attacks, the Huns scored a hit on Sully's No. 3 engine, setting it on fire, which soon grew in fury as he dropped out of formation. Soon the fire had burnt a large section of the wing away and in no time the right wing folded back along the fuselage and Sully plummeted down [into Terschelling harbour] for his last landing. The crews in the other planes watched helplessly as his plane disintegrated in the air and fell into the sea like a burning rag. Two men were seen to jump out and float towards the sea in their parachutes. A third man jumped but his chute trailed out behind him, never seeming to open fully. Their fate is still unknown. [Lt Albert W Glass was the only survivor but he had to have a leg amputated after being rescued.]

A little while later another Fw 190 came in on a head-on attack aiming at Cargile's plane. Either through accident or design, as he went to turn away, his wing clipped the wing and then the right tail fin of Cargile's B-24, knocking both off. The Fw 190 [possibly Fw Fritz Koch of 12 Staffel JG1, who was apparently killed by fire from a 68th Squadron Liberator] seemed to fold up and then go into its last dive. With part of his wing gone the big B-24 dropped away like a fluttering leaf, finally going into a tight spin, its fate sealed. None of the crew was seen to jump. Capt Wilkinson, a very swell fellow and friend, was the navigator in Sullivan's ship. As the attack continued many of our ships were shot up, but no more were knocked down. Capt O'Brien, also of the 68th, had a waist gunner and

44

bombardier killed and his navigator wounded. Nearly every ship had a hole in it somewhere, Billings having a shell come through the cabin between him and his co-pilot. Everyone was sobered up by this raid and we're beginning to realize that war is no picnic.

Gunners claimed 22–14–13 enemy fighters. Again the figures were inflated: JG1, for instance, lost just seven Fw 190A-4s and Bf 109G-1s with four pilots killed.

Another change in Luftwaffe tactics saw the first use of night fighters of NJG1 against American formations on 4 February, when eighty-six bombers attacked Emden, Hamm and Osnabruck. It was believed that the heavily armed Bf 110 night fighters would bolster the day fighter arm and prove effective against American day bombers. Hptm Hans-Joachim Jabs led eight Bf 110s of IV./NJG 1 into action against the B-17s. Jabs was a seasoned combat veteran who had his first taste of action during the Battles of France and Britain when he served as a 'Zerstörer' ('Destroyer') pilot in Bf 110s with ZG76. He quickly became one of the leading fighter pilots in the Bf 110 day fighter force with seven aircraft shot down during the Battle of France and another twelve Spitfires and Hurricanes over England during the summer of 1940. For these excellent feats of arms, bearing in mind that the Bf 110 was clearly outdated in daylight air combat by 1940, he was decorated with the Ritterkreuz in October 1940, and thereupon successfully led his 6./ZG76 during the campaign in Crete. His Staffel became 9./NJG3 in November 1941, and on completion of night fighter training Jabs became an operational night fighter pilot. He went on to claim his first night kill in June 1942 and was appointed Staffelkapitän of the élite 11./NJG1 at Leeuwarden in November 1942. By the end of 1942 he had shot down four RAF night bombers.

Jabs, therefore, was well qualified to lead the Bf 110s against the American combat boxes, on 4 February, for the first time. Although Jabs, Ofw Grimm and Uffz Naumann claim three B-17s shot down in the ensuing combat – among which was *El Lobo*, a 305th BG B-17 flown by Lt Cornelius Λ Jenkins, with five men killed – IV./NJG1 paid dearly. All eight Bf 110s were badly damaged; two made belly-landings on Ameland and near Leeuwarden. For the coming night, none of these aircraft would be serviceable to combat the RAF night bombers. The 305th BG lost a second B-17 when a Fw 190 slammed into *What's Cookin' Doc?*, flown by Lt William K Davidson. All the crew were killed. Three more B-17s, two from the 91st BG and one from the 303rd,

45

were lost on the mission. Fw 190s of JG1 claimed ten B-17s shot down for the loss of two pilots, Oblt Walter Leonhardt (Stkap of 6./JG1) and Uffz Rudolf Mayer (12./JG1).

Bad weather intervened and it was not until 16 February that the bombers could go all the way to their target, at St Nazaire. Two B-24Ds of the 44th BG were lost when they collided over the Channel. III./JG2 and 9./JG26 made aggressive attacks on the bomber formations and four bombers were shot down. Lt Otto 'Stotto' Stammberger led 9./JG26 and hit one Fortress in the cockpit. He saw it fall from formation but was then hit in the hand and he had to dive away. Another spell of bad weather prevented any missions being flown by the 8th Air Force until 26 February when Bremen was the target for the day. The 44th Bomb Group taxied out at Shipdham in sombre mood. The day before, the 66th Squadron had suffered the loss of popular pilot Captain 'Wild Bill' McCoy and his crew when their Liberator lost its tail assembly at 4,000ft during a training flight. Immediately after, the Liberator went into a flat spin and dived into the ground, killing everyone on impact. For the Bremen mission the 66th Squadron sent out six aircraft, including *Sad Sack*, flown by 1/Lt Robert H McPhillamey and 1/Lt Wilbur E Wockenfuss and crew, and *Maisie*, which as usual was being flown by Howard Adams and Stanley McLeod. McPhillamey and Adams had recently flown their B-24s to Langford Lodge in Northern Ireland for modifications, and while they waited had spent an enjoyable two days in Belfast 'taking in a show and window shopping'. As they taxied out at Shipdham, Adams' mascot, a little wooden doll of the same name, swung gently from the cabin windshield in front of him and his co-pilot. The crew had also found room for Robert Perkins Post, a *New York Times* war correspondent, the only one of seven in the 'Writing 69th' who had asked to fly with the Eightballs on the mission.

At airfields on the Continent, Luftwaffe fighter pilots lay in wait for the Liberators and B-17 Flying Fortresses. Once again night fighter crews too were ordered to stand by. At Leeuwarden thirty-year-old Hptm Ludwig Becker, Staffelkapitän of 12./NJG1 and a great night fighting tactician with forty-four night victories, waited to fly his very first daylight mission. Becker had scored his first kill on 16 October 1940 when he downed a Wellington of 311 Squadron RAF, and in 1941–42 he had developed into one of the leading 'Experten' in the Luftwaffe night fighter arm. He not only shot down forty bombers in 1942 but also taught the new and young crews from his experiences. To them Becker was an inspiring fatherly figure. The 'Night Fighting

Professor', as he was dubbed, was instrumental in introducing the Lichtenstein AI radar into the night fighter arm in 1941. Most of the night fighter aircrew were sceptical about this new gadget – they liked to rely on the 'Mk I Eyeball' – but Becker took the lead and had one of the still experimental sets installed in his Do 217Z night fighter at Leeuwarden aerodrome. Guided by the revolutionary radar, he shot down no less than six RAF night bombers between 8/9 August and 29/30 September 1941. Most of his colleagues and the Luftwaffe High Command were now convinced that the AI radar was an invaluable new asset in the night battle against the British bombers, and the Lichtenstein went into mass production shortly after. In the course of 1942, most of the Luftwaffe night fighters were equipped with the AI.

Shortly before taking off from Leeuwarden in a formation of twelve Bf 110s, again led by Hptm Jabs, in pursuit of the American daylight raiders Becker was informed of the award of the Oak Leaves to his Knight's Cross which had been bestowed on him on 1 July 1942, after his twenty-fifth night victory, for his leading role in the development of the night fighter arm. Completely at ease and master in the night battle against the British bombing offensive, Becker fell victim to the gunners of B-17s and B-24s of the 1st and 2nd Bomb Wings.

At 1135 hours IV./JG1 had taken off from Leeuwarden and intercepted the B-17s and B-24s. They returned, claiming two shot down but had lost Becker's Bf 110. Almost an hour earlier, Lt Heinz Knoke and eleven other pilots in I./JG1 took off from Jever–Wangerooge. They returned having shot down five B-17s and B-24s (they claimed thirteen bombers!). Among the Fortress groups the 91st BG lost two and the 305th BG three B-17s. About fifteen minutes from Bremen Lt George E Stallman's B-17, the lowest in the entire formation, came under attack from two Bf 109s. They made several passes and the Fortress took hits in the right wing and No. 4 engine, knocking the ship out of formation. A burst of flak hit Stallman's B-17 as he tried in vain to catch up with the 305th BG formation over Wilhelmshaven and the crew were ordered to bale out. The other two ships in the 305th BG that were lost belonged to Captain Trippet and Lt Benson.

The Liberators too were set upon by I./JG1. The German fighters had begun their attacks some thirty miles off the coast and they were so determined in their mission that the attacks would continue all the way into the target. *Night Raider*, also called *Heavenly Hideaway*, a 93rd Bomb Group B-24D flown by Capt Beattie H 'Bud' Fleenor, limped away from the target area with a supercharger out, flak holes in its fuselage, and a pair of useless tail guns which had frozen tight after only eight rounds. Fleenor's B-24 was attacked again and again. T/Sgt Lou Szabo, waist gunner, said later: 'A Fw 190 came towards us. His wings were pure red. I could almost see the lead coming point-blank. I froze on to the trigger. His left wing dropped off – he went hell-bent into the water. But he'd fired first and hit Jung [S/Sgt Robert P Jungbluth, the radio operator] and me. I knew Jung was hurt worse than I was. I looked up and saw part of his arm hanging above the window, looked around and saw his side intact. The 20mm blast had ripped Jung's arm from his body, and the shrapnel had hit us both.' Szabo had over eighty pieces lodged in his body. Incredibly, *Night Raider* made it back to crash-land at Ludham, Norfolk with a badly wounded crew, no hydraulic system, punctured tyres, a fifteen-inch hole in the right tail flap and 177 .30 and 20mm cannon shell holes in the aircraft. One ground crew man said, 'This one shouldn't have come back.' Either Uffz Heinz Hanke of 9./JG1, in a Fw 190, or Uffz Wennekers of 2./JG1, in a Bf 109, had claimed the apparently doomed B-24 as their first victory.

Sad Sack, a 44th BG ship captained by Robert McPhillamey, was also shot down by one of these two pilots. McPhillamey wrote later: 'They picked me off shortly before we reached the IP. Two engines were shot out and on fire. The oxygen was shot out and there was a fire in the bomb bay. Controls, elevators, wings etc., were also badly hit and the plane became inoperable.' Wilbur Wockenfuss adds: 'We could see the coast of Sweden and opted to try for it but it soon became apparent to all of us that it was hopeless.' Under these conditions McPhillamey gave the order to bale out. 'At the time that all of this was happening we were flying near 30,000ft but couldn't go any higher to avoid the prop wash of the B-17s. 2/Lt Rexford W Lippert, the navigator, was killed instantly in the plane by a 20mm shell which decapitated him. S/Sgt Robert P Garmon, waist gunner, was hit in the knee just as he baled out. Sgt Alberto O Salvo, the belly gunner, was hit in the shoulder and chest, and in several other places, but managed to bale out with the rest of us. He died in a hospital shortly thereafter. After the crew was out (I thought) I started to leave as well but our engineer, Sgt Eugene Rudiger, had passed out from lack of oxygen and was blocking the exit. I must have beaten and abused him very badly when trying to get past him. I finally made it and was about to jump when something stopped me. I thought, "My God! I can't leave the engineer." I reached back and grabbed him by the collar of his fur flying jacket and backed towards the bomb bay, falling out and dragging him with me. I saw him later on the ground and it looked like he had been through a meat grinder. I never did tell him that I had almost beaten him to death trying to get past him. I reasoned that he must have regained consciousness on the way down and pulled the rip cord.'

Since the island of Texel, when the Liberators had first come under attack, *Maisie* had dropped behind, so 2/Lt Wayne Gotke, navigator, had spent most of the time working with position reports trying to get short-cuts filled into the flight to allow Howard Adams to gain and catch the rest of the formation. Gotke was to recall later: 'We fought off the planes with very minor damage until we almost reached Oldenburg, then all hell broke loose. However, I am reasonably sure no one was injured up to this point. When we were almost to Oldenburg, fighters hit us from all sides.' Heinz Knoke drew closer, and takes up the story: 'I must have opened the throttle subconsciously. I can distinguish the individual enemy aircraft now. Most of them are Liberators. They look as if their fat bellies were pregnant with bombs. I pick out my target. "This is where I settle your hash, my friend," I mutter. I shall make a frontal attack. The Yank is focused in my sights. He grows rapidly larger. I reach for the firing buttons on the stick. Tracers come whizzing past my head. They have opened fire on me!' T/Sgt Robert K Vogt, the engineer and top turret gunner, had swivelled his turret into the line of Knoke's fighter and taken aim. From the nose Wayne Gotke and S/Sgt James W Mifflin, assistant radio man, also let loose with their .5 calibres. Only Sgt William Welsh, the belly gunner, who passed out from lack of oxygen, was unable to open fire. Gotke thought that as far as he knew 'he never regained his senses'. Knoke was unharmed by the return fire from *Maisie*. Now it was his turn: 'Fire! I press both buttons, but my aim is poor. I can see only a few hits register in the right wing. I almost scrape the fat belly as I dive past. Then I am caught in the slipstream, buffeted about so violently that for a second I wonder if my tailplane has been shot away. I climb up steeply and break away to the left. Tracers pursue me, unpleasantly close. Blast all this metal in the air! I come in for a second frontal attack, this time from a little below. I keep on firing until I have to swerve to avoid a collision. My salvos register this time. I drop away below. As I turn my head, flames are spreading along the bottom of the fuselage of my Liberator. It sheers away from the formation in a wide sweep to the right. Twice more I come in to attack, this time diving from above the tail. I am met by heavy defensive fire.'

In the heat and turmoil of battle, confusion reigned aboard the devastated Liberator. Wayne Gotke claimed later that 'Robert Vogt, the engineer and top turret gunner, shot down the first fighter (*sic*) and I shot down the next one (*sic*) but not until he had sent 20mms into the nose and cockpit. Sgt Mifflin shot down the third (*sic*) from his waist position. At this point my left gun jammed and I know at least two planes made direct hits on our nose and flight deck. Someone, I am not sure who, was hurt on the flight deck, and I was hit twice in the nose of the ship operating a jammed gun. 2/Lt Bill Hannan, bombardier, was riding in the nose with me and was uninjured up to this point. He had passed out twice from lack of oxygen [crimped oxygen supply hose] and I had replaced his mask and straightened the hose to bring him back to normal. Engine Nos. 3 and 4 had been hit and were on fire.'

Knoke's shells had indeed found their mark but the B-24 gunners had not hit the incoming fighter. The only shudders Knoke was experiencing were those caused by the recoil from his two cannons and 13mm guns. He watched his cannon shell bursts rake along the top of the fuselage and right wing of the doomed Liberator. He hung on to the stick with both hands. Knoke wrote: 'The fire spreads along the right wing. The inside engine stops. Suddenly, the wing breaks off altogether. The body of the stricken monster plunges vertically, spinning into the depths. A long black trail of smoke marks its descent. One of the crew attempts to bale out but his parachute is in flames. Poor devil! The body somersaults and falls to the ground like a stone. At an altitude of 3,000ft there is a tremendous explosion, which causes the spinning fuselage to disintegrate . . .'

Wayne Gotke was working on his guns when, all at once, 'it seemed as if someone pushed me from behind, and all went black. I woke up falling through space and I pulled my rip cord, but with no results! So I reached back and tore the back off my chute and quickly pulled as much of the material out as possible until it all opened. My last look at our altimeter in the ship was at 26,000ft.' Knoke recounts the events following the Liberator's crash:

Fragments of blazing wreckage land on a farm 200 or 300 yards from the Zwischenahn airfield, and the exploding fuel tanks set the farm buildings on fire. In a terrific power dive I follow my victim down, and land on the runway below. I run over to the scene of the crash. A crowd of people are there, trying to fight the fire in the farmhouse. I join in the rescue work and bring out furniture, animals and machinery from the burning buildings. Smoke blinds and chokes me, my flying suit is scorched by the flames, as

I drag a fat pig out by the hind legs, squealing like mad, from the pig-sty, which is completely gutted by fire. The farmhouse and barns are saved. Strewn all over the cow field lies the wreckage of the Liberator. The explosion threw the crew out in mid-air. Their shattered bodies lie beside the smoking remains of the aircraft. One hundred yards away I find the captain's seat and the nose wheel. A little doll, evidently the mascot, sits undamaged between the shattered windows of the cabin.

One hour later I land at Jever. My men carry me shoulder-high to the dispersal point. That was my fourth victory, on my 164th mission . . . I cannot help thinking about the bodies of the American crew. When will our turn come? Those men share, in common with ourselves, the great adventure of flying. Separated for the moment by the barrier of war, we shall one day be reunited by death in the air.

Two men had survived from the doomed Liberator. Wayne Gotke was picked up after 'dangling between two trees about twenty feet in the air for about twenty-five minutes', afraid that if he unbuckled he would fall badly. 'It was at the first-aid station that I saw S/Sgt Mifflin. Also there was Lt Wockenfuss, the co-pilot of the other ship that was shot down.' Wockenfuss had landed about a hundred yards from the main gate of a German Army camp where he was met by dozens of excited soldiers. He had said 'Hello' in his best German and one of the Germans responded, 'Hello! For you the war is over!' He had lived in Cleveland, Ohio for seventeen years! The Germans told him that the enlisted men from the crew had landed safely and were being interned. McPhillamey landed near a small village close to Oldenburg and was captured immediately after a couple of shots were fired in his direction. He ran into Mooney, Wockenfuss and two others of his crew at a police station in Oldenburg. Gotke continues: 'Wockenfuss said he had seen Captain Adams' leather jacket and it appeared the man had been killed. The Germans had obtained the ship's loading list from the jacket and asked me about a Robert P Post, the *New York Times* correspondent who was flying with us. I gave them no information whatsoever as my orders were to say nothing in the hope that if men were at large their chances of getting home would be better. The Germans asked questions about Donald Bowie, one of the gunners, and Hannan, and from that I believe these two men could not be identified. I am under the impression that all the bodies were not found, or if found, could not be identified. Positive identification of the body of Robert Post was never made. His father, Waldron K Post, continued to search for his son's grave or official verification as to the disposition of Robert long after the end of the war, but with no apparent success.'

Bremen was the last mission of the month for the Eightballs. February had been a bad month for the 66th Squadron, which had lost three ships and their crews. Ironically, the hardest loss to come to terms with was McCoy's, who had perished in an accident, not at the hands of the Luftwaffe. Combat losses were to be expected and, although not liked, were accepted as part of the game of war.

CHAPTER 3

SCOURGE OF THE 'VIERMOTS'

Twenty-two-year-old night fighter pilot Lt Dieter Schmidt-Barbo had joined 8./NJG1 in September 1941 at Twente airfield near Enschede on the Dutch-German border. As with many young and enthusiastic but inexperienced night fighter crews, he only got a few opportunities to prove himself in the Himmelbett night fighting system – the most experienced and successful crews were usually assigned to the 'best' Himmelbett zones where they kept accumulating their 'Abschüsse'. Keen but green men like Schmidt-Barbo had to wait or patrol in those zones which were seldom flown through by the RAF bombers. In the spring of 1943 the round-the-clock bombing of western Germany presented an opportunity to pilots like Schmidt-Barbo to score his first victory, albeit in daylight, against American bomber formations. Schmidt-Barbo recalls:

Because the German Fighter Arm at this time was engaged mainly in operations over the Eastern Front, and had only a few units at its disposal in the west, we were at this time called in to repel these American attacks. This meant that we had to be at readiness both day and night, and our aircraft constantly had to be modified. Well, we usually were much too late to take off and intercept the Americans. However, on 4 March, it was a different story.

10.30 a.m. I am still in bed when I receive a call from Werner Rapp (who on this day is our unit's officer in charge of day fighting). 'The whole Squadron on "Sitzbereitschaft" [cockpit readiness]!' I inform Gustel Geiger of this message. He tells me, 'What nonsense! We won't catch them anyway and we'll be too late as usual!'

'Well, we'll get out of bed anyway!'

The Chief, Hptm Lütje, has not arrived yet and I phone Werner and ask him if he has arrived with him. Werner is very excited. 'Yes, yes, I've just spoken to him. Aren't you out yet? The Americans will arrive shortly over the airfield. Twenty bombers! End of message!'

Well then, I'll be off. Perhaps I will see them after all. I drive off on my motorcycle, meet Hptm Lütje on my way; he is fetching the aircrews, having slept at the Station HQ. Our aircraft are prepared for the mission. The ground crew technicians have been at work already. I phone Werner once again from the Operations shed and ask him if we should proceed with getting strapped into our machines.

'Yes, where are you for God's sake? How much longer will it take you to get ready; how many crews are at their aircraft?'

'Four.'

'Good, over and out!'

I am now as eager as can be! When all the crews have arrived, I phone once more.

'At last! Yes, of course, everybody get strapped in! Over and out!'

Today I will fly the Kurfürst-Siegfried, a Bf 110G-4. I call in a ground crew member who explains to me the counter of the MG-151 machine-guns and get strapped in as I've done so many times before. Suddenly, I hear on my left side, where the Chief is standing, the roar of his engines, but from the Operations shed no orders have come to take off yet. To be on the safe side, I switch on everything, and there from the left they sign to 'start engines'. When I switch on the engines the thought flashes through my head: 'Keep your fingers crossed and hope no gremlins are in the engines.' The Chief already taxies in front of me. I queue behind his tail. Becker is still in the hangar and I can't see other aircraft. Out on the airfield it's a bit chaotic – in front of us a plane of the 9th takes off. Behind him cross two from the 7th, then one more from the 9th, clouds of dust billowing and the feeling that at last something is going to happen! There, the Chief is accelerating. Should I take off together with him? I hesitate a bit too long and now have my work cut out to get out of his slipstream and the cloud of dust which his plane throws up, but I manage it. I tuck in with him and we fly in the direction of 4-Berta – of the other two only one, Heinzelmann, has managed to take off, as we find out later.

We climb steadily. Over the radio we hear wild chattering but soon this is solved too and we clearly receive the orders from ground control; we have set course for 'Caesar'. The Chief sets course, and there we hear 'Leo's' calm and steady voice: 'Mailcoach [course of the enemy aircraft] 300 or 330.'

I don't listen very carefully to what he says. It is only important to the Chief anyway. Suddenly, he waggles his wings and is speeding up. Something must be going on! I look ahead, but in vain. Our speed is increasing all the time, course north-west. We can already see the Zuider Zee in the distance. Then, all of a sudden I hear over the R/T: 'From Karin

1, message understood. We can still see them.' I ask Schönfeld: 'Karin, that is us three, isn't it?'

'Yes.'

'But I can see zero!'

'Me too.'

Then all at once I see them, in front of us and a little to the right. They are almost over us already. They are cruising along 2,000 metres higher than us, quite a lot of them, four-engined, in close formation. A flight of three on the right outer side of the box, which are not as closely tucked in as the rest, formed vapour trails, which in turn formed black streaks against the blue sky – a very powerful sight. Slowly, we get closer, and now we can see them well. They are Boeings, painted brown on top, which look like dorsal fins. One of them is trailing a bit.

The lone formation that was intercepted in the Texel area comprised sixteen B-17s of the 91st Bomb Group led by Major Paul Fishburne in B-17F 42-5139 *Chief Sly II* of the 322nd Squadron. They had taken off from Bassingbourn and should have formed part of a large force of seventy-one B-17s which were bound for Hamm, but due to very bad visibility over East Anglia and the North Sea, the Groups did not find each other. Fishburne had then taken the decision that the 91st would continue to Hamm alone. (The 303rd and 305th Bomb Groups turned south and successfully bombed the Wilton Feyenoord docks near Rotterdam. The twenty-one B-17s in the 306th Bomb Group aborted the mission and twenty returned to Thurleigh with bombs on board. Captain William Friend's B-17 was badly damaged and set on fire by Uffz Flecks and Uffz Meissner, both of 6./JG1, at 1025 hours, and fell out of formation. The crew probably jettisoned the bomb load while under fighter attack: nine bombs hit two schools and two houses at Den Briel near the Hook. Four Dutchmen were killed, and between sixty and seventy children were dead or missing. The fire took hold and Friend gave the order to bale out over the sea. Seven parachutes were counted yet no survivors were ever reported.)

Fishburne's formation, having bombed Hamm whilst under fighter attack all the time, were returning over Friesland Province in northern Holland when they were attacked by Lt Schmidt-Barbo and his fellow night fighter pilots. As he approached the 91st BG B-17s he saw a single Me 110 already approaching the formation from the rear. Schmidt-Barbo continues:

Our fighters have arrived at last – one or two carry out head-on attacks and streak straight through the formation and the bombers tuck in even more closely together. Heinzelmann is still flying behind me and now we're at the same height as the formation, sixteen in all. Occasionally, the fighters press home their attacks, but they don't attack in close formation. From behind, another one or two Me 110s have arrived at the scene, and one of the 'Amys' that trailed a bit has regained his position in his box. The three of us slowly but steadily fly over the formation and overtake the bombers.

'We will go in for a head-on attack.'

'Understood. Understood.' We are ready. Every now and then I squint at the Boeings. They are now to the right, behind and underneath us. The leading bombers are taking pot shots at us. One can see the threads of the tracer bullets. The weather is fine, a bit hazy but the sky is cloudless. A little while ago the haze in front of us looked like clouds and the 'Amys' descended to get shelter in the clouds, but it was nothing.

In the meantime we have arrived over the mouth of the Zuider Zee, just to the west of Texel, time 11.30 a.m. The Chief is curving towards the formation. I turn with him and there I already have the 'Amys' in front of my nose. We go in a bit from the right to the left. The automatic gunsight is on. Full throttle, and there we go in. I immediately have one in my sights. Aim is in front of him. Press the tit! The guns roar and dust flies around. The tracer curves away over him. Aim a little lower. Press the tit again and I race past him already. There is the next one. Aim precisely. Cracking and banging. Dirt flies around in the cockpit, into my eyes. This time the tracers disappear in his fuselage and wing roots and I flash past. I see no one in front of me any more. What next? One instant I don't know where to head to. There I see in front of me a Me 110 breaking off and curving down. I follow him. The fat one [Schönfeld] gave them a burst with his twin pop guns when we curved away; twenty-eight bullets!

'Are you still alive?'

'Yes.'

'No damage?'

'No.' With me everything is OK. Both engines still running smoothly. Can't see any hits. Great. I look over my shoulder. I'm now underneath and to the right of the formation. As we flew through the formation, I saw one of the leading bombers peeling off and plunging towards the earth, as if to crash-land on Texel. In front of me I see a pair of Me 110s, without flame dampers as far as I can see, so they are from Leeuwarden [IV./NJG1, led by Hptm Jabs and Sigmund]. Where the Chief is, I can't tell. A short distance off Texel, one bomber plunged into the sea. A column of black

56

and white smoke still hangs over the ripples in the water. Another one has sheered off from the formation. I see him to the left and underneath me. Just when I decide to finish him off, I watch how an Me 110 in front of me raced up to the aircraft, and at the same time several Fw 190s also went into the attack, so there is no need for me to share in this! There is no one left near the formation. The Me 110s have also disappeared. We get in touch with the Chief. He will touch down at Bergen. His engines were damaged, but this was not caused by hits during the engagement; the driving unit of the fuel pump had crammed into the engine, so he has to have an engine change.

The B-17 gunners put up stiff resistance in the face of overwhelming odds. Hptm Jabs of IV./NJG1 and his three wingmen finished off a straggler, which had repulsed at least thirty attacks before finally going down. Hptm Lütje then claimed a B-17 at 1131 hours and, shortly after, four Me 110s had finished off another. These were probably B-17F 42-5370 flown by Lt Henderson, and B-17F 41-24512 *Rose O' Day* captained by Lt Felton. Both these B-17s crashed in the sea west of Texel and Den Helder respectively, at 1128 and 1134 hours. The battle raged on for another ten minutes, and B-17F 41-24464 *Excalibur* captained by Lt Brill finally fell victim to a Bf 110, probably of IV./NJG1 flown by Lt Köstler. Brill succeeded in ditching the heavily damaged bomber in very rough seas some forty miles west of Texel, and although it broke in two, the crew managed to get out safely and enter their dinghies. In a six-hour struggle with the high seas, three of the crew drowned before the seven survivors were picked up by an ASR Walrus.

Major Fishburne and Capt James Bullock, his navigator, were both awarded the DFC for successfully leading and completing the mission, and Lt Brill and Lowry, both of whom drowned after ditching their B-17, were posthumously awarded the DFC. The Germans did not escape unscathed. American gunners claimed thirteen destroyed, three probables and four damaged. In fact, both III. and IV./NJG1 lost an Me 110. The attacking Fw 190s of II./JG1 and JG26 suffered no losses. Lt Schmidt-Barbo sums up: 'This was the only daytime mission of the IIIrd Gruppe in this period which resulted in an encounter with the enemy. Losses: Uffz crew Heintszch/Hendel; possibly they were one of the Me 110s that had approached the formation from behind on their own. As the proceedings had clearly shown, our Me 110 which was specially equipped for night fighting duties was much too slow and cumbersome for daytime missions. And especially our crews, apart from the double burden of daytime and night-time missions, were completely inexperienced in daylight air combat. Thus, it was practically suicidal to attack such a formation of Boeings from behind as we were used to do at night. Still, only the death of Hptm Becker during such a daylight attack on 26 February, slowly led to the insight by the "powers that be" that the losses amongst the highly skilled night fighter crews were much too high in comparison to the possible, meagre results. So, after this day, we were not called upon to combat these formations of bombers penetrating our airspace at daytime.'

On 6 March the Eightballs flew their fiftieth mission with a diversionary raid on a bridge and U-boat facilities at Brest while the Fortresses hit the port of Lorient. All ten Liberators returned without mishap. Things were looking up for the B-24s. Mission No. 51 followed on 8 March, when fourteen Liberators of the 44th BG, and some from the 93rd, took part in a raid on the Rouen marshalling yards to divert attention from the B-17s attacking another marshalling yard, at Rennes. Three squadrons of RAF Spitfires and, for the first time, the 4th Fighter Group's P-47C Thunderbolts escorted the bombers. Crews had been told of their involvement at briefing and, understandably, reacted favourably to the news. 1/Lt Leo O Frazier, navigator in 1/Lt Robert W Blaine's crew in the 67th Squadron, wrote later: 'It looked like an easy mission with fighter protection.' It was probably the first good news the ill-fated 67th Squadron had, having begun missions from England with nine crews, but now down to just three original crews.

1/Lt James E O'Brien from the 68th Bomb Squadron started out leading the Eightballs in *The Rugged Buggy* with Lt-Colonel James Posey, the future 44th BG Commanding Officer, aboard, but one of the gunners passed out through lack of oxygen and O'Brien was forced to return to base. Captain Clyde E Price of the 67th Bomb Squadron in *Miss Dianne* took over the Group lead, and 1/Lt Bob W Blaine moved up to the deputy lead. It was just after this that their troubles started. Fw 190s of JG26 attacked from head-on. Unfortunately for the bombers, the Spitfires had met heavy opposition from the Third Gruppe of JG26 led by Major (later Oberst) Josef 'Pips' Priller and the Eightballs were forced to fend for themselves. At first crews mistook the Fw 190s of the Second Gruppe for Thunderbolts because of their similar radial engines. All too late they realised they were not P-47s but the dreaded yellow-nosed Fw 190s, otherwise known as 'The Abbeville Kids'. The fighter attack on the Flying Eightballs was led by Oblt Wilhelm-Ferdinand 'Wutz' Galland, brother of Generalmajor Adolf Galland, who led his Fw

190s of II./JG26 in a tight turn to go 'von Schnauze auf Schnauze' (snout to snout).

The sky was like a black cloud of fighters. *Miss Dianne* and Lt Blaine's B-24s went down immediately. Only three gunners survived from Price's ship, which crashed in flames at Totes at 1404 hours with the bombs still in their racks. S/Sgt Kenneth L Erhart was to write later: 'We were hit by Fw 190s as well as by flak, amidship. Needless to say, with oxygen and hydraulic lines damaged, fire was inevitable. The bale-out bell was sounded. The ship was well aflame. Due to the nose attack, the flight deck personnel did not make it out. I assisted Sgts Iris Wyer and Duane Devars out the right waist window, and also checked on Sgt Fleshman, but he was already dead. [Devars and Wyer were captured a day or two later.] I baled out of the right waist window, and, upon hitting the ground, saw Lt Morton P Gross, the bombardier, coming down. His whole abdomen was ripped open and he died in my arms, with the German soldiers looking on. Lt Gross told me to take his watch and give it to his mother, but the Germans took the watch away from me.' Leo Frazier aboard Blaine's B-24 was to recall later: 'The reason we went down is that we were hit by fighters of Göring's Flying Circus from about two o'clock high, with a cannon shell exploding in the cockpit.' Blaine's ship had been singled out by Uffz Peter Crump. Crump had fired a long burst at the B-24 from long range and could clearly see a number of hits in the cockpit area. He dived away in a split-S, then saw to his horror that he was immediately in the way of Blaine's jettisoned bombs. Crump managed to miss them in a tight turn but lost sight of his target and could not say which of the falling aircraft was his kill. (Blaine's B-24 crashed at Barentin at 1405.) He saw one of the doomed Liberators crash in a patch of trees north of the Seine, but without a witness, Crump would not be awarded confirmation of his victory. Instead, it went to Ofw Roth. Frazier adds. 'I am sure that the co-pilot, Lt Roetto, was killed instantly, but Bob Blaine lived long enough to ring the bale-out alarm. I was the only one that baled out. I was told that the airplane went into a flat spin that caused centrifugal force, preventing the others, if alive, from jumping.'

The Spitfire escort finally showed up in time to prevent further losses. Even so, two Liberators barely made it back to Shipdham. *Peg*, a 93rd BG Liberator, which was attacked by Oblt Johannes Naumann of II./JG26, limped back across the Channel and crashed at Bredhurst, Kent.

On 12 and 13 March, 44th and 93rd Bomb Group Liberators flew diversions for the Fortresses. Then on 18 March General Ira Eaker ordered a maximum effort: seventy-three Fortresses and twenty-four Liberators, the highest number of bombers so far, to attack the Bremer Vulkan Schiffbau shipbuilding yards on the Weser, a few miles north of Bremen. The yards were ranked the fourth largest producer of U-boats in Germany.

At Jever at 1412 hours operation orders for I./JG1 arrived telling the Bf 109 pilots to intercept and attack a formation of heavy bombers approaching the coast of Germany: Heinz Knoke and his comrades had been practising for a few days previously on bombing the tight formations of American bombers from above with 100lb bombs – this was an idea that Lt Gerhardt had come up with in late February 1943. In the early morning of 18 March, Gerhardt and Knoke made a practice flight off Heligoland with each dropping four 100lb bombs on a sack which was towed by a Ju 88; Gerhardt's third bomb was a direct hit and the idea became a reality. However, the 'Alarmstart' (scramble) on 18 March gave the pilots of 5./JG1 too little time to arm their fighters with bombs, and so Knoke decided to attack with guns only on this occasion.

At 25,000ft Lt Heinz Knoke and his fellow pilots made contact with the American formation in the Heligoland area. Knoke led his flight in close formation in head-on attack on the Liberators of the Second Bomb Division. He opened fire on a B-24 flying low right in the 93rd Bomb Group formation. It was *Hot Freight*, flown by 1/Lt Howard E 'Tarzan' Kleinsteuber, which immediately caught fire and fell away to the right like a crippled beast. Knoke pursued it, attacking from the rear, then from head-on. Suddenly, at 1514 hours, *Hot Freight* exploded, hurling wreckage through the sky. Knoke hurled his Fw 190 into a power dive to escape the flying engines and debris and only just managed to miss the falling fuselage of the doomed Liberator which fell into the sea ten kilometres south-east of Heligoland. It was Knoke's fifth victory.

In his diary Knoke says that his friend Dieter Gerhardt's first Liberator 'went down a few minutes before'. In fact, he claimed it at 1537 hours off Heligoland. This could have been *Eager Beaver*, a 93rd BG B-24D, which although badly hit and seen to drop from formation with a smoking engine, made it back to England. Frank Lown, the pilot, was nearly killed when three rounds missed his head by only inches. The crew of *Shoot Luke* (with which Lown had been co-pilot before getting his own ship), flown by George Murphy, accompanied Lown's B-24 home. They too were hit by 20mm cannon fire. S/Sgt Paul B Slankard, the tail gunner, was blasted through the top of his turret by a direct hit from a 20mm shell. He survived, thanks to emergency medical attention given by his crew. Both Liberators made it back to Hardwick and Slankard made a full recovery. Gerhardt, however, did not survive. He was shot down moments later attacking a second 'Viermot'. Though he managed to bale out he died of his wounds in his dinghy. Major John 'The Jerk' Jerstad, who led the 93rd Bomb Group this day, reported that they were under attack from fighters for one hour and forty-five minutes.

Near Heligoland, the B-17s came under attack from the Luftwaffe and the leading 303rd Bomb Group formation of twenty-two aircraft bore the brunt of most of the enemy fighters' venom. During the bomb run the Group also came in for some concentrated and accurate flak. One 303rd BG bomber, with a 92nd BG Group crew flying it, was lost. Capt Harold Stouse brought a badly damaged *The Duchess* home to Molesworth with the dead body of Lt Jack Mathis, the lead bombardier. He was hit during the bomb run by a flak explosion which shattered the nose compartment. His right arm was almost severed above the elbow and he sustained deep wounds in his side and stomach but he got his bombs away before he succumbed. Mathis was posthumously awarded the Congressional Medal of Honor, America's highest military award, for 'conspicuous gallantry and intrepidity above and beyond the call of duty'.

Vegesack was officially described as 'extremely heavily damaged'. The bombers had dropped 268 tons of high explosive smack on the target and later photographic reconnaissance revealed that seven U-boat hulls had been severely damaged, and two-thirds of the shipyards destroyed.

On 22 March eighty-four Liberators and Fortresses attacked U-boat yards at Wilhelmshaven. This day Lt Heinz Knoke carried a 500lb bomb on the underbelly of his Bf 109G, which he dropped in action for the first time, in the midst of a formation of Fortresses. He observed a wing break off from one of the B-17s and it scattered two others. (One B-17 belonging to the 91st BG failed to return from the raid.) 1/Lt Jim O'Brien and Major Francis McDuff, 68th Squadron Commander, led twelve Liberators of the 44th BG in *Rugged Buggy* behind five B-24s of the 93rd BG. Colonel Ted Timberlake, who was leading the 93rd in *Teggie Ann*, narrowly escaped death when a 20mm shell entered the cockpit and missed him by only a few inches. When the Liberator returned to Hardwick there were no less than 368 holes in the aircraft. Jim O'Brien described the mission as 'hot as my first' and later counted twenty-nine separate holes in *Rugged Buggy*. *Maggie*, flown by Capt Gideon 'Bucky' Warne in the 67th Squadron, was damaged by flak over the target area and slowly lost altitude on the return. Lt Robert J Walker, the navigator, wrote: 'We were coming home from Wilhelmshaven when the ship was badly shot up by German fighters. Shortly after several attacks on us, the ship was shot up so badly that we all had to bale out, in spite of the fact that we were out a bit over the North Sea. We all came down in the vicinity of Alte Mellum Island, but into the water. Sgt Klug, the left waist gunner, and I were the first two picked up by a ship headed for Heligoland. Apparently, all others drowned, or died of exposure in that frigid water before rescuers found them.' (Oblt Sommer of I./JG1 is credited with this, his second, victory.) The second B-24 lost was *Cactus*, flown by 1/Lt Virgil R Fouts of the 506th Bomb Squadron. He and his crew were flying their first mission. Lt Pancritius of 8./JG1 is credited with shooting the B-24D into the sea off the coast of Holland, as his third 'kill'.

On 28 March seventy heavy bombers attacked the Rouen–Sotteville marshalling yards. Then three days later, on 31 March, when VIIIth Bomber Command raided the wharfs and docks area at Rotterdam, four of the six bomb groups which set out were recalled because of strong winds and thick cloud. *Ooold Soljer* and *Two Beauts* in the 303rd BG were lost in a mid-air collision. Thirty-three heavies hit the dock area. Many of the B-17s, blown off course by strong winds and bad visibility, missed their objectives completely and killed 326 Dutch civilians when their bombs hurtled down into the streets of Rotterdam. JG1 intercepted the returning 305th BG formation and made one pass before their fuel was expended. Peter Crump attacked *Southern Comfort* and it caught fire between the No. 1 and No. 2 engines. Hugh Ashcraft managed to fly the B-17 to England where the crew abandoned the Fortress safely. It crashed at Wickham Bishops. A 93rd BG B-24 flown by 1/Lt Bill F Williams of the 409th Bomb Squadron was shot down by Oblt Otto Stammberger of Fourth Staffel, II/JG26. Williams crashed into the sea shortly after 1245 hours, sixty miles off Ostend. There were no survivors.

Bad weather grounded the Eighth until 4 April, when the target was the Renault factory in the Billancourt district of Paris. Before the war the Renault works had been the largest producer of vehicles in France and now the Germans were using it to turn out military trucks and tanks. Their output was estimated at 1,000 trucks, tanks and armoured cars a month. On the night of 3/4 March 1942 the RAF had destroyed the plant but the Germans had rebuilt it in nine months by using slave labour. They had even managed to increase production to 1,500 vehicles a month.

During the morning Fortresses took off from the Bedford area while the 44th and 93rd BGs flew a diversionary mission. It took two hours for the four B-17 groups to complete assembly before a total of ninety-seven Fortresses departed the rendezvous point at Beachy Head. However, when landfall was made at Dieppe only eighty-five Fortresses remained, twelve having aborted through malfunctions. For once the sky was clear and blue and many of the Spitfire escort fighters could be seen quite plainly. Others were simply vapour trails in the upper reaches of the atmosphere. From their altitude of 25,000ft, crews could see the black mass of Paris apparently cradled by the long curved arm of the River Seine, ninety-five miles in the distance.

At 1414 hours the Fortresses were over their target and 251 tons of high explosive rained down on Paris. Flak was moderate and not too accurate and crews were able to pick out the Renault works despite the industrial haze which covered much of the city. Most of the eighty-one tons that landed square on the factory were released by eighteen B-17s of the leading 305th formation, led by Maj McGehee in *We The People*, flown by Capt Cliff Pyle. Before the last group had left the target the whole area was blotted out by a thick pall of smoke reaching to 4,000ft. Unfortunately, the groups in the rear of the formation were not as accurate as the 305th had been and many bombs fell outside the target area causing a number of civilian casualties.

JG2 failed to intercept the bombers but five minutes after the target between fifty and seventy-five fighters of JG26 began attacks on the formation, which lasted all the way to Rouen. JG26 made repeated frontal attacks, sometimes by four and six fighters at a time. *Available Jones*, flown by Morris M Jones, and three other B-17s in the 364th (low) Squadron of the 305th BG were shot down, two of them falling to the guns of Hptm 'Wutz' Galland of II./JG26. At 1433 the Spitfire escort reappeared to provide withdrawal support but five of their number were shot down in a seven-minute battle without loss to the Luftwaffe. The gunners aboard *Dry Martini 4th*, piloted by Capt Allen Martini, were credited with the destruction of ten enemy fighters, a record for a bomber crew on a single mission. In all, American gunners claimed forty-seven enemy fighters destroyed. The real losses were two German pilots killed and one wounded. After the raid, photographs smuggled back to England by the French Resistance showed that the Renault works had been severely damaged.

When he returned to Thurleigh after the Paris mission, 2/Lt Robert W Seelos of the 368th Squadron, 306th BG, was suffering with ear problems and he sought out Doc Shuller. Seelos recalls:

> He said I had a head cold and the pressure at high altitude was making my ears ache. He said I was grounded for a few days. For medication I went to the officers' club, and after a couple of drinks I felt all right again. Then the usual unwelcome announcement came over the loudspeakers: 'All armament personnel report to the flight line.' This meant they were loading them up again for another mission the next day. Then, somehow, the word leaked out that the mission would be a short milk run. Naturally, I figured I shouldn't miss the chance to get my nineteenth mission in, leaving me with only six more to go. So I immediately went to Doc Shuller and had him 'unground' me. I advised my Squadron commander that I was ready to go, but that I didn't have a navigator. [Seelos had lost a waist gunner, one bombardier, two navigators and a co-pilot on his previous eighteen missions.] He said not to worry; a replacement crew had just arrived from the States that night, and I could have the navigator.
>
> The next morning after briefing I had the crew all in place, the engines warmed up and waiting for the red flare to signal us to start taxiing – but still no navigator. Just before the signal, a command car skidded around the corner and let out the new navigator, who was pulled up into the nose. We started to taxi immediately. I didn't even get introduced to my new crew member. I learned later that his name was James E Murray, and that he had been married just prior to leaving the States.

Seelos's B-17, *Montana Power*, was one of eighteen in the 306th BG, which departed Thurleigh at 1245 on 5 April. The 368th Squadron flew lead, the 423rd high and the 367th 'Clay Pigeons' flew low. An American war correspondent, writing in the *Saturday Evening Post* said that the 367th Squadron reminded him of a bunch of clay pigeons. The name had stuck! (Between October 1942 and August 1943 the 367th suffered the heaviest losses in VIIIth Bomber Command.) The 306th were led by Lt Col Jim Wilson and Capt John Regan in *Dark Horse*. Brigadier-General Frank Armstrong, Commander, 1st Bomb Wing, flew aboard this aircraft as an observer. Altogether, 104 bombers were despatched. Their target was the ERLA VII aircraft and engine repair works at Mortsel, near Antwerp.

One 306th BG B-17 turned back at 1435 just before reaching the English coast after a cylinder head broke and supercharger buckets blew off. A second turned back at the English coast at 1436 because No. 4 engine went out and the aircraft could not keep up. Altogether, twenty-

Above: General Kammhuber visiting II./NJG2 at Leeuwarden airfield in the first half of 1942. *Left to right:* Ofw Paul Gildner; General Kammhuber; Hptm Lent. *(Coll. Heinz Huhn via Ab A. Jansen)*

Left: Flight Lieutenant John Price, air gunner, age twenty-one, 150 and 104 Squadron Wellingtons 1941–1943. *(John Price)*

Wellington III X3662 'P' of 115 Squadron, RAF Marham with thirty-six operations recorded on its nose. Some 599 Wellingtons made up the bulk of the Cologne raid on 30/31 May 1942. *(IWM)*

Above: Stirling I N6086 LS-F *MacRobert's Reply* of 15 Squadron, which made its last operational sortie on 29 January 1942, overflies RAF Wyton. Some eighty-eight Stirlings were used on the thousand-bomber raid on Cologne on 30/31 May 1942. *(Theo Boiten)*

Left: Ofw Heinz Vinke, 54 Nachtabschüsse with 5./NGJ2 and 11./NJG1 1941–1944, during some 150 sorties. At 0032 hours on 3/4 June 1942 near 'Het Kuitje', one kilometre south of Den Helder, Vinke shot down Stirling Mk I W7474 HA-K of 218 Squadron. P/O James Carscadden, pilot, P/O John R. Webber, pilot, P/O John Douglas Insch, observer, F/Sgt Harold C.F. Broadbent DFM, WOP/AG, and air gunners – F/Sgt Leo Joseph Farley, Sgt Norman C.F. Sibley, and Sgt Leonard J. Smith – were killed. Vinke was awarded the Ritterkreuz on 19.9.43 and Eichenlaub on 24.4.44 (posthumous). *(Coll. Ab A. Jansen)*

Below: Avro Lancaster Mk I R5689 of 50 Squadron RAF photographed in August 1942. This aircraft was destroyed in a crash at Thurlby while returning from a Gardening sortie on 18/19 September 1942. *(Flight)*

Sergeant Neville Hockaday *(centre)*, pilot of *F for Freddy*, a 75 RNZAF Squadron Wellington, who flew his second Op on the night of 29/30 June 1942 when the target was Bremen. Michael Hughes, WOP/AG, is far left. *(Peter Hughes)*

On 26/27 July 1942 a Halifax of 158 Squadron piloted by P/O F. S. White *(centre)* was shot down by a night fighter and ditched in the North Sea with both starboard engines on fire. The four crew in the cockpit area of the Halifax were killed. The three survivors were spotted sixteen hours later by a German seaplane which picked them up and flew them to Nordeney. *Left to right:* P/O Eric 'Syd' Johnstone, navigator (PoW); F/Sgt D. Mc. G. Blott RCAF, rear gunner (PoW); Sgt C. B. Bridgewater, mid-upper gunner (PoW); P/O F. S. White (MIA); Sgt A. G. Mogg, bomb aimer (MIA); G. Archer, navigator from another crew; Sgt F. W. Holmes, WOP/AG (MIA). *(Syd Johnstone)*

Bf 110 night fighters of 6./NJG1 in the 'pioneering days', 1941. The machine nearest the camera is flown by Oblt Reinhold Eckardt, Gruppenadjudant and ace with the twelve Abschüsse by the end of 1941. Eckardt was KIA on 29/30 July 1941 north-east of Melsbroek, Belgium after shooting down his twenty-second victim. He baled out after being hit by return fire, got entangled on the tail of his Bf 110 and was killed in the ensuing crash. *(Coll. Rob de Visser)*

Halifax B.II Series I W7676 of 35 (Madras Presidency) Squadron. This aircraft was lost on the night of 28/29 August 1942 during a raid on Nürnberg. (*Flight*)

B-17E Flying Fortresses of the 97th Bomb Group prepare to take off. This group flew the first US heavy bomber mission from England on 17 August 1942 and came up against the 'Abbeville Kids' of II./JG26 for the first time two days later (*USAF*)

Fw 190 A-3 of II./JG1 at Schiphol airfield in the summer of 1942.
(Coll. Rob de Visser)

Lt Heinz Knoke of I./JG1 who was successful against the Liberators of the 44th BG on 26 February 1943.
(via Eric Mombeek)

El-Lobo of the 305th BG which was flown by Lt Cornelius A. Jenkins on the 4 February 1943 mission when they were shot down by a Bf 110 of NJG1. Jenkins and four crew were killed. The élite night fighter unit was pressed into day action against VIIIth Bomber Command during February, often with disastrous results.
(via Bill Donald)

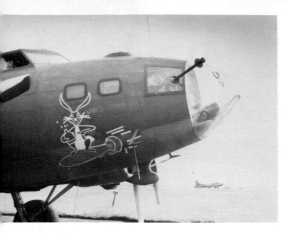

B-17F 42-425060 *What's Cookin Doc?* of the 305th BG which was lost when a Fw 190 collided with it on 4 February 1943. All the crew, including the pilot, Lt William K. Davidson, were killed. *(via Bill Donald)*

1/Lt Cliff Pyle's crew of *We The People* in the 305th BG at Grafton Underwood. *Back row, left to right:* Arthur Laskowski; Mulvana; Russell K. Weller; William K. Davidson (KIA 4.2.43); Cliff Pyle. *Front row:* Edgar S. Nicholls; Vernon D. Myrion; Harold J. Fedora; L. G. McCoy; Paulich. *(via Bill Donald)*

'The fire spreads along the right wing. The inside engine stops. Suddenly, the wing breaks off altogether. The body of the stricken monster plunges vertically, spinning into the depths . . .' *(USAF)*

Above: Back at Bassingbourn, 91st BG crews inspect the damage to their B-17. *(USAF)*

Above: B-24D D-1-CO *Night Raider* of the 93rd BG, which was badly shot-up by fighters on 26 February 1943 and crashed at Ludham, Norfolk on return from Bremen.

(via Mike Bailey)

Hptm Josef 'Pips' Priller, Kommandeur, III./JG26, who on 9 October 1942 shot down B-17F 41-24510 *Snoozy II* of the 367th Squadron, 306th Bomb Group, even though he identiified it as a Liberator!

Right: Captain Howard L. Adams, pilot of B-24D-5-CO 41-23777 *Maisie* in the 66th Bomb Squadron, 44th Bomb Group, which was lost on 26 February 1943.
(via Steve Adams)

Above: Robert Perkins Post, a *New York Times* war correspondent, the only one of seven in the 'Writing 69th' who asked to fly with the 44th BG on 26 February 1943. The others flew aboard B-17s.
(Jim Hamilton)

Below: On 14 May 1943 attacks by German fighters and disruption caused by incendiaries dropped from higher flying B-17s (taken from a 306th BG Fortress) accounted for this scattered formation flown by the B-24D Liberators of the 44th BG crossing the target at Kiel. *(USAF)*

one Fortresses and Liberators turned back due to various mechanical problems before reaching the enemy coast. The 306th headed almost due east across the Channel to the Belgian coast, near Ostend. Seelos noted:

> Obviously our diversion hadn't worked. The Germans were forewarned of our arrival. We were the lead group, and they were already attacking us [Fw 190A-4 and A-5s of JG26]. I would guess that we were about halfway between the coast and Antwerp when I took a direct hit in the prop dome of my No. 1 engine [caused by flak from Flak Abteilung 295]. It was running wild, and, with the feathering mechanism destroyed, there was no way I could do anything about it. With the old style props and the drag from the No. 1 engine, I had to use full power on the other three engines to stay with the group, which seemed to me to be in anything but a tight formation.
>
> At least three other planes were in trouble and trying to hang in there for more firepower and protection. I called the group lead ship and told them to slow down, that we were in trouble. I got no response. For some reason I kept thinking – if only our old Squadron commander, Bill Lanford, was leading the group, he would have slowed it down and tucked the cripples in like an old mother hen, and would possibly have got us all back at least as far as the Channel. By now I was so mad and busy trying to keep going to the target, I really didn't have time to get scared or worry that we weren't going to make it.

The 306th bore the brunt of the head-on attacks, which continued all the way to the target. In the words of a later report to the Commanding General, 1st Bomb Wing, 'Enemy aircraft concentrated head-on attacks on lead group, evidently under orders to break up attack at all costs before bombs were away. Probably most determined attack and hottest fight seen by our forces in this theatre. Lead group reports forty to sixty enemy aircraft, mostly yellow-nose Fw 190s. We claim 5–3–2.'

The III Gruppe had taken off to intercept the Fortresses in the Ghent area. Just before 1510 hours the Kommandeur, Hptm Fritz Geisshardt, and his Stabs Flight encountered the B-17s. Geisshardt attacked a B-17, coming in from the right and to the side and from above. He went charging in again from the same direction, but was hit in the abdomen by return fire from the B-17s. He was able to make a wheels-up landing in his Fw 190A-4 on the airfield at Ghent at 1515 hours but died from loss of blood early the following morning. Geisshardt had been decorated with the Knight's Cross with Oak Leaves for his 102 confirmed victories.

At around the same time, *L'il Abner*, flown by Lt Clarence Fischer, was hit by flak over Ghent en route to the target and finished off by Major 'Pips' Priller. The crew managed to bale out before the Fortress exploded in the target area. It was Priller's eighty-fourth victory. Lt Kelly Ross's aircraft was badly hit on the way into the target by cannon and machine-gun fire from Hptm 'Wutz' Galland. After the No. 2 engine was shot out Ross gave the order to bale out. All except the tail and waist gunners survived. It was Galland's thirty-eighth victory.

The Fortress piloted by 1/Lt William H Parker was shot down north of the Scheldt at 1538 hours by Ofw Adolf 'Addi' Glunz of IV./JG26 who claimed it as his thirty-second victory. Parker, James E Gross, radio operator, both waist gunners, and the ball gunner were killed. Navigator Paul Spaduzzi's parachute was popped open by the force of the explosion. Lt Charles Thelen, the co-pilot, pushed the bale-out bell. Tail gunner Leonard O'Brien left his turret and passed the two dead waist gunners. When he reached the flight deck he found engineer John Creatore in the pilot's seat and Spaduzzi in the co-pilot's seat vacated by Charles Thelen. Creatore and Spaduzzi told O'Brien that they were going to fly the B-17 to France but when Creatore tried to turn the crippled bomber it did a full roll and entered a spin to the left. O'Brien, Thelen and Milbourn baled out. Their B-17 spun in near Ainteloord, fifty kilometres north of Antwerp.

At 1535 hours north of Antwerp Oblt Otto Stammberger, Staffelkapitän of 4./JG26, found a faltering B-17 squarely in his sights. It was *Montana Power* which, after having lost its No. 1 engine, had dropped from formation during the bomb run. Stammberger raked the B-17 from head-on with a burst from his four cannon and two machine guns. Bob Seelos says: 'Just after our bombs were released I took a direct flak hit in the No. 4 engine. I immediately made a flat left turn in hopes that the group lead would try to pick me up as they made their turn off the target at least a half mile ahead of me. But they seemed to be heading full power for the coast. In the meantime the German fighters were spraying the hell out of us. I had hopes of reaching the Channel and trying to ditch in the water, but the No. 4 burst into flames. I told co-pilot Alex Kramarinko to tell the crew to bale out at once.'

Stammberger had to pull up quickly because the Fortress suddenly nosed downward. He watched the survivors bale out and saw the pilotless ship carry on for a short time before finally crashing at Kalmthout. It was his fourth victory (three hours later he shot down a Spitfire near Dieppe). By the time Seelos got out he was well away from the others:

I came down on the edge of the town of Wuustwezel, Belgium. As I was descending I could see I was going to go through the top of a tree. I braced myself and gritted my teeth – so hard that I bit through my cheek. The chute collapsed and I hit the ground so hard that I was knocked out momentarily. When I came to I was looking into the eyes of a perfect doll of a Belgian girl – long braids, blue eyes, wooden shoes. Blood was coming out of my mouth, and she thought I had been shot and was bleeding internally. She was trying to find the bullet hole and I had a hard time convincing her there wasn't any. When I was finally able to get to my feet, I had her hide the parachute in the brush. I then tried to tell her I wanted to get the hell out of there and hide someplace. But just then about a dozen German soldiers appeared with their little machine-guns. I wasn't about to try to run or do anything foolish. They proceeded to march me to their headquarters at the local city hall. A crowd of Belgian people were gathering and following us and giving me the V for Victory sign, much to the annoyance of the Germans.

The blonde girl (I later found out her name was Elsa Moors) stayed right behind me all the way to the city hall. I had eased my escape kit from my pocket and managed to give it to her without the Germans noticing. Just prior to reaching city hall, I slipped off one of my dogtags and gave that to her also. The following morning, my family in Montana received the standard MIA telegram. When no more word was received after more than a month, my family was about to give up hope. On Mother's Day, the blonde girl was in Brussels and went to the equivalent of our Western Union. Using the address from my dogtag, she sent this cablegram to Mrs Seelos, Philipsburg, Montana, USA: 'Dear Auntie, Robert was here visiting, was in very good health, and sends his love to his darling relative.' Unbelievably, the message got through, untouched and uncensored. It was one fantastic Mother's Day gift to my mother. She called the War Department, and they informed her that they still had no information about me but they would check with the Swiss Red Cross. They called back shortly that my name was on the latest PoW list.

Seelos went to Stalag Luft III. Seven crew managed to evacuate the doomed ship but the top turret gunner, a waist gunner and Lt Murray were killed. In a bomb group reputed for its high turnover rate, Murray had the shortest tour of all in the 306th BG – a matter of hours only. Kramarinko and S/Sgt William E Baker evaded capture and together reached Spain, only to be caught and handed over to the Germans.

Dark Horse was hit by cannon fire from a Fw 190 attacking head-on during the bomb run, but Lt-Col James Wilson, the 306th BG CO, managed to bring the Fortress home safely to Thurleigh aided by Capt Robert Salitrnik, the lead navigator, who had been critically wounded when he was hit in the leg by fragments from a can of .50 calibre ammunition which exploded when hit by 20mm fire from a Fw 190 during a head-on attack. Salitrnik received four pints of plasma on arrival at Thurleigh and was out of shock the next day but developed gas gangrene on 15 April and died the next day.

Well-aimed bombing was not possible due to the persistent fighter attacks, which forced many bombers off course. This serious situation was aggravated by problems with the Norden bombsights in the 303rd (and 44th) Bomb Groups, and the eighty-two B-17s that got their bombs away consequently dropped most of them on Mortsel where over 3,000 houses were destroyed killing 936 inhabitants and injuring 1,342. Only four bombs hit the ERLA VII works, which killed 229 workers, with another seventy-eight missing. The ERLA Werke however suffered little damage and within a few weeks aircraft and engine repairs were back to the normal level.

On 13 April, P-47Cs of the 4th Fighter Group were joined by the 56th and 78th Fighter Groups for the first time when they became operational with P-47C-2 Thunderbolts. A *Rodeo* (fighter sweep) by one squadron from each group was flown to St Omer in the Pas de Calais with the aim of luring the 'Abbeville Kids' into combat, but the Luftwaffe fighters did not show. Two days later the two new groups met the Luftwaffe for the first time. On the evening of 15 April the 4th put up twelve P-47s, led by Major Don Blakeslee, and the 56th and 78th each put up twenty-four aircraft. They tussled with Fw 190A-4s of II./JG1 over Ostend and three Fw 190s were claimed destroyed. In fact the German unit suffered no losses. Two P-47s and their pilots were lost as a result of engine failures.

On 16 April, the 8th's first mission since Antwerp, fifty-nine B-17s bombed Lorient for the loss of a single B-17, and eighteen Liberators from the 44th and 93rd Bomb Groups hit Brest. The Eightballs came through unscathed but the heaviest fighter attacks by JG26 seemed to be aimed at the 'Travelling Circus', who lost four B-24s to Fw 190s attacking from the rear of their formation at the target. 1/Lt Frank Hodges and his crew in *Liberty Lass* were the first to go down, followed by the crew of *Ball of Fire Jnr*, flown by Frank Lown (Hodges and Lown were captured and sent to Stalag Luft III). Capt Bud Fleenor and crew (who had crashed at Ludham on 26 February) in *Missouri Sue* went

68

down in the Channel after the bombardier had baled out over France, while *Judith Lynn* also went down, and Lt Packer nursed the crippled *Yardbird* back to England and crashed at St Eval.

Next day, 17 April, a record 111 bombers set out for the Focke Wulf factory at Bremen, but intense fighter attacks by an estimated 105 fighters of JG1 and 11 were encountered on the bomb run and fifteen Fortresses were shot down. JG1 and 11 claimed to have shot down sixteen B-17s of the Bremen force. Another was brought down by flak. Ten of the ships lost came from the 306th BG, while the 401st Squadron of the 91st BG lost all six of its Fortresses.

In April four new Fortress Groups, the 94th, 95th, 96th and 351st, increased the numbers of bombers of the 8th Air Force in Britain. Despite inflicting serious losses, the situation regarding the defence of the Reich had become so bad that by the spring of 1943 Luftwaffe night fighters were put into action against American day formations whenever the latter flew without escort. Heavy German losses were thereby sustained, owing to the night fighter habit of going in close before attacking, tactics which proved very costly when met with the heavy defensive fire of the day bombers, and which soon led to the prohibition of day operations for key night fighter crews. German High Command refused for a long time to credit the depth of the penetrations achieved by American escort fighters and night fighters continued to be sent up on what were suicide operations. It became necessary for Generalmajor Galland himself to take off and obtain personal confirmation before Göring would believe the situation.

On 1 May, fifty-six bombers in two waves attacked St Nazaire. On 4 May sixty-five bombers hit the Ford and General Motors plants at Antwerp, accompanied for the first time by P-47s of the 4th and 56th Fighter Groups who provided fighter escort up to 175 miles. Meanwhile, more than thirty B-17s and B-24s flew diversionary feints towards the French coast. These succeeded in drawing over 100 German fighters away from the main force, which returned without loss. It was not until 13 May that the 8th went out again, when 119 bombers, the numbers swollen by the inclusion of the 94th, 95th, 96th (which failed to complete the mission) and 351st Bomb Groups for the first time, attacked the Avions Potez aircraft factory at Meaulte and St Omer–Longuenesse airfield. Three B-17s, including a 305th BG ship captained by Harold C Pierce of the 365th Squadron, were shot down; Pierce and three crew were killed. 'Stotto' Stammberger was shot down by an RAF Spitfire. He had to exit his Fw 190 when the fuel tank exploded, but his parachute failed to open fully and he was seriously injured on landing. He would not return to action until October.

Next day, 14 May, 196 bombers made simultaneous attacks on four targets. The principal attack was by the 1st Bomb Wing on the Krupp shipyards at Kiel while the 96th and 351st Bomb Groups were to bomb Courtrai airfield and the 94th and 95th Bomb Groups, the Ford and General Motors plant and locks nearby at Antwerp. Large numbers of Spitfires and P-47s were on hand to escort the bombers. The Kiel force included twenty-one Liberators of the 44th BG, which brought up the rear of the B-17 formation. By the time they crossed the coast 109 Fortresses and seventeen B-24s remained. At the target the mission developed into chaos when the B-17s unloaded their incendiaries through the Liberator formation, causing them to scatter. The Luftwaffe seized their opportunity and made repeated attacks on the rear of the Liberators and shot down five B-24Ds. Three of them, *Miss Delores*, which was hit by flak and finished off by fighters, *Annie Oakley* and *Little Beaver* came from the 67th Bomb Squadron while *Rugged Buggy* came from the 68th Squadron and *Wicked Witch*, the 506th Squadron. *Scrappy*, a 66th Squadron ship, made it back to Shipdham where the crew baled out after 1/Lt John Y Reed, the pilot, and 1/Lt George W Winger, the co-pilot, set course on auto-pilot for the North Sea before they too baled out. The Liberator was shot down over the sea by Spitfires. Eight other B-24s were damaged, twelve men were wounded while *Margaret Ann* returned to base with one gunner mortally wounded and three seriously wounded. *Ruth-less*, piloted by Lt Frank Slough in the 506th, was very badly damaged but made it back, although Slough finally had to crash-land in Northern Ireland because Shipdham was so congested that it could not take any more aircraft in trouble. Three B-17s also were lost.

The attack on Courtrai fared better. It was so heavily damaged by bombs dropped by the 96th and 351st Bomb Groups that III./JG26 was forced to move to Lille–Nord. On the bombers' return east of Ypres they were attacked en masse by fighters. II./JG26 shot down two B-17s of the 351st BG. Flak bracketed the 94th and 95th Bomb Groups at Antwerp and the Fw 190s, and at 1330, over the island of South Beveland, Fw Peter Crump of 5./JG26 shot down B-17 42-3115 of the 95th BG captained by J E McKinley. It spun out of formation at only 2,500ft and all the crew were killed. A 78th FG P-47 (one of three Thunderbolts lost) and a Spitfire were also shot down by pilots of JG26 but the German unit lost two pilots to return fire from the bombers and Hptm Karl Borris,

Kapitän of 8 Staffel, was forced to bale out at 22,000ft after coming off worse against a bomber. He was fortunate to survive when his parachute failed to open properly. A fourth Fw 190 was shot down by the 78th FG. Altogether, VIIIth Bomber Command lost eleven aircraft, while sixty-seven fighters were claimed shot down.

On 15 May, 135 bombers bombed shipping targets at Emden, Heligoland and Wilhelmshaven. Next day a fighter sweep by 117 P-47s of the 4th, 56th and 78th Fighter Groups over northern Belgium resulted in combat action when they met the fighters of JG1 in the Vlissingen area being led by the Geschwaderkommodore, Major Hans 'Fips' Philipp, an ex-JG54 'Experte', who had assumed command of JG1 on 1 April. Philipp claimed a P-47 as his 205th 'Abschuss' at 1312 hours, followed one minute later by another 'Jug' shot down by Oblt Koch as his sixteenth kill. (Philipp was killed in action on 8 October 1943 during air combat with B-17s and escorting fighters, after having claimed a B-17 for his 206th and final victory.) Colonel Arman Petersen, 78th FG CO, destroyed one Fw 190 and two more fell to the guns of his Group. In fact, there was only one victim, Gruppenführer of II./JG1 Hptm Dietrich Wickop, who had thirteen victories to his name, including three B-17s. Next day 118 bombers attacked Lorient while a smaller force bombed Bordeaux. On 19 May, 102 bombers hit Kiel and on 21 May, 123 bombers attacked Wilhelmshaven. German fighters attacked using rockets. With the increase in attacks on the north German coast, on 23 May III./JG26 flew to Cuxhaven – Nordholz to reinforce JG1, III./JG54 and JG11 against the USAAF attacks. On 27 May only eleven bombers hit St Nazaire but on the 29th, 147 bombers managed to drop their bombs on the U-boat pens there. It was the last raid by the 8th during the month.

In June General Ira Eaker was able to send the 1st and 4th Wings on two-pronged attacks against north German targets at Emden, Kiel, Bremen, Wilhelmshaven and Cuxhaven on a single day. On 11 June the B-17s of the 1st and 4th Wings set out to bomb Bremen but the target was covered with a solid layer of low cumulus clouds down to about 5,000ft and they also partially covered Wilhelmshaven, the secondary target, so Cuxhaven was bombed instead. About twenty fighters attacked the low groups in the 4th Wing but it was the 1st Wing that suffered the greatest onslaught, at their secondary target at Wilhelmshaven. During the bomb run the leading 303rd BG formation was bracketed by a severe flak barrage. Col Chuck Marion, the Commanding Officer, lost two engines and following aircraft had to manoeuvre violently and reduce speed dramatically to avoid a collision.

71

Just at that moment the Luftwaffe took advantage of the now scattered formation and made repeated head-on attacks. One B-17 was rammed by a Fw 190 that failed to pull out in time.

The 379th BG, flying only its second mission, bore the brunt of the attacks, as Col 'Mo' Preston the CO, recalls:

The enemy fighters, as expected, first appeared as the lead wing of B-17s approached the shoreline just north of the target. The fighters came in large numbers; probably several hundred. As expected, they climbed to the bombers' altitude and then a little higher as they pulled on out to the right front of the bomber column a mile or so. Then they broke off in groups of four to six and swung around to a diving turn to deliver their attack from the front. They concentrated on the low group of those at the head of the column, which as it happened was the 379th Group.

The fighters approached upright until they reached a point about one half mile to the front, then they rolled on their backs, fired their guns and rockets and dived towards the earth. The little puffs of 20mm shells exploding were clearly visible as the fighters approached from up front. As soon as one bunch of fighters made its pass and disappeared earthward, another bunch would roll in for its run at the B-17s. And they kept coming and coming, on and on. They attacked all during the bomb run and the subsequent reassembly and they continued the attack until the bombers crossed the coastline. Then the attacks stopped, probably because all their ammo was spent. A very typical engagement, though perhaps untypical in its severity, and an effective one.

The 379th lost six aircraft [the 8th lost eight B-17s in all] or one third of its strength. Our gunners claimed many dozens of fighters destroyed. A strange thing: we always claimed to inflict great losses on the enemy and in the tally sheets back in the 8th Air Force HQ. I'm sure we destroyed the Luftwaffe many times over. Yet in my personal experience, whereas I saw many B-17s shot down by enemy fighters – perhaps a score or more – and occasionally enemy fighters destroyed by friendly escort fighters, I never once saw a fighter destroyed by a B-17 gunner – not once. And I am personally convinced that bombardment gunnery was a very ineffective weapon. It was certainly no match for the fighter.

On Sunday 13 June 102 heavies attacked Bremen while a smaller force bombed Kiel. In addition, during the morning the 56th Fighter Group (which had claimed its first victory the day before) flew a diversionary sweep off the Belgian coast at 27,000ft. They chanced upon

II./JG26 and over Dixmuide Col Hubert 'Hub' Zemke, the CO, shot down two of the Fw 190s, and Lt Robert Johnson got a third before the German pilots knew what hit them. Ogfr Zenker was killed in the P-47 attack. In the afternoon forty-four Thunderbolts of the 78th Fighter Group flew their sweep over Ypres and St Pol. II./JG26 shot down two of the P-47s for no loss. The B-17s, meanwhile, headed for their targets in north-east Germany, hoping that their two-pronged attack on Kiel and Bremen would split the Jagdflieger. It failed, almost all the German fighters forsaking the 1st Wing's attack on Kiel to concentrate on the seventy-six 4th Wing B-17s attacking Bremen. Among the eight losses in the 95th BG, which led the 1st Wing at Kiel, was the command aircraft flown by Captain H A Stirwalt and which carried Brigadier General Nathan B Forrest. He was the first American General to be lost in combat in Europe. JG26 lost another leader and ace when Hptm Kurt Ruppert, Kommandeur of III./JG26, was killed when his parachute straps snapped after he baled out at high speed. At the time of his death Ruppert had twenty-one kills to his credit. This day the 4th Wing lost four B-17s to flak at the target. Nine more B-17s fell to the guns of black Ju 88s which attacked the returning 4th Wing formation while they were still some miles from the East Anglian coast.

On 22 June, the 8th made its first large-scale attack on the Ruhr, when 182 heavies bombed the chemical and synthetic rubber plant at Hüls. Once again elaborate diversionary measures were put into operation with two planned 'spoof' formations making feints over the North Sea. Unfortunately one of the diversions, a formation of twenty-one B-17s of the 100th BG (making its theatre debut this day), was delayed because of ground mists and other problems and played no major part in the proceedings, while the 381st and 384th Bomb Groups (which were flying their maiden missions) fell behind schedule and failed to rendezvous with Spitfire and Thunderbolt fighters which were to escort them to the Ford and General Motors Works at Antwerp. This lapse placed the forty-one B-17s at the mercy of II./JG26, which had refuelled after an earlier raid by RAF medium bombers, and head-on attacks succeeded in shooting down four of the B-17s, two from each group. The survivors made their bomb run on Antwerp and were met on the return by fighters of the 4th and 78th Fighter Groups who provided withdrawal support. They claimed seven fighters for no losses. Meanwhile, the Hüls force had severely damaged the plant but at a cost of sixteen B-17s, including one of eleven multi-gun YB-40s which flew with the 303rd BG, which was downed by flak. Thirteen of the B-17s were claimed shot down by JG1, with four more 'Herausschüsse' (Luftwaffe fighter pilots' term for Allied bombers which were attacked, and which had to leave the protection of their formation; a bomber was thus 'shot out', became a straggler and was easy meat for the fighters).

On 25 June, 167 heavies bombed targets in north-western Germany. Cloud hampered bombing at Hamburg, the main objective, and split up the formations and scattered some of the groups in the sky – an open invitation to fighter attack. Eighteen B-17s, including six from the 379th BG, were shot down by fighters. Cloud interfered on the twenty-sixth also, when 246 B-17s were despatched to bomb Triqueville airfield and an aircraft factory at Villacoublay in the Paris area. Five B-17s, all from the 384th BG, were shot down by Fw 190s, including one machine which fell to the guns of Major 'Pips' Priller, Kommodore of JG26, over Dieppe on the return. JG26 also intercepted the forty-nine P-47s of the 56th Fighter Group near Forges, France as the Jugs arrived to provide withdrawal escort for the bombers. Five P-47s were shot down without loss to JG26. Lt Robert Johnson had a fortunate escape when a Fw 190 which pursued him and pumped 20mm shells into his Thunderbolt, HV-P *All Hell*, was forced to break off out of ammunition. With a wave and a shake of the head, the German pilot rocked his wings in salute and broke off, perhaps thinking that the stricken P-47 would never make England anyway. Johnson, fortunately, did, and he put down safely at Manston.

At Thurleigh, a party had been planned in honour of Capt Raymond Check, an original 306th BG pilot from Minot, North Dakota, and very popular member of the 423rd Squadron, who was on his twenty-fifth and final mission. He was going to marry a Red Cross nurse the very next day. Lt-Col J W Wilson, his original Squadron commander, returned to Thurleigh to fly the mission from the left-hand seat while Lt William Cassedy, Check's regular co-pilot, flew as one of the waist gunners. *Chennaults Pappy III* touched down and pulled off the runway on to the grass. Puzzled, Capt Adrian M Poletti, chaplain, and Capt Manning, who were standing in front of the ambulances, drove over to the B-17 as two men dropped out of the nose and motioned to them. With electrifying finality they said, 'Check's dead!' During the bomb run a German fighter attacking out of the sun had raked the cockpit with 20mm cannon fire. One shell had exploded just above Check's head. He had been killed instantly. Col Wilson stayed with the controls despite being badly burned until the rubber on his oxygen mask melted on his face. His hands were so burned that he could not let go of the wheel. Finally, Cassedy came up from the waist and helped Wilson. Luckily, they were carrying Maj George Peck, a visiting surgeon who wanted practical experience, and had it not been for his work on Col Wilson, he might well have died. A cake was baked for Check and his name was inscribed on top. When Check's ship flew into the field with Cassedy at the controls, there was not a man on the field who felt like eating the cake or having a party. Cassedy was awarded the DFC and Wilson the DSC.

During July, in an attempt to bring more firepower to bear on the B-24 and B-17 formations, both the Fw 190A and Bf 109G had their armament increased substantially during the month. The Bf 109G-6/R6 now carried three MG 151 cannon in addition to its two MG 151 13mm machine-guns, and the Fw 190 now carried two Rheinmetall MG FF-M-20 cannons in addition to its two MG 151s. During July also, the Fw 190A-6, equipped with two MG 151 20mm cannon in place of the MG-FF-M, became operational in the Jagdgruppen.

Despite continuing losses the 8th Air Force grew in size with the addition of more groups and on 17 July Eaker was able to send a record 322 bombers to Hannover. At about the same time as the RAF mass attacks on Hamburg in July 1943, the 8th AF again began the first of its really heavy daylight attacks and ever-increasing penetration. In the beginning the German defences had achieved good results against these. The flak, by operating in massed Grossbatteries, had been very effective, especially when daylight attacks were carried out in clear weather allowing visual ranging, and the newly established 'Zerstörer' heavy fighter organisation especially distinguished itself. After a short while however, its operation in the original form no longer seemed possible because it was so strongly tied down by the rapidly rising number of USAAF escort fighters.

On 24 July, a week-long series of American heavy bomber raids, later called 'Blitz Week', went ahead, beginning with a raid by 208 B-17s on Heroya and Trondheim in Norway. Next day 218 bombers attacked Hamburg and Kiel. JG1 and 11 accounted for most of the nineteen bombers that failed to return with fifteen 'Abschüsse'. On 26 July, 146 bombers attacked Hannover and Hamburg and again JG1 and 11 accounted for most of the twenty-four bombers shot down. After stand down on 27 July the 8th despatched over 300 bombers on the twenty-eighth in two forces to bomb German targets, but bad weather interfered with the mission and only forty-nine bombed the aircraft works at Kassel, with twenty-eight hitting the Fw 190 factory at Oschersleben. JG1 and 11, many using rockets, shot down the majority of the twenty-

75

two bombers lost. However, US fighters accounted for nine German aircraft for the loss of just one Thunderbolt. In fact, these two Jagdgeschwadern lost twenty Fw 190s and Bf 109s with three pilots killed and eight injured.

After attacking U-boat yards at Kiel and the Heinkel aircraft factory at Warnemünde on 29 July, the 8th despatched 186 bombers to Kassel on the thirtieth. Their route took them over Woensdrecht airfield, home for part of II./JG1, and the scene of an ineffective attack by eleven B-26 Marauders that morning (an attack on Courtrai–Wevelgham was also abandoned). II./JG1 took off from Woensdrecht and intercepted the bombers, followed by 8./JG26 from Lille–Nord. Two of the B-17s were shot down for the loss of one fighter. The Fortresses carried on to the target, where 134 bombed. Waiting for them on their return were the fighters from all four of the Jagdflieger defensive zones. Near Apeldoorn II./JG26 attacked, sending two B-17s down in flames for the loss of three Fw 190s. I./JG26 also claimed two B-17s shot down for the loss of one fighter. Like cavalry to the rescue, 107 American fighters of the 4th, 56th and 78th Fighter Groups arrived on the scene to prevent further losses. (They carried auxiliary tanks for the very first time this day, which greatly enhanced their range and undoubtedly contributed to the severe German fighter losses.) They claimed twenty-four fighters shot down, including three, the first triple victory in the ETO, by Maj Eugene Roberts of the 78th Fighter Group. Capt Charles London, also of the 78th FG, was credited with downing two fighters. No JG26 fighters were lost, so the victories probably were at the expense of JG1 and JG11.

For its part, the 8th lost twelve bombers and six fighters. The 78th FG lost its second CO within a month when Lt-Col Melvin F McNickle was shot down at 1030 hours. Whilst severely injured, he was made PoW near Ravestein in Holland. His wingman, Lt Byers, was shot down and killed near Elden in Holland a few minutes before his CO went down. At least twenty-four Luftwaffe fighters were lost over Holland on this day: JG1 lost eight Fw 190 A-4s and A-5s destroyed with another three severely damaged when their pilots crash-landed their Bf 109G-6s after being damaged in air combat; JG2 lost seven destroyed; JG11 one Bf 109G-6 destroyed with another five G-1s and G-6s between fifteen and eighty per cent damaged; JG26 had four write-offs and JG54 lost another four. In all, eight Bf 109s and sixteen Fw 190s were destroyed. Ten Jagdflieger were killed and two went missing; another nine fighter pilots were injured. Two of these fighters, both of JG26, were shot down in air combat with Spitfires and B-26s in the early morning during the Woensdrecht airfield attack. The remaining twenty-two Luftwaffe fighters lost were all victims of the fierce dogfights with P-47s and in attacks with the B-17s. The next day groups were stood down. In a week of sustained operations, the 8th had lost about 100 aircraft and ninety combat crews.

Its strength replenished, on 12 August 243 heavy bombers were despatched unescorted to targets in the Ruhr. Some twenty-five bombers, eleven of them claimed by I. and II./JG26, were shot down. Undeterred, over 300 bombers were sent to attack targets in Holland and France on 15 August. Friendly fighter support, notably by the P-47 Thunderbolts, was described as 'excellent' and the Jagdgruppen stayed mostly on the ground. Two days later, on 17 August, it was quite a different story. The 8th had no long-range escort fighters for deep penetration raids into Germany so when Eaker despatched 315 B-17s in a two-pronged attack on the VKW ball-bearing factories at Schweinfurt, and the Messerschmitt factory at Regensburg, the Jagdgruppen, and especially the Zerstörergruppen, were able to break up the American daylight bomber formations with almost consummate ease while the single-engined fighters picked off the stragglers and cripples.

In an attempt to minimise attacks from enemy fighters, the Regensburg force was detailed to fly on to North Africa after bombing the target while the Schweinfurt force returned to East Anglia. Over Eupen at 1620 hours the 56th FG met the survivors returning from Schweinfurt and waded into the German fighters which had dogged them throughout the terrible mission. Zemke's Wolfpack claimed seventeen fighters, including six Fw 190s. One of these was a II./JG26 machine flown by Major 'Wutz' Galland, Kommandeur of II./JG26, who was killed. His Fw 190A-6 crashed at Hees-Vlijtingen, west of Maastricht. Galland was possibly shot down by Capt Walker Mahurin. Four fighter groups had been scheduled to escort the Regensburg force but only the 353rd Fighter Group, which was flying its first mission, was able to rendezvous with the B-17s, but the overburdened P-47s could not hope to protect all seven groups in the line of bombers which stretched for fifteen miles. American losses, mostly as a result of German fighter attacks, were severe. Altogether, twenty-four Fortresses were shot down on the Regensburg mission while the Schweinfurt force lost thirty-six. If nothing else the Schweinfurt–Regensburg débâcle reinforced the need for a long-range escort fighter that could accompany bomb groups deeper into the Reich.

At the end of September 1943, apart from the single-engined Bf 109 and Fw 190 day fighters, B-17 and B-24 crews now faced over 150 Bf 110Gs and Me 410A-1/B-1s in five Zestörergruppen. The P-47D, with the installation of a 108-gallon belly tank, could escort the bombers as far as Duren on 4 October when 282 bombers hit Frankfurt, Wiesbaden, and Saarbrucken, and kept losses down to just twelve bombers. However, on 8 October, when more than 350 bombers attacked Bremen and Vegesack again, the several attempts to reduce the effectiveness of the Jagdgruppen in north-western Germany failed. A diversion mission by B-24s was flown and the 1st and 3rd Wings approached the target from two different directions in an attempt to fool the German controllers, but these ruses, and the use of airborne 'Carpet' radar jammers aboard some of the B-17s for the first time, were not enough to prevent the loss of thirty B-17s. P-47s, before they had to return, low on fuel, took on Geschwaderstab JG1 over Nordhorn and accounted for Geschwaderkommodore Major Hans Philipp. Oberst Walter Oesau, previously Jagdfliegerführer 4 Brittany, and forbidden to fly operationally, assumed command two days later. 'Gulle' Oesau had destroyed ten aircraft during the Spanish Civil War and now had one hundred victories, and he had received the Knight's Cross, Oak Leaves and Swords. Oesau did not survive the war either. He was shot down and killed on 11 May 1944 south-west of St Vith in his Bf 109 G-6, having gained 117 'Abschüsse', of which fourteen were American 'Viermots'.

On 10 October, 264 heavies set out on a direct course for Münster. This was intended so that P-47s could escort the bombers all the way to the target. However, when the 352nd FG turned back as planned at 1148, their place, which should have been taken by the 355th FG, went unfilled as the latter group remained fog-bound in England. At 1453 hours, just nine minutes from the target, the fighter attacks began. First to attack were the single-engined fighters, which paused only when the flak opened up at the approach to the target. They resumed their attacks again after the Zerstörers waded in with rocket attacks to add to the carnage. Worst hit were the unlucky 13th Wing comprising the 95th, 100th and 390th Bomb Groups. It took just seven minutes to tear the 'Bloody Hundredth' formation apart, losing a dozen B-17s, while the 390th lost eight out of eighteen despatched, and five out of the twenty 95th BG B-17s despatched also failed to return. Only the intervention of the 56th FG prevented further losses. Lt Robert Johnson destroyed two fighters to become an ace and was joined by Major David Schilling and by

Captain Walter Beckham of the 353rd, both of whom downed their fifth fighters on this mission. In all, thirty B-17s were either shot down or written off in crashes. Fourteen were claimed shot down by JG1 and 11, with another eight 'Herausschüsse' and two P-47s shot down (one of the jugs by Oblt Knoke as his eighteenth victory). The Americans claimed 180 fighters shot down, 105 claims being submitted by the 13th Wing alone. (The Luftwaffe had lost twenty-five fighters, including nine Bf 110s and Me 410s and seven Fw 190s and Bf 109s of JG1, with four pilots killed in this Geschwader.)

Still without suitable long-range fighter cover, on 14 October 230 B-17s were sent to Schweinfurt again. Fw 190A-5/R6s and Bf 109Gs of JG1, JG3, JG26 and JG27, which carried two underwing 210mm WGr 21 rocket tubes, and Bf 110s of the Zerstörergruppen blasted and scattered the tightly packed Fortress formations and made many easy prey for single-engined fighters. Altogether, sixty Fortresses were shot down, seventeen more were written off in crashes and another 121 required extensive repair. The losses were softened by press reports that 104 German fighters had been shot down, but the true figure was actually thirty-eight from the 340 single- and twin-engined fighters that attacked the Fortresses.

The American losses and a spell of bad weather restricted the 8th to just two more missions in October. Meanwhile, desperate attempts to improve the range of the few Thunderbolts in the ETO were carried out. The 200-gallon flush ferry tank provided for early P-47C and D models was unsuitable for combat, and there were not enough seventy-five-gallon drop tanks available. A British-made 108-gallon tank made of pressed paper could be used under the fuselage or two could be fitted beneath the wings, increasing radius of action to 350 miles and 445 miles respectively. The tanks, first used on 12 August, caused a number of problems, including the inability of an aircraft with tanks attached to climb above 20,000ft.

In 1942 the 8th Air Force had lost all its P-38 Lightnings when they went to North Africa with the 12th Air Force. The decision must have been bitterly regretted for it was not until 15 October, the day following the Schweinfurt disaster, that the Lightning re-entered combat in England when the 55th Fighter Group at Nuthampstead became operational on the P-38H. The 'H' had a combat radius of 400 miles. During early November 1943, individual squadrons of the 20th Fighter Group, which had been busy working up on the P-38H at King's Cliffe since August, flew missions as a fourth squadron in the 55th. They would not fly their first full Group mission until 28 December 1943. General Eaker knew that his deep penetration missions were finished without a proven long-range escort fighter. 'At this point nothing was more critical than the early arrival of the P-38s and P-51s,' he said.

The P-38 was not the total solution for long-range fighter escort duties. That would only come with the introduction of the P-51B Mustang, but when this magnificent fighter finally entered combat with the USAAF, on 1 December 1943, it was as a tactical fighter with the 354th Fighter Group, 9th Air Force. The first 8th Air Force group to receive the Mustang was the 357th Fighter Group, stationed at Raydon, Essex. They flew their first escort mission on 11 February 1944, and in March that year P-51Bs would fly to Berlin and back for the first time. The Mustang was the straw that would break the back of the Jagdgruppen (the twin-engined fighters of the Zerstörergruppen in particular were no match for the P-51), but in December 1943 the crews in the B-24 and B-17 groups were, for the most part, still very much on their own against the Luftwaffe.

Chapter 4

Chivalry in the Clouds
Charles L Brown

AAF Station 117, Kimbolton, England, 20 December 1943.

It was cold, a pervasive, numbing cold. The fire in the small stove, used to heat our combat crew's Nissen hut, had died out and the very damp, demonic cold of an English winter night penetrated the walls, blankets, clothing, and even the flesh, ending in a bone-chilling misery. Perhaps the effect was enhanced somewhat by a deep-seated fear which had yet to find a full measure of expression. The time was near 4.30 a.m. and what moments of sleep had been possible were dominated by vivid nightmares relating to combat against the Japanese. When my mind began to function in a semi-awake condition, I realized that my fear, to a large degree, was based on wondering how I would perform during my first mission as a pilot/aircraft commander of a B-17 and crew on an impending bombing mission over *Germany*, not Japan.

It was almost a relief when the hated wake-up orderly made his appearance. Dressing in combat flying gear was accomplished rather quickly due to the cold and a desire to have breakfast and get to the briefing as soon as possible. Even though there was plenty of time, there seemed to be some type of urgency compelling me to hurry. Breakfast was quick and quite sparse, as my nervous stomach butterflies preferred black coffee to solid food. We moved rapidly on to the briefing room already crowded with combat crew and briefing personnel.

As we entered, there were subdued conversations and an air of false bravado, and attempts at humour were prevalent among the crews. After a few minutes there was sudden silence and then everyone came to attention even before the command ATTENTION! was heard. Colonel 'Mo' Preston, CO of the 379th BG, and who was also to be the Air Group Commander for the mission, said a few words of encouragement, with emphasis on explicit instructions to keep the formation tight. He then drew back the curtain and our target of Bremen was identified. Our

Group's specific target was to be a Fw 190 plant in one of the outlying districts of the city. I was somewhat relieved, since I had just flown my first combat mission to the port area of Bremen on 13 December, at which time I flew as pilot for one of the deputy Group leaders. Although I felt apprehensive about combat, I also felt confident that, barring a disaster, I could handle the requirements of combat as a B-17 pilot/aircraft commander.

The briefing continued with the intelligence officer pointing out flak areas to avoid en route and finishing with the fact that Bremen was protected by over 250 flak guns manned by what was known as the 'OCS' [Officer Candidate School] for flak gunners; in other words, the best. We would also be subject to attack by between 500 and 750 German fighters. American and RAF fighter cover was scheduled to be available all the way to the target and return, if we were on time. The Group combat formation was to consist of the lead, high and low squadrons, each made up of one three-ship lead element followed by a second four-ship or diamond element for a total of twenty-one aircraft. My crew was to fly No. 3 (left wing slot), second element, low squadron, or what was more commonly called 'Purple Heart Corner', for well-documented reasons. Not much of a morale booster for a first trip, but a normal position for inexperienced combat crews. We certainly qualified there. Weather at take-off was forecast to be 5/10ths to 8/10ths cloud cover with restricted visibility; meaning a longer and more dangerous climb and assembly process. Due to the low clouds, we were briefed to assemble in formation at 7,000ft on the Kimbolton radio splasher [beacon]. Weather was forecast to be from 3/10ths to 5/10ths cloud cover with tops at 20,000-plus feet en route and 7,000 to 8,000 feet in the target area. After the general briefing, the navigators and bombardiers attended short specialised briefings, conducted respectively by the Group Navigator and Group Bombardier.

The briefings finally ended and we proceeded to the various supply points to sign for special combat items such as survival gear, escape and evasion materials, mission codes, weapons etc. We then had a short truck ride to the dispersal site where our first assigned aircraft, *Ye Olde Pub*, B-17F 42-3167, awaited our arrival. After having flown dozens of different aircraft in the previous five months of combat training as a crew, this was finally to be our very own 'lady'. For a pilot, each new aircraft he flies is somewhat like a first date with a new girl. All girls have certain similarities, but in the final analysis, each one is different and requires different handling techniques. Airplanes are a lot like that.

Perhaps that is why, regardless of the actual name, an airplane is always a 'lady', at least when you first meet.

After removing our equipment from the truck, I introduced myself to the crew chief with the normal, 'How's she doing Chief?'

'Pretty good sir, but No. 4 was running rough when we fired her up. She smoothed out after warm-up and seems OK now. I would watch her though.'

'Thanks, Chief,' was all I could think of.

'Sir, are you going to be the regular crew on this ship?' the Chief asked.

'If she treats us right, I sure hope so. We need a good friend and maybe she can do the job,' was my response.

'Lieutenant, take care of our baby,' was the Chief's final comment as I started my walk around inspection of the aircraft. I concluded with, 'Chief, I'll treat her like my own, and you can be sure of that.'

'Thanks Lieutenant,' and so ended the conversation.

During the walk-around inspection of our aircraft, I suddenly realised how proud I was to be allowed to fly this magnificent machine. She had a wingspan of over 103ft, was 75ft long and weighed in excess of twenty-four tons without either bomb or fuel load. She was equipped with four Wright Cyclone radial engines rated at near 1,200hp each or near 5,000 total hp. She could fly over six miles high, carry up to six tons of bombs, cruise at over 200mph at altitude and stay airborne for over eleven hours. Normal fuel load was in excess of 2,700 gallons and she was equipped with eleven .50 calibre machine-guns for protection. A thing of beauty as well as a mighty war machine designed to fight a new type of combat high in the skies. The many patches on this beauty's surface, revealed by the shaft of light from my flashlight, confirmed that she had been there before. She, at least, was a veteran. I felt a certain comfort in that.

After I had finished my external inspection, I put my gear aboard and completed the internal portion of the inspection. The guns had all been secured in place, spare ammunition was placed in strategic positions and the oxygen supply and availability at all stations was verified. The twelve bombs, each weighing 500lb for a total of three tons of high explosives, filled what appeared to be a modest-sized bomb bay for such a large aircraft. The bombs looked ominous just hanging on the racks. The bombardier carefully examined each shackle to ensure that one would not drop prematurely either on the ground or due to turbulence in the air.

After the internal inspection, I left the aircraft and went into the tent used by the ground crew, to relax for a few minutes and have yet another cup of coffee to quieten my protesting stomach. Suddenly, I experienced a quiet, almost tranquil feeling, and my thoughts wandered. I remembered that I had just celebrated my twenty-fifth birthday about two months before on 24 October. In actuality, it had been my twenty-first birthday, as on our first meeting in order to impress my crew and give them confidence in my ability, I had told them that I was four years older, and up to that point they had had no reason to question my reported age. My dominant thought or worry was how I would perform in a true combat emergency with the lives of nine other men and myself dependent upon my ability. The full impact struck me that I was now the senior pilot and aircraft commander, and would have to make the final decisions. It was a bit frightening!

I thought of the individual members of my crew – 'the quiet ones', as we had been dubbed by our training provisional Group Commander. 'Pinky' Luke, our co-pilot, and I were both from rural backgrounds, and normally only made noise when somebody stepped on us a little too hard. Hugh 'Ecky' Eckenrode, our tail gunner, Lloyd Jennings and Alex 'Russian' Yelesanko, our waist gunners, Richard 'Dick' Pechout, our radio operator, 'Frenchy' Coulombe, our engineer and top turret gunner, and Robert 'Andy' Andrews, our bombardier, were also quiet and reserved. That left Sam 'Blackie' Blackford, our ball turret gunner, and Al 'Doc' Sadok, our navigator, neither of whom could be classified as either quiet or reserved. They became the crew defenders when we were unjustly reproached or our honour or capabilities were questioned. A good mix of personalities allowing a close bond to develop beginning with our initial assignment as a training crew back in July. I was very proud to have them as my crew and my adopted family.

Shortly after re-entering the cockpit, the first of a series of signal flares arced through the ground haze, indicating that it was time to start engines. The first three engines started without problems. Our crew chief was right, however, as No. 4 engine did run rough for the first few minutes. The quiet of the airfield was now shattered by the rolling thunder of ninety-six large radial engines, capable of producing thousands of horsepower, being brought to life. The semi-darkness was pierced by the exhaust flames and the poor visibility was further restricted by the smoke from the starting engines. The smell of oil, gasoline and smoke now penetrated our cockpit as we too prepared to taxi.

Taxiing to the take-off point was quite a chore as the taxiways were narrow and the wings and engine nacelles of the aircraft overlapped on either side of the taxiway. There was no room for passing, and falling in line in the proper position was a must. Due to the limited runway length, only three aircraft could line up on the runway at the same time. Starting with the group leader as No. 1, the other aircraft lined up according to their position in the formation. Except for the three spares, we were to be second from last, or No. 20 on take-off. The green flare was still in the air when the Group leader started to roll for take-off. Each thirty seconds another pilot started his take-off roll and approximately ten minutes later I applied power to all four engines and we began to move. Take-off in any aircraft is an exciting moment for the pilot, but taking off for the first time with a full bomb and fuel load on a combat mission was nothing short of awesome. The double doses of adrenalin due to both the sheer excitement of take-off and the fear of a bomb-laden take-off mishap brought on an extra-sensory awareness of my surroundings and circumstances along with the realisation that, up to this point, learning to fly had been a challenge, somewhat like a game. This was no training mission; the guns, bullets and bombs were real. The game was over. Although the runway seemed excessively rough due to the extra bomb and fuel loads, we quickly gained speed on our take-off roll. As the elevator trim was co-ordinated with a slight back pressure on the control column, we gently lifted off the runway and began a climbing right turn to follow our lead aircraft.

Despite the poor visibility, we were able to keep the aircraft in front of us in sight until we formed into flights and squadrons while we also assembled into the Group formation. We had completed take-off by 0842 and by 0940 had formed the Group at 8,000ft; the other two groups completed our Wing formation of sixty aircraft. High cloud build-up prevented following the scheduled assembly route as we climbed and other combat Wings fell in, in trail behind us as were the lead Group for our Wing and for the entire VIIIth Bomber Command. As we turned to miss some of the towering clouds, we could see many of the aircraft behind us. The vast number of almost 500 bombers presented a spectacular and reassuring sight. They were ours and we were not alone.

Due to the clouds, we were five minutes late as we left the English coast just south of Great Yarmouth at 1039 and 24,000ft. We were still five minutes late as we entered the enemy coast at Texel Island at 1105 at 27,000ft. Our original squadron of seven planes had lost three planes due to aborts for mechanical malfunctions and we had moved into the No. 3 slot on the left wing of the Squadron Leader. The No. 4, or diamond, slot remained filled by our former flight leader. With one other abort from the lead squadron, our combat group was now down to seventeen aircraft. The cloud cover over the continent was scattered to broken with most clouds topping at under 10,000ft.

Friendly fighter escort of P-47s and P-51s was excellent until we reached the initial point for the bomb run at 1132 at 27,300ft. During the bomb run of approximately ten minutes, we would cover over thirty miles in essentially a straight line, with some minor diversionary course changes, while maintaining level flight. Although the procedure gave our lead bombardiers adequate time to set up the bombsights and correct for wind drift, smoke and cloud obstructions etc., it also gave the German defence units time to identify our target, flight path, and altitude – the key ingredients to destroying us by anti-aircraft fire and/or fighters.

As we were leading the strike force, there were no aircraft in front of us and all we could see was the rapidly expanding black cloud from flak bursts which gradually became a black oily carpet as we got closer to the target. A veteran combat pilot had told me that you were in serious trouble when you were close enough to see and distinguish the orange and red centres of the flak bursts! About two minutes before bombs away, immediately in front of us, I saw several of what appeared to be fantastically beautiful, deadly, black orchids with vivid crimson centres. I knew we were in trouble.

'We're hit! We're hit!' Both Andy and Doc in the front compartment were on the intercom simultaneously. 'The nose section has been hit and almost destroyed. There's a large hole.'

Pinky and I also had problems as the oil pressure suddenly dropped in No. 2 engine and we initiated engine shutdown procedures. The rapid descriptive comments of both Andy and Doc slowed down as though synchronised with the No. 2 propeller speed as they saw it stop in a feathered position. As I attempted to apply more power to the remaining engines, No. 4 ran away. At that point, the aircraft suddenly lurched skyward just as Andy called out the welcome 'Bombs away!' report. With the sudden shedding of three tons of weight, I thought perhaps we could remain in formation. However, this was not possible as with No. 2 shutdown, we also had to start shutdown procedures on No. 4 to bring it back into a useable power range. Just as the Group started a left turn of the target, both the No. 4 aircraft in our squadron (our original flight leader) and our own aircraft fell out of the Group formation, but we continued flying side by side. Suddenly, both left engines and the left wing section of the other aircraft were enveloped in flames as it went into a steep dive.

86

'I didn't see any chutes, did you?' was the question raised by Blackie, Andy and Doc.

'No, damn it, no!' was the only response. We could not maintain enough speed to stay in sight of the formation; we were now alone as we became a 'cripple' with a feathered engine and a 'straggler'. Either condition normally attracted German fighters somewhat like blood attracts piranha or sharks.

There was little delay. 'Enemy fighters, ten o'clock; bandits, twelve o'clock,' called out Doc, Andy and Frenchy as the intercom came alive with multiple reports of sightings of German fighters at various locations in front of us. I quickly looked up from the instrument panel to see eight Fw 190s forming a line slightly above and just ahead of us. Just then Ecky our tail gunner, called out, 'Enemy fighters, six o'clock!'

'How many?' I asked.

'Five 109s are queueing up and I see two more climbing,' he replied.

'Let me know when they start their attack,' I said.

'Bandits attacking ten o'clock' was heard just as Frenchy opened fire with the twin fifty-calibre guns in the top turret and Doc opened fire with the gun in the nose, both trying to shoot down two Fw 190s approaching in a co-ordinated attack from the ten and twelve o'clock positions. As I saw the wings of the first fighter light up with machine-gun and cannon fire, I pulled up and headed directly toward the attacking fighters on a collision course with the one attacking from twelve o'clock. Just as they broke off their attacks by rolling over and diving, 'Fighters attacking, six o'clock level,' was reported by Ecky in the tail, along with, 'Get them somebody, my guns are jammed!'

'My God, they won't fire!' was the next intercom exclamation heard from Blackie in the ball turret. The information regarding the jammed guns combined with the sound of the machine-gun bullets and exploding cannon shells striking the aircraft increased the level of my fear to sheer terror.

'Denver One, Denver One, Mayday, Mayday, Mayday! This is Goldsmith under attack south of Wilhelmshaven – need assistance!' It was the only brief message I could transmit on the fighter frequency. There was no response from our fighter escort and I switched back to intercom. This was my last radio call as the radio room was hit shortly thereafter.

After the first fighter passes I found that the controls of No. 3 engine had been shot away. However, the oil pressure and engine temperature remained stable and the engine continued to produce fifty to sixty per cent power. Total loss of the No. 3 engine would have precipitated complete disaster. Despite the good fortune of being able to keep the No. 3 engine producing at least partial power, some type of drastic survival action was immediately required. Due to the frozen and/or otherwise malfunctioning weapons, the only defensive guns available were the twin guns operated by Frenchy in the top turret and the single gun in the nose operated by Doc or Andy. With these limitations in mind, I began to turn our nose into each attacking fighter and for a few minutes became a four-, or more appropriate, two-and-a-half-engined fighter aircraft with three forward-firing guns as our offensive weapons. The fact that we appeared to be attacker rather than the one being attacked seemed to throw the German fighter pilots off their routine. As a consequence, due to our climb, dive and turn manoeuvres, they were given shorter aiming and firing runs, faster rates of closure, and our violent manoeuvres kept them somewhat off balance.

Despite our best and most desperate efforts, however, we were hit hundreds of times by the machine-gun bullets and several 20mm cannon shells. Fortunately, the extreme manoeuvres to avoid certain destruction did not result in additional casualties on our aircraft. There were moments in which I became angry and forgot that many of the crew were not held in place by belts, and in the case of the waist gunners, they could be thrown or fall from the aircraft through the open windows. In one instance, we executed a severe bank of near eighty degrees by turning into a group of five fighters queueing up for attack from the rear. To say that my flying techniques were influenced by the survival instinct in this cacophony of sound, fear and turmoil would be gross understatement. Many of the details were more effectively captured by the following pertinent excerpts from their diaries reflecting the different views of Doc in the nose and Blackie in the ball turret. Doc wrote:

> We were then on our bomb run rushing towards a black carpet of flak in front of us, and suddenly without warning, out went our Plexiglas nose and our No. 2 engine. A minute later bombs were away. Before we knew what happened our formation left us on a wide steep turn which swung us out too far and we couldn't catch up with one engine gone. It then struck me that we were a cripple, a straggler and certain prey for the enemy, without much hope of returning. However, there wasn't too much time to delve into this very deeply as the Me 109s and Fw 190s began boring in and the pilot was yelling for a heading home.
>
> I felt like a one-armed paperhanger trying to figure out the safest

heading home which would not take us over many flak areas, and at the same time I was scraping the frozen Plexiglas so that I could keep an anxious vigil on the enemy attackers. Somehow, I gave the pilot a heading and got enough ice off the window to see a Fw 190 bearing in at about one o'clock, close enough to spit on; black belches of smoke coughing out of his wing and his wing lighting on and off like a neon sign gave me the general idea that he was shooting at us and not for fun. I trained my fifty calibre and let go with a long burst and, due to his proximity, I couldn't miss. As he snap-rolled to give us his bulletproof belly as a target his engine burst into flames, but I don't know whether he went down or not as I wasn't interested due to my shaking knees.

At that moment our tail gunner's voice rasped over the interphone, 'Fighter coming in, six o'clock. Get him somebody, my guns are jammed.' Our pilot went into a violent manoeuvre in an effort to spoil the aim of the attacker. Just about this time our top turret gunner, T/Sgt Frenchy Coulombe, shot a Fw 190 out of the sky which had come in about eleven o'clock and high.

It was bitter cold up there (somewhere about sixty degrees C below) and with a wide gap in the Plexiglas nose, an icy blast kept pouring in, making my hands and feet bitter cold. But in spite of that cold, I felt myself sweating uncomfortably.

Listening over the interphone I understood that about five enemy fighters were queueing up ready to make a pass at us at about six o'clock, and what with only the top turret guns operating in that direction, all the others were frozen and inoperative. I then prepared to meet my destiny and soon our airplane was rocking all over the air with 20mms exploding and sounding like hail on a tin roof. Every time our plane made a wild gyration I thought surely everybody in the rear of the airplane was dead, including the pilot. The silence on the intercom was more terrifying than the sounds of exploding shells.

Blackie observed:

I became aware of how bitter cold it was! My feet had absolutely no feeling. My heated shoes had malfunctioned. The first Me 109 to come in on the tail, I remember having trouble with my range finder (which was located under my left heel) because I couldn't feel it. Then, without a doubt, the biggest surprise of my life: when I depressed both thumb buttons, the guns did not fire! Had I forgotten to turn the gun selector switches on? No! Had I overlooked putting a round into each of the chambers? No! Looking quickly at the left and right gun: my God! The guns were frozen metal to metal with a build-up of frost all over them that was three eighths to half an inch thick! The worst sound was the repeated dry click of the solenoids and the guns not firing!

So what do you do? I tied my gut in a knot, said a quick prayer, and looked right at each fighter coming in, hoping they would think I had live guns. They were not fooled.

The intercom was very active with everyone calling at the same time. The Me109s and the Fw 190s were coming in from all directions. I realised somewhere during all of the confusion that we were not getting any more reports from the tail gunner and thought his intercom had been damaged. During the heavy fighter attacks, there were twelve to fifteen combined Me 109s and Fw 190s coming in on us, and why not? They had cut us out of the formation by flak and they had a cripple to eliminate by fighters. Each wanted credit for one more B-17. They all attacked for several minutes. I later learned that during part of our violent manoeuvres, S/Sgt Lloyd Jennings, one of our waist gunners, spent much of this time trying to treat the mangled leg of S/Sgt Alex Yelesanko and prevent him bleeding to death. The severe cold was one blessing in that a portion of his leg was deliberately frozen to assist in stopping the flow of blood.

At some point during our continuous twisting, turning, climbing and diving manoeuvres, the attacks finally ended and the fighter escort of P-47s reappeared. We had not seen friendly fighters since just prior to bomb release. During a few minutes of normal flight, I attempted to ascertain the casualties and full damage to the aircraft. Somewhat later, as I looked out the right window, there, flying very close formation with his wingtip only about three feet from our wingtip, was an Me 109. For a moment I thought that I had lost my mind and if I briefly closed my eyes it would disappear. I tried – he was still there. I later pointed him out to Pinky who had returned from the rear. The German pilot nodded but Pinky and I were in a state of shock and did not return the greeting. Although the German pilot appeared relaxed, I was most uncomfortable and felt that at any time he would unleash some type of new German weapon to destroy us and our aircraft. Somehow, all of the briefings and combat training sessions had omitted to inform us as to the proper protocol or reaction when a German fighter pilot wanted to fly close formation with us. I finally surmised that he was probably out of ammunition, but I was amazed at his curiosity and daring in flying that close to even a badly crippled enemy bomber.

At that point, only a single gun in the top turret was functioning out of the original eleven guns on the B-17F, with the other weapons in the 'guns down' or inoperable condition. I was also able to get Frenchy to return to the cockpit and join Pinky and myself in observing the audacious German pilot. Now we had three wide-eyed American airmen in the cockpit plus Blackie in the ball turret going eyeball to eyeball with one German pilot. (Blackie adds: 'He was closing in at a *very slow rate* from the low rear. Finally, he came up on our wing, so close that his wing actually overlapped ours. I kept my dead guns trained on him. We looked directly at each other. He was also looking inside the plane. The pilot motioned with his right hand as if to say, "I salute you. I gave you my best and you survived." With that he went into a dive down to his right and disappeared. There was something different about this fighter. First of all it was quite dark in colour. There was also quite a large round bulge just to the left and in front of the cockpit area, which about a month later intelligence personnel at the 379th identified as a new supercharger installation.') After a few more seconds, my nerves could stand it no longer and I asked Frenchy to get back to his turret and point his guns at the German pilot. When the fighter pilot saw the engineer's head appear in the top turret, he saluted, rolled over, and was gone. An abrupt end to one of the briefest, but most unusual encounters in the short history of the heavy bombardment as a major weapon of war.

Just as we were leaving the enemy coast to head back, losing altitude due to problems with three engines, Blackie climbed out of the ball turret and saw Jennings trying to administer morphine to Yelesanko: 'It would not flow due to the fact that it was so cold it had turned into a gel and would not come out of the tube. I immediately crawled back to the tail gunner to see if I could help. There was no hope. He had been mortally wounded by 20mm fire. I had a flashback to when he was calling out an attack from nine o'clock level by a Fw 190. The front of his guns were smoking and flashing; all at once, there was silence and the tail gunner never spoke again. My next effort was the radio room, where it actually looked like the inside of a cheese grater. Richard Pechout, the radio operator, who appeared to be in a state of shock, was still trying to make radio contact with our fighters using the damaged equipment, with his gloves off. We later found out he had had his gloves off for some time.'

The moment of decision had arrived. The aircraft was badly damaged with the No. 2 engine totally inoperable, the No. 3 engine operating at about fifty to sixty per cent power and the No. 4 engine, damaged by flak, tried to run away [overspeed] periodically and every time the throttle was touched. At this point we had between one and a half and two and a half engines operable. The co-pilot spent most of his time trying to keep the No. 4 engine functional and in a workable rpm range. The rudder did not respond and the elevators were slow in their reaction. With the large hole in the nose, the aircraft seemed to be swimming through heavy air, grossly overweight for the available power and very slow to respond to any control pressure. Attempting to fly a straight path was like trying to guide a water-soaked log in a swift moving stream. Lateral movement was difficult due to loss of rudder control and maintaining altitude in our river of air was impossible due to insufficient power and partial loss of elevator controls. By experimenting I established that we could remain flying, but with drastically reduced airspeed, and with a slight, but constant, loss of altitude. By dropping the left wing a few degrees and using trim tabs, we could maintain a relatively straight but slightly descending flight path. The question was, could we remain in the air long enough to cross the unyielding North Sea, a distance of approximately 250–350 miles?

An assessment of casualties indicated that Eckenrode was dead, Yelesanko was in a critical condition with a major leg wound (which later required amputation), Blackie was unable to walk because of frozen feet, and Pechout could not use his hands. The decision had to be made as to the possibility of trying to limp back to England or bale out. A crash-landing was never seriously considered since we were under strict instructions that if a crash-landing became necessary as a last resort, we were to destroy the aircraft and activate the explosive charge in the SECRET Norden bombsight. Since it appeared that in addition to Eckenrode, three more of the crew would not survive a parachute jump into northern Germany in the winter, and possibly all of us would perish in a crash-landing, I decided I would fly back over land to let any of the crew bale out who wished to do so, and I would then try and fly the aircraft back to England. Fortunately, each of the uninjured crew members chose to remain on board and, disregarding the questionable odds, try to make it to England. The fact that they would be needed to assist in keeping the aircraft airborne and care for the casualties played a large part in their decisions. They had trained as a crew and they decided to remain a crew, whatever the outcome.

Despite the extreme cold, all of my clothing was soaked with perspiration when the air contacts ended. As my body temperature returned to normal, the oxygen mask froze to the perspiration and blood (from a nosebleed) on my face until we reached a lower altitude and the mask could safely be removed.

Out over the North Sea we finally had free movement in treating the wounded and injured crewmen. We stayed fairly close to the enemy shore in the event we had to shut down another engine and execute a crash-landing. Although the aircraft seemed to fly slightly better in the more dense air at the lower altitude, the fact that even the slight descent was constant was still terrifying. Numerous bombers flew high over us and several friendly fighter aircraft, mostly P-47s, flew down near us during our crossing. We believed that they were keeping ASR informed of our flight path and position, plus giving us encouragement with thumbs-up signals as many rocked their wings in passing. The lower we dropped, the more ominous the North Sea appeared in its dull grey mantle interspersed with large whitecaps indicating strong wind and high waves. As we gradually lost altitude, we began throwing out excess weight, including moveable guns, ammo, ammo cans and miscellaneous equipment.

My concern increased to near panic proportions as we passed through 500ft without sighting land. We all started to breathe again as we came over the English coast at about 250ft. A pair of P-47s approached from the rear, and flew by each side of our aircraft, climbed to about 1,000ft and soon began to circle, just as we were looking for an open field suitable for a crash-landing. Just below the circling fighters we spotted an airfield to our immediate front. I lightly rocked our wings to the P-47s to acknowledge their help. The crew was able to get the gear down and start cranking the flaps down, just as I started flare out. Pinky cut the ignition switches on engines three and four and our landing, essentially without flaps, was completed with No. 1 the sole operating engine.

Despite the lack of effective brake or rudder control, and by a minor miracle, the aircraft remained relatively straight as we stopped, still on the runway. The fighter pilots had apparently alerted the tower and we were immediately surrounded by emergency vehicles and personnel. The four casualties were removed and I finally dropped to the ground, both figuratively and literally. Both Pinky and I had fought non-existent rudder controls across the entire North Sea and now my legs would not hold me upright. Being unable to stand and with a few spots of residual blood from the nosebleed on my face, the medics kept trying to put me on a stretcher. I was finally able to wipe away the remaining blood spots and convince them that I was not wounded and could, in fact, stand up. This I proceeded to do and was then able to walk rather well until I surveyed the damage to the aircraft. Upon examining the tail section, my legs again became quite weak when I realised that there was no rudder control possible due to the severe damage to both the rudder and vertical stabiliser and that both elevators had been damaged and one horizontal stabiliser was almost destroyed. I now understood why the control responses had been sluggish! In addition to the three damaged engines, every major component of the aircraft had suffered severe damage. The Plexiglas nose section was almost gone. There were hundreds of flak and bullet holes and one large hole possibly left by an 88mm anti-aircraft shell which had miraculously passed through the wing without exploding. The radio compartment was almost destroyed and the mid-section of the aircraft had suffered extensive damage. The aircraft was described by one military onlooker as a 'flying wind tunnel that looked like it had been designed by a Swiss cheese manufacturer'.

We had landed at Seething, an air base near the coast of East Anglia, and occupied by an American B-24 unit, the 448th Bomb Group [which had arrived at the end of November and which would fly its first combat mission on 20 December 1943]. After brief visits with intelligence personnel and the unit commander [Col James M Thompson], I went back to the aircraft. It seemed as though every camera in England was focused on what appeared to be an unflyable aircraft. As a badly crippled bomber, operating with a maximum of three functional defensive guns, we had survived attacks by between thirteen and fifteen German fighters as well as a harrowing return flight to England across the deadly North Sea. I realised that survival of the flak damage, our survival of the fighter attacks, our return flight, the timely assistance of our 'little friends' the P-47 pilots, and my own decisions enabling the successful completion of our mission, had been guided by a higher power.

During the interrogation and questions by the intelligence personnel and a subsequent conversation with a unit commander at the East Anglia recovery base, reference was made to recommending me for the nation's highest military award. At that point, I was too numb for the full effect to sink in, and although I later day-dreamed about it, I never mentioned it to my crew members since it would essentially be a crew award, and I did not want to give them false hope. This proved to be the proper decision.

After being assigned three replacement crew members, we finally completed our next mission on 7 January 1944. From that point until our final mission on 11 April 1944, I fantasised about receiving the highest award and along with my crew returning to the United States to sell war bonds and do public relations tours. The dream had been that if the award was made, there would be no more combat for our crew and hence no more dead or wounded crewmen. By the time we finished the tour, I realised that even if it had been recommended, the award had somehow fallen through the cracks and that, discounting severe and disabling wounds, nine of the original crew plus three replacement crew members had survived combat and *that* was the ultimate reward. (In addition to the Purple Hearts, I did recommend, and as I recall, S/Sgt Hugh Eckenrode was posthumously awarded the DFC for remaining at his frozen guns until his death to warn of impending fighter attacks.)

Robert L Harper, Assistant Intelligence Officer in the 448th BG at Seething, who assisted in removing the casualties (but who was not involved in the crew interrogation), advised that shortly after the landing, *Ye Olde Pub* was classified SECRET and the taking of photographs was prohibited. No explanation was given for the high security classification. Analysis of the mission details transmitted by the 448th BG to the 379th BG disclosed a number of errors, omissions and possible misrepresentations. *Significantly*, there was no mention made, under 'Crew Observations and Unusual Tactics', of the action by the single German fighter pilot who had completed a perfect tail attack on a crippled enemy bomber and then gave a salute as a final act of camaraderie/respect, even though this unusual event constituted a court martial offence. In fact the News Report stated that after the air battle, 'Thunderbolts picked up the stricken B-17 again, hovering over it like a group of doctors over a wounded patient, *and brought it back over the Channel . . .*'

Charles Brown has a strong feeling that when the recommendation for award of the Medal of Honor, or a lesser award, went forward, the most unusual actions of the German pilot in sparing their lives and escorting them out of Germany were included. Instead of a positive reception the response was totally negative.

Charles Brown never forgot the encounter and in January 1988 Bob Harper, who post-war had become a successful teacher, architect, and commercial artist, voluntarily recreated the final airborne encounter between *Ye Olde Pub* and the black 109. During 1986 Brown initiated an extensive international search in an attempt to locate any of the surviving German pilots from that encounter. In 1989 he wrote an article about it for the German fighter pilots' association. On 10 January 1990 Lt Franz Stigler, former Oblt in 6./JG27, responded by letter from his home in Surrey, British Columbia (he had emigrated to Canada in 1953), and after considerable investigation, it was confirmed that Stigler was the pilot of the lone Bf 109 who did not attempt to finish off the helpless B-17.

Stigler was born near Regensburg on 21 August 1915. He started flying gliders in 1927 (age twelve) and soloed in a Fw 44 powered bi-wing aircraft in 1933. (His instructor was Ritter von Greim, who became the last Luftwaffe commander in World War Two when he replaced Hermann Göring in April 1945.) Stiegler then flew primarily multi-engined aircraft with Lufthansa, the German national airline, until 1940, when he joined the Luftwaffe. In action he flew mostly fighters, especially the Bf 109 series. He flew combat in North Africa, Sicily, Italy and central and western Europe. At various times a Staffelkapitän of three Staffeln – 6., 8. and 12./JG27, he was credited with twenty-eight confirmed victories in JG27 and over thirty probables during World War Two.

Stigler had already downed two B-17s that day and his Bf 109 was being refuelled when Brown flew over the edge of his airfield. The German pilot immediately cut short the refuelling and went after the B-17. Upon catching up with the bomber he positioned himself to fire on the Fortress from the rear (Stigler's fighter was fully armed at the time of the encounter; he was not out of ammunition as previously thought by Brown's crew). When the tail gunner did not raise his guns and there was no defensive fire from the bomber Stigler went closer. As he came alongside and surveyed the damage he could hardly believe what he saw. 'The B-17 was like a sieve and there was blood everywhere,' he recalls. 'I could see the crew were having a terrible time dealing with their wounded and struggling to stay in the air. I was amazed that the aircraft could fly. I saw two wounded men on board, rather than just the airplane, which was our normal target. It was one thing to shoot an airplane, but in this case I saw the men. I just couldn't do it. I thought to myself, how can I shoot something like that? I cannot kill these half dead people. It would be like shooting at a parachute.' Stigler later described the Brown aircraft as 'the most badly damaged aircraft I ever saw which was still flying.'

At least twice he turned his fighter into the front of the bomber in attempts to get Brown to turn back into Germany and surrender. After Brown had ignored his efforts he decided to escort the B-17 out over the

Above: On 4 May 1943, sixty-five bombers hit the Ford and General Motors plants at Antwerp, accompanied for the first time by P-47s of the 4th and *(pictured)* 56th Fighter Groups. *(Coll. Bill Cameron)*

Below: Uffz Schönrock of 4 Staffel JG1 who claimed two B-17s shot down on 17 August 1943, 'The Day of the Fighters', poses for the camera in front of his Fw 190 A-4 at Woendrecht. *(Eric Mombeek)*

B-17 42-5077 *Delta Rebel II* of the 91st BG, which was lost on 12 August 1943 when it was captained by 2/Lt Robert W. Thompson. *(USAF)*

B-17s of the 306th BG weave their way through heavy flak over Schweinfurt on 14 October 1943. Altogether, the group lost ten Fortresses, the second highest loss in the First Division.

(Gordon and Connie Richards)

Left: B-17F 42-30727 of the 306th BG piloted by Lt William C. Bisson in the 376th 'Clay Pigeons' Squadron, was lost on the Schweinfurt raid of 14 October 1943.

(Gordon and Connie Richards)

Below: The first P-51Bs to serve in the ETO were assigned to the 354th FG, 9th Air Force, while the first 8th Air Force Group to receive the Mustang was the 357th FG at Raydon, Essex, who flew their first escort mission on 11 February 1944.

Crew of *Ye Olde Pub*, 379th BG, October 1943. *Back row, left to right:* T/Sgt B. O. 'Frenchy' Coulombe, engineer/top turret; Sgt Alex 'Russian' Yelesanko, waist gunner; Sgt R. A. 'Dick' Pechout, radio operator; Sgt Lloyd H. Jennings, waist gunner; Sgt H. S. 'Ecky' Eckenrode, tail gunner; Sgt S. W. 'Blackie' Blackford, ball turret. *Front row, left to right:* Lt Charlie L. Brown, pilot; Lt S. G. 'Pinky' Luke, co-pilot; Lt A. 'Doc' Sadok, navigator; Lt R. M. Andrews, bombardier. *(Charles L. Brown)*

The then unknown Bf 109 pilot of 6./JG27 gives a final salute after sparing *Ye Olde Pub* from certain destruction, leaving pilot Charlie Brown to fly the wrecked B-17 back to England and safety.
(From a painting by Bob Harper)

P-47 42-8369 of the 61st Fighter Squadron, 56th Fighter Group. The friendly fighter escort of P-47s and P-51s on 20 December 1943 was excellent until the IP. *(via Mike Bailey)*

Colonel Maurice 'Mo' Preston *(right)* CO, 379th BG at Kimbolton. *(USAF)*

Above: Bf 109G-6 R3 of 9./JG27 in flight. *(Heinz Nowarra)*

Left: Charlie Brown celebrates completing his tour at Kimbolton on 11 April 1944 with a swig of 'mountaineer tea'. *(Charles L. Brown)*

Right: Oblt Otto Stammberger, Staffelkapitän, 4./JG26, who on 5 April shot down *Montana Power* of the 368th BS, 306th BG, flown by 2/Lt Robert J. Seelos. Stammberger was seriously wounded by RAF Spitfires on 13 May 1943. *(Bundesarchiv)*

Fw 190 A-3 of 5./JG1 at Katwijk airfield, Holland, in 1943. *(Coll. Rob de Visser)*

Above: Ofw Karl Georg Pfeiffer *(right)* of IV/NJG1 who shot down F/Sgt David Mills' Stirling on 27/28 May 1943, pictured at Leeuwarden with Ofw Scherfling *(top)* and Ofw Vinke, foreground. *(Coll. Karl Pfeiffer, via Rob de Visser)*

Above left: Hptm Reinhold Knacke, Staffelkapitän 1/NJG1, KIA 3 February 1943 near Achterveld, Holland after having scored forty-four victories. He was the first Nachtjagd pilot to shoot down a Mosquito, on 28/29 July 1942. *(Coll. Ab A. Jansen)*

Left: Twenty-two-year-old Sgt Stanley 'Peter' Moore, mid-upper gunner, 218 Squadron Stirling, MIA 27/28 May 1943. *(Jim Moore)*

Below: Stirling 'A' of 218 Squadron at Downham Market in 1943. *(via Harry Barker)*

Halifax II Series 1A X-X-Ray BB324 of 10 Squadron which was lost on a raid on Mulheim on 22/23 June 1943. *(via Tom Thackray)*

Right: Lt Gerhard Dittmann, pilot, 12./NJG1, KIA 18 August 1943. He destroyed two B-17s, on 25 and 26 July 1943.
(Coll. Elsbeth Dittmann, via Ab A. Jansen)

Left: Franz Stigler

Avro Lancaster shot down near Terschelling Island. *(Coll. Hille van Dieren)*

Oblt (later Oberst) Hans-Joachim 'Hajo' Herrmann, initiator of 'Wild Boar' night fighting in May 1943, and creator of Rammkommando Elbe in early 1945. *(Coll. Werner Zell)*

Ofw Heinz Vinke and Uffz Rudi Dunger enjoying a meal at Bergen/Alkmaar in 1943. Vinke had lost his crew in combat on 17/18 August 1943 when Bob Braham of 141 Squadron shot down his Bf 110G-4 Wrk Nr 4874. Dunger, who lost his pilot on the same night, crewed up with Vinke, and was killed on 26 February 1944 by RAF Spitfires during an ASR operation off Dunkirk. At the time of his death Vinke had fifty-four night victories in some 150 sorties. *(Coll. Ab A. Jansen)*

Left: Uffz Rudi Dunger, bordfunker IV./NJG1, who on 17/18 August was rescued from the sea after his Bf 110, piloted by Fw Kraft, was shot down by Bob Braham. *(Coll. Ab A. Jansen)*

Right: Fw Karl Schödl, bordfunker, IV./NJG1, MIA 17/18 August 1943. *(Coll. Ab A. Jansen)*

North Sea, hoping the pilot would turn towards Sweden, only about a half-hour flight away. However, after clearing some islands Brown turned towards England, instead of Sweden. Stigler then thought, 'Stupid guy, I hope he makes it home and gets medical help for his crew.' Then, in one of those rare moments of compassion in an otherwise brutal war, Franz Stigler did an extraordinary thing. He saluted, rolled his fighter and departed. It was a decision that could have resulted in severe punishment, possibly even execution, had his superiors known.

Stigler ended the war as technical officer of General Adolf Galland's famous Jagdverband 44 of 'Experten' (aces), flying the Me 262. He was credited with 487 combat sorties, was wounded four times, and was shot down seventeen times: four by fighters, four by ground fire, and nine times by American gunners on bombers. He baled out six times and rode his damaged aircraft down eleven times.

Stigler met with Brown and two of the surviving crew members, Sam Blackford, the ball turret gunner, and Dick Pechout, the radio operator, during the 379th BG Association Reunion, at which the ex-Luftwaffe ace was a guest of the Association. Brown and Stigler, not surprisingly, have remained friends ever since.

CHAPTER 5

RAF BOMBER OFFENSIVE: 1943

After a certain respite in the winter of 1942–43, in the spring of 1943 AM Harris ordered large concentrated RAF attacks on the Ruhr. Since the thousand-bomber raid by the RAF on Cologne on 30 May 1942, which inaugurated a new era of mass attacks, and up until the Window attacks on Hamburg in July 1943, the German night fighters had succeeded in inflicting heavy losses on RAF bomber forces, whose tactics of staggered approach, involving a period of long duration (one to one and a half hours) over the target, were ideal for the successful operation of the Himmelbett system. Some notable Nachtjagdgeschwader pilots, though, had been lost during the winter battles. Among these were three NJG1 'Experten': Hptm Reinhold Knacke, who was lost on 3 February after having scored forty-four victories (he was KIA after having shot down two Viermots on this night and crashed in his damaged Bf 110 by return fire from his forty-fourth victim); Oblt Paul Gildner, on 24 February, who had amassed forty-six victories (he crashed near Gilze–Rijen airfield due to an engine fire and was killed); and Hptm Ludwig Becker who, it will be remembered, was lost on 26 February after having also scored forty-four victories.

Lt Dieter Schmidt-Barbo, meanwhile, was still waiting to get his first victory of the war and in March 1943 he was given an opportunity, as he explains:

> During 1942–43 the British often penetrated with single, low-flying aircraft over Holland to drop sabotage equipment, weapons, and at times also secret agents to aid the Resistance in their fight against German troops. Dutch liaison people called in the material by radio and the dropping zones were marked by three or four simple lamps. For some time the Abwehr had succeeded in turning the whole thing around and the radio traffic was now almost completely controlled by German posts. Thus, the material, including the agents, could be collected immediately at the dropping zone. In order to make sure that the whole game looked real, we received orders from time to time to shoot down one of the Special Operations machines.

The whole exercise was difficult for us insofar as it was hard to track down machines by radar because of their low flying height. And for the same reason, our connection by radio with the GCI station often largely fell out. These missions were therefore relatively unattractive for the 'old hands'. For us 'young hands', however, they were a welcome practice.

On the night of 24/25 March my name appears on the battle order for this type of mission. We are briefed on the place and time of the established drop and we take off as soon as the intruder is confirmed. It is shortly after midnight. As expected, the radio connection with the GCI controller fades out relatively soon; the last message we receive is that the aircraft is homeward bound at a height of 200 metres. We proceed at a height of some 100 metres in the direction of the Zuider Zee and beneath us – the night is not too dark – we see the newly reclaimed land to the eastern side of the Zuider Zee. Then suddenly my navigator/wireless operator discovers him above us – definitely four-engined.

I sneak up on him from behind, a short burst in the left wing. I can see hits registering but despite the low level at which we fly, he immediately peels off to the right, and levels off just over the water. I can only still chase him because of a fire in his left engine, the glow of which reflects on the water. Immediately after everything is dark; over and out? A red Very light which a few minutes later is fired into the sky from the spot confirms that it has certainly crashed.

Therefore we are deeply disappointed when on our return at the Operations Room we are greeted with the news that the intruder's outward flight has been reported over northern Holland. Empty-handed again!! I gather I have, out of inexperience and for fear of being detected myself, opened fire at much too long a range and especially with much too short a burst! With the obvious mixed feelings we drive to our quarters and try to sleep.

At dawn I am rudely awakened by the phone: 'My congratulations on your first kill.'

'Are you trying to pull my leg?' On the other end of the line is my friend Werner Rapp, who is duty officer and still in the Operations Room. He informs me that the crew of seven have in the meantime been picked up in their dinghy between Enkhuizen and Stavoren, so the aircraft did crash! The report on the outward bound machine was the second enemy aircraft in this night!

As far as I know, this Halifax must still rest relatively unscathed on the bottom of the Zuider Zee west or north-west of the former island of Urk.

Schmidt-Barbo's first victory in fact was Halifax HR 665 of 138 Squadron that had taken off from Tempsford for dropping at three different DZs. F/O Chow was at the controls and on board were two secret agents, Gerbrands (codename 'St John') and Bergman ('Andrew'), and a load of containers with supplies for the Dutch Resistance. Two containers were successfully dropped near Limmen twenty-five kilometres north-west of Amsterdam and then F/O Chow set course for Friesland where the two agents were to be dropped. When flying low over the Zuider Zee they were hit in the left wing by Schmidt-Barbo's gunfire at 0036 hours. Bergman was killed by the burst of fire and the aircraft was so heavily damaged that Chow had no option left but to ditch in the sea east of Enkhuizen. The crew managed to escape from the aircraft before it sank and set sail in their dinghy but were soon picked up by the Germans. A second SD Halifax, also from 138 Squadron, successfully completed its mission with two drops in Holland, at 'Lettuce 10' and 'Parsnip 5' with F/O Rutledge at the controls. The Halifax safely returned to Tempsford.

A few months after his first victory, Dieter Schmidt-Barbo was appointed Staffelkapitän of 8./NJG1, and his star rose rapidly. By the end of 1943 he had nine kills to his credit. On 13/14 January 1944, he succeeded in bringing down a Mosquito. During 1944 he proved himself to be an expert night fighter pilot and claimed three kills on one night on more than one occasion: on 22/23 April (his nineteenth to twenty-first kills); 3/4 May (twenty-third to twenty-fifth); 22/23 May (twenty-seventh to twenty-ninth) and 28/29 July (thirty-third to thirty-fifth kills). Barbo was awarded the Knight's Cross on 27 July 1944, after thirty-two night victories. As Oblt Schmidt-Barbo, he left 8./NJG1 for 9 Staffel of the same élite night fighter wing, again as Staffelkapitän. By the war's end he had risen to Hauptmann, flown 171 operational sorties and claimed forty British aircraft, all at night.

In 1942, when the RAF began attacking targets within a period of thirty to forty minutes, the narrow night fighter zone in the west was quickly penetrated, and at the same time only a few fighters came into actual contact with the bomber stream. Flak, emplaced in single batteries, was unable to cope with the concentrated attacks by the RAF. The carefully practised system of concentrating several batteries' fire on a single target broke down because so many aircraft appeared over the target simultaneously. As a result of all this, the night fighter zone in the west had to be rapidly increased in depth and extended to Denmark in the north and to eastern France in the south. Operational control had to be developed whereby two or more night fighters could be brought into action in any one night fighter area at the same time. In addition, bombers over the target had to be attacked by fighters as well as flak, and the flak had to be consolidated into large batteries near the targets and concentrated at the most important targets. Above all, accuracy had to be increased by developing a large number of radar range-finders.

While the changes took time to become effective, the numbers of aircraft shot down were relatively small. However, there were opportunities for the German night fighters to exploit, like on the night of 25/26 May 1943 when 759 bombers were despatched to bomb Düsseldorf and twenty-seven bombers were shot down. The raid failed because bad weather made target marking difficult. Sgt Ken Dix, navigator aboard Wellington X HE202 Z-Zebra of 431 (RCAF) Squadron, recalls: 'As the navigator I was concerned when I saw that our flight path took us one and a half miles north of the German night fighter base at Venlo. I said they could orbit their beacon and pick off bombers behind the main stream. But no route change was made. On the runway the port engine would not start and the other bombers went off. Usually we were the lead machine as a specially selected crew. We carried 4,000lb of incendiaries to drop within less than ten seconds of the flares from the Pathfinder Force aircraft going down on the target, usually from as near to 18,500ft as we could reach with a full bomb load. But it was twenty-two minutes before we got the port engine going. So it left us well behind the main stream of bombers. The machine did not climb well enough and had not enough speed. So we flew to Hornsea on the coast, and flew across the North Sea to Ijmuiden. Then we headed between the flak zones of Soesterberg and Hertogenbosch on our way to the Track Indicator Markers laid by the pathfinders. We had just seen it and were on the correct track when Sgt Harry Sweet in the rear turret shouted, "Fighter!" He immediately fired his four Browning machine-guns.'

The fighter, a Bf 110, was flown by Oblt Manfred Meurer, Staffelkapitän of 3./NJG1 from Venlo. (Hptm Meurer was killed in action on 21 January 1944, by which time he had amassed no less than sixty-five 'Nachtabschüsse'.) At the same time as Harry Sweet opened fire, Meurer fired his cannons and hit the Wellington along the starboard beam from the tail as Sgt Bob Barclay, the pilot, took evasive action. Ken Dix continues: 'The cannon shells had hit hard. They stopped just by my Gee radar set. The voice intercom failed, then our flashing intercom buttons also went off. Sgt Jeffries, the WOP/AG, was behind the main spar ready to launch the flare for our picture after the bombing

run. He was killed. The aircraft was blazing with the port engine hit and on fire. We were spinning round and down. I managed to get my chest chute into my new harness. I couldn't go back to Sgt Jeffries because of the fierce flames driving me back. I went to the cockpit. The front hatch was open but F/O Bert Bonner, the bomb aimer, and Bob Barclay, the pilot, had baled out. They could have tried to contact us but the system had been hit. I had flown the aircraft when we were on exercises and I had also been on a pilot's course in Florida before becoming a navigator, so I decided to try and fly the Wellington back to base. I got into the pilot's seat and the Wellington at first answered the controls. I turned to fly north-west back to England then dived to try and put the flames out. It was going well when suddenly the control wires, hit by cannon fire, broke. I had no control so, reluctantly, I had to bale out. I pulled the rip cord and the turning Wellington just missed me. I saw it hit the ground.'
(Dix and Barclay were made PoW. Dix's Wellington was one of three RAF bombers which Meurer shot down on this night; in May 1943, he claimed fourteen 'heavies' shot down.)

On 27/28 May 1943, a 218 Squadron Stirling crew, skippered by F/Sgt David Mills, a twenty-three-year-old married man from Hayes, took off from Downham Market near King's Lynn on their first operation. There were two New Zealanders on the crew: twenty-two-year-old F/O William Fitzgerald, navigator, and twenty-one-year-old F/Sgt Geoffrey Alan Mathias, bomb aimer. The wireless operator was Sgt Henry Thomas George Hubbard, a twenty-one-year-old from Cromer, Norfolk. Finally, the rear gunner was P/O Bernard True, a twenty-two-year-old Yorkshireman. They had been joined on 22 April 1943 by twenty-two-year-old Stanley Moore as their mid-upper gunner and Sgt Stanley Smith, flight engineer, who was from Yeadon, near Leeds, married and the oldest man in the crew at twenty-eight. They all had just four weeks to get to know each other and to come to terms with the problems of the conversion from the twin-engined Wellington to the giant four-engined Stirling. Stanley Moore had been on leave when his first crew were lost on operations and was on sick leave recovering from mumps when his second crew failed to return from an operation. Jim 'Dinty' Moore, Stanley's twenty-three-year-old brother, a WOP/AG on Bostons in 88 Squadron, recalls what happened:

> They were briefed to lay magnetic mines in the shipping lanes off the island of Terschelling. By comparison with raids against the cities of the Third Reich, this type of operation, known throughout the RAF as 'gardening',

was deemed to be less dangerous and suitable for an inexperienced crew.

I know how I felt after a briefing until the time we climbed into the aircraft for an operation. The tension affected all of us. You couldn't stand still, you told stupid jokes and laughed loudly at other pathetic attempts at humour. There is a regular procession to the toilets, a condition we used to refer to as 'operational twitch'. You are really hyped up all because, although you would never admit it to a soul, you are scared. However, once you are in the aircraft, the engines are started and you feel OK as you are able to concentrate on the job in hand. Stanley, unlike most "Sprog" aircrew, had experienced life on an operational squadron which was suffering heavy losses in 1941, so he can have had no doubt as to the dangers ahead. I simply cannot imagine what must have been going through his mind as he waited to go out to the aircraft, though I do know it must have taken a special brand of courage to climb aboard their aircraft when the time came.

At 2250 hours they were seen to take off and the ground crew settled down to await their return. No word was heard from them, the time for their return came and passed so that by morning it was evident they had been lost. The Squadron adjutant arranged for telegrams to be dispatched to anxious relatives telling them their loved ones were MISSING IN ACTION. During the past three years I had become conditioned to the loss of many of my fellow aircrew, some of whom had been close friends, yet nothing had prepared me for the shock I felt on reading this brief message. It is almost impossible to describe the trauma which the phrase MISSING IN ACTION can cause to the recipient of the message. I was to learn that over the years, but you never ceased to wonder what had happened and to hope that somehow Stanley had survived.

My mother, who could speak German, listened regularly to the broadcasts by 'Lord Haw Haw' from Germany, in the hope that she would hear Stanley's name amongst the list of those reported as prisoners of war. She also wrote to the Squadron adjutant and through him wrote to the relatives of the other members of the crew and kept in touch with them for quite a while. Six months later, as was Air Ministry policy, a second telegram was received by our parents informing them that Stanley must now be officially presumed dead. Even this failed to extinguish their hope that this was wrong and by some miracle he was still alive.

In January 1991, to my utter astonishment, Theo Boiten, then a twenty-six-year-old student at Groningen University in the Netherlands, was able to tell us that Stanley and his crew were shot down by a Bf 110 of IV./NJG1, whose pilot was a young Rhinelander, Ofw Karl Georg Pfeiffer and his radar operator/air gunner, a youngster called Willi Knappe. So far they had shot down four Allied bombers. [By the end of the war Pfeiffer had increased his tally to eleven victories.] At midnight they took off on a patrol. At 0058 hours they reported shooting down a Stirling into the sea north of Terschelling, a 'victory' which was confirmed. Pfeiffer recorded this incident in his logbook, although he claims he can no longer recall any further details of the attack.

On the night in question, 560 bombers took part in operations over north-western Europe. Of these, twenty-four failed to return, but only one was a Stirling and this was engaged on minelaying operations. Further, the point where the aircraft was shot down was where they had been briefed to lay their magnetic mines. Therefore, there can be no doubt as to the identity of the aircraft shot down by Pfeiffer. My initial reaction to this information from Theo Boiten was one of shock but, in due course, I came to terms with this revelation. Now, at least we know how Stanley gave his life in what he believed to be a righteous cause. He and his crew, like so many others, can rest in peace knowing their names, unlike ours, will forever be remembered at Runnymede. We will always remember Stanley as the lively, freckle-faced twenty-one-year-old who was our best man at our wedding in 1943.

By the early summer of 1943 the only effective tactical measure against the German night fighter defence available to Air Chief Marshal Harris and his staff officers was the saturation of the German GCI system by concentrating the RAF bomber routes through relatively few GCI areas or through zones in which few or no GCI stations existed. The German response to this measure was to proceed with the thickening and extension of the GCI system. This was carried out with satisfactory results and, on average, fairly heavy losses were inflicted on RAF Bomber Command by the German Air Force.

Losses to the main force had reached such proportions (275 were shot down in June) that when 'Bomber' Harris launched the first of four raids, codenamed 'Gomorrah', on the port of Hamburg on 24/25 July, Bomber Command was at last given permission to use Window. Although Window had been devised in 1942 its use had been forbidden until now for fear that the Luftwaffe would use it in a new 'Blitz' on Great Britain. These strips of black paper with aluminium foil stuck to one side and cut to a length (30cm by 1.5cm) were equivalent to half the wavelength of the Würzburg ground, and Lichtenstein airborne interception, radar. When dropped by aircraft in bundles of a thousand at a time at one-minute intervals, Window reflected the radar waves and 'snowed' the tubes.

Window was carried in the 791 bombers which set out for Hamburg. Led by H2S PFF aircraft, 728 bombers rained down 2,284 tons of HE and incendiaries in fifty minutes on the dockyards and city districts of Hamburg, creating a fire-storm which rose to a height of two and a half miles. Dispensing Window was not that scientific an operation, as Len Bradfield, bomb aimer in a 49 Squadron Lancaster flown by Johnny Moss, recalls: 'On the trip to Hamburg Ernie Roden, our flight engineer, threw it through the cockpit window. It splattered the mid-upper turret and stained it with black streaks. Also, the open window blew the navigator's charts to glory. (On the next trip, to Essen, we had a little chute cut in the bomb aimer's compartment).' For some, scientific delivery it might not have been, but effective it certainly was. Only twelve bombers, or just 1.5% of the force, were lost at Hamburg. The advantages enjoyed by Kammhuber's Himmelbett system, dependent as it was on radar, had been removed at a stroke. Window neutralised the Würzburgs and short-range AI and completely destroyed the basis of GCI interception. Controlled anti-aircraft fire was almost completely disrupted at night and fixed box barrages only remained possible. The new British tactics also combined the use of PFF, the massed bomber stream, and new target-finding equipment (H2S). This combination resulted in total chaos to the German night fighter defence system, which was unable to obtain a true picture of the air situation and unable to control its night fighters. (Over four nights in July/August 1943 3,000 bombers dropped 10,000 tons of HE and incendiary bombs to devastate half of the city and kill an estimated 42,000 of its inhabitants.)

After the fourth raid on 2/3 August, a million inhabitants fled the city. Albert Speer, Minister of War Production, warned Hitler that Germany would have to surrender after another six of these bombing raids. Being paralysed by Window, the Nachtjagd and Flakwaffe had been unable to offer any significant resistance to these attacks. On average, British losses during these Hamburg raids had been no more than a mere 2.8%, whereas in the twelve months previously, losses had risen from 3.7 to 4.3%.

The measures immediately undertaken to overcome this jamming met with some measure of success by the end of the year and ranging was again possible, although the quality of the locating was inferior. Moreover, since H2S permitted the bombers to find their targets in heavy cloud, raids no longer always took place on moonlit nights and the effectiveness of Objektnachtjagd, the one technique available to the Germans, was much restricted. Window also imposed an additional strain on the ground radar reporting organisation. In an effort to overcome this, the German Air Force converted many of its now almost useless GCI stations into aircraft reporting stations. It also devised a new organisation designed to intercept IFF and H2S and Monica transmissions from the bombers, thus creating a new source of plotting information. The greatest potential dangers of this organisation were removed when Bomber Command prohibited such transmissions in areas where they were of more use to the Luftwaffe night fighters than to the bombers.

For short periods after the introduction of Window the Luftwaffe did overtake Bomber Command's tactics and inflicted heavy losses, but constant employment of new tactics and new counter-measures usually left the Germans one step behind. Window helped give crews in Bomber Command a new-found sense of confidence. Johnny Moss's crew in 49 Squadron, for instance, felt that they could overturn the odds which arithmetically gave them no chance of completing a tour of thirty operations. Len Bradfield, the bomb aimer in the crew confirms:

When we first began flying Ops in March 1943 losses were averaging five per cent a night but we believed we were special and would survive. We were sorry other crews didn't make it back but we accepted that this was the way things were. We didn't think it could happen to us. We were an above average crew and expected to go to Pathfinders after our tour. On return from leave in August our spirits were high. Casualty figures had got significantly lower. It came as a sharp jolt when the crew we had trained with failed to return from the raid on Mannheim on 8/9 August. Next day, 10 August, however, was a beautiful day. The NFT went well. When we saw the fuel and bomb loading for *B-Baker* we decided it would be a longish operation.

After the flying supper we went to briefing. The target was Nürnburg with the MAN diesel factory at Fürth being the aiming point. As it was in south Germany the route was over lightly defended territory as much as possible. Climbing to a height of 21,000ft on track, we crossed the enemy coast at Le Treport, then flew on over France, directly to Nürnburg. Window was dropped at intervals on entering German airspace north of Trier. There was about 8/10ths cloud with tops at 14,000ft, which meant we would be silhouetted from above by the bright moonlight. We knew we were in trouble and we generally weaved to give a maximum sky search.

All of a sudden, at about 0030 hours, near Wolfstein (south of Bad Kreuznach and north-north-west of Mannheim, where we could see the glow from our bombing the night before), we were attacked by a night fighter. Terry Woods, the mid-upper gunner, spotted the incoming attack and shouted, 'Bandit five o'clock high!' I abandoned scrabbling about on the floor dropping Window and stood at my guns (being 6'1½" I could work the turret better standing than sitting). Cannon and tracer fire hit our port wing and port outer engine, setting both on fire. Terry returned fire, followed by Ronnie Musson in the rear turret before he was put out of action because of the loss of the port outer which produced hydraulic power for his turret.

As our attacker broke away over the nose, I got in a short burst from the front guns. It was a Ju 88. Johnny started taking violent evasive action to blow out the fire. Sammy Small, the WOP/AG, was standing in the astrodome co-ordinating the defences as we had practised. Almost at once Ron Musson, the rear gunner, called out a second attack. It began at six o'clock level, dead aft. All hell was let loose. Shells were exploding, crunk, crunk, crunk, against the armoured doors and the 4,000lb cookie in the bomb bay. There was a smell of cordite and fire broke out in the bomb bay and mainplane. I dropped down to the bomb aimer's compartment and could see the fire raging in the bomb bay. I told Johnny and he gave the order to jettison. I did. The attack was still in progress. The Ju 88 was holding off at 600 yards, blazing away. He didn't close.

The fire persisted and Johnny gave the order to bale out – 'Abracadabra, Jump, Jump!' From beginning to end it had lasted perhaps one and a half seconds but it seemed like slow motion. The order was acknowledged, except for the rear gunner. I got my parachute on and pulled up, twisted and dropped the front escape hatch in order to bale out. Ernie Roden, the flight engineer, and David Jones, the navigator, were coming down the bomb aimer's bay. I dived out and fell clear, and delayed opening my chute until I was below the cloud. I could still see red and yellow tracer flying by. It is possible that Ernie and David were hit when they baled out. As I broke cloud I could see several small fires which reinforces the idea that *B-Baker* exploded.

On the ground I chucked my lucky woolly golliwog away. It was nothing personal (I had carried him on all my eighteen Ops) but I thought it had failed me. He hadn't because later, when I was captured, when I asked about my crew I was told 'Fünf Tot' (five dead). Johnny Moss was the only other survivor, probably blown clear when the Lancaster exploded. A Luftwaffe NCO told me that three four-engined bombers had been brought down in a ten-kilometre circle by his unit. At Dulag Luft interrogation centre I thought about the attack and concluded that we had been shot down by a professional, a real 'tradesman'.

Victories such as these cheered the Nachtjagd crews and until such time as the German scientists could evolve counter-measures against Window, temporary measures had to be found. This emergency provided an immediate opportunity for Oblt Hans-Joachim 'Hajo' Herrmann, a bomber pilot, and one of the foremost blind flying experts in the German Air Force, who had been agitating for a long time without success for permission to practise freelance single-engined night fighting. Herrmann had reasoned that enemy bombers could be easily identified over a German city by the light of the massed searchlights, pathfinder flares and the flames of the burning target below. By putting a mass concentration of mainly single-engined fighters over the target, his pilots could, without need of ground control, but assisted by a running commentary from a Zentraler Gefechtsstand (Central Operational Headquarters), visually identify the bombers and shoot them down. A Fühlungshalter (shadowing) aircraft, usually a Ju 88 or Do 217, would fly in or near a penetrating bomber stream and keep the plotting room at the Zentraler Gefechtsstand informed on course, height and speed of the bombers. In about May 1943 Herrmann had begun trials at Jüterbog in the use of the Bf 109G6 as a night fighter. On 27 June he transferred his activities to Blind Flying School No. 10 at Alteburg, where he gathered together some experienced pilots and began forming a Kommando using twelve Fw 190-A fighters fitted with 300-litre (sixty-six-gallon) drop tanks. As a result of his suggestion, Helle Nachtjagd was again tried, in July, and, after the first trials in Berlin and the Ruhr proved successful (twelve RAF 'heavies' were shot down on 3/4 July over Cologne), was put into operation over the whole of Germany. This procedure, termed 'Wilde Sau' (Wild Boar) for short, called for close co-operation by the night fighters and the flak over the target, and a dependable control of single-engined night fighters throughout wide areas. Co-operation was achieved by visual signals and by radio. Flare paths and a system of radio beacons was established. The single-engined night fighter was particularly favoured by virtue of its high rate of climb to participate in this primitive form of night fighting the Germans were now forced to adopt.

Herrmann's pilots were a motley collection, loosely organised and rather like guerrilla bands in their attitude to authority, composed as they were of volunteers drawn from all sections of the Luftwaffe, including highly qualified ex-bomber pilots and even pilots in disgrace seeking reinstatement. They were equipped with the Focke Wulf 190A-5/U2 and the Bf 109G-6/U4N. Additional FuG 25a and FuG 16ZY radio equipment, and the FuG 350 Naxos-Z radar-receiving set, which could pick up H2S radar emissions from up to thirty miles away, were installed.

The éclat of their early success was undoubtedly achieved by Herrmann's original band of ex-bomber pilots, whose individual scores were considerable and who continued to secure victories as long as they survived. Oblt Friedrich-Karl "Nose" Müller of JG300, for instance, claimed 29 Viermots and a Mosquito destroyed in just 52 Sorties. The vast majority of the single-engined night fighter pilots had no such tale of success to tell, but lived on the reputation and glory of the skilful few. Such was the immediate success of Wilde Sau that in September they were expanded into three Geschwader named JG300, 301 and 302, under Major Kurt Kettner, Major (later Oblt Helmut Weinreich and Major Manfred Mössinger, respectively. In line with the swashbuckling nature of the entire enterprise, Herrmann conducted his operations without the slightest regard for losses. Only when the last of the best pilots had been expended and bad weather set in, late in 1943, it became quite a normal occurrence for as many as twenty-five Wilde Sau aircraft to be lost out of sixty engaged. Wastage on this scale continued into the winter of 1943/44. On 15 February 1944 Jagddivision 30, the Divisional staff which controlled the three Geschwader, was scrapped and shortly afterwards the remnants of Herrmann's three Geschwader were subordinated to Jagdkorps I and retrained for day fighting.

The first night attack to cause serious anxiety to the German High Command now took place in August 1943, and during the same month, the USAAF attacked the German aircraft industry for the first time by day. The ineffectiveness of the air defences caused an upheaval in the highest echelons of the German command system and, as a result, Generalleutnant Josef Schmid, whom it was intended to place in command of the day fighter units of Fliegerkorps XII under Kammhuber, was ordered to report on the state of the fighter defences. Schmid was particularly struck by the eccentric organisation of Command, which seemed to belong to two separate worlds – Luftflotte 3 covering France, and Fliegerkorps XII covering Germany and the Low Countries. The gravity of this position was strongly impressed upon him on the night of the RAF raid on the top secret rocket research establishment at Peenemünde on 17/18 August 1943 when he happened to be at Deelen in Holland, where, owing to the failure of a division in the Luftflotte 3 area to report on the air situation, the target of the raid was not known until the following day.

The bombing of Peenemünde, carried out by 596 heavies in moonlight to aid accuracy, was orchestrated for the first time by a master bomber. The necessity for concentrated attack against the bomber stream not only over the target but also during its outward and homeward flight, was carried out for the first time by the procedure of ground control throwing stronger night fighter formations against the bomber stream. Called 'Zahme Sau' (Tame Boar), or Pursuit Night Fighting, it had been developed by Oberst Victor von Lossberg of the Luftwaffe's Staff College in Berlin and was a method in which the (Himmelbett) ground network, by giving a running commentary, directed its night fighters to where the Window concentration was at its most dense. Thus, night fighting had developed from a closely radar-controlled operation in small night fighter areas, to an operation over large areas. For night control of formations, an extensive system of navigational aids, including radio, flares, searchlights, and anti-aircraft flare signals, was established. The tactics of Zahme Sau took full advantage of the new RAF methods. Night fighters were fed into the bomber stream as early as possible, preferably on a reciprocal course; the slipstream of the bombers provided a useful indication that they were there. Night fighters operated for the most part individually, but a few enterprising COs led their Gruppen personally in close formation into the bomber stream, with telling effect (Geschlossener Gruppeneinsatz). By this means full advantage was taken of the excellent 'Y' navigational control system, which escaped jamming throughout the war, but which owing to its limited number of channels was restricted to use by individual reconnaissance aircraft and formation leaders.

Although the ground controllers were fooled into thinking the bombers were headed for Stettin, and a further 'spoof' by Mosquitos aiming for Berlin drew more fighters away from the Peenemünde force, some forty Lancasters, Halifaxes and Stirlings, or 6.7% of the force, were shot down. On 17 August the upward-firing cannon installation codenamed 'Schräge Musik' (Slanting Music), was first used successfully. This device, invented by an armourer, Paul Mahle, of II./NJG 5, comprised two 20mm MG FF cannon mounted behind the rear cockpit bulkhead of the Bf 110 and Ju 88 night fighters and was arranged to fire forwards and upwards at an angle of between seventy and eighty degrees. Gefr Hölker of 5./NJG 5 shot down two bombers and Lt Peter Erhardt destroyed four more.

Since the late summer of 1943 British bombers could be 'homed in' on their H2S set by the Naxos Z (FuG 350) 'homers' fitted to German night fighters, and Flensburg (FuG 227/1) could home in on the British Monica tail-warning device. Meanwhile, since the end of 1942 RAF night fighters had been able to 'home' on to the radar impulses emitted by the FuG Lichtenstein (AI) radars in the 490 megacycles band by using the Serrate receiver. (Serrate, which could only home in on the Lichtenstein AI radar and only if the sets were turned on, had first been used by 141 Squadron Beaufighter FVIs on 14 June 1943. That night, the CO, W/C 'Bob' Braham DSO, DFC*, and his radar operator, F/O W J 'Sticks' Gregory, DFC, DFM, claimed a Bf 110 destroyed. (The first victories to be credited to Mosquitos fitted with Serrate occurred on the night of 28/29 January 1944, when a Bf 109 and a Bf 110 were shot down.)

On the night of the Peenemünde raid Braham and his radar operator, 'Jacko' Jacobs, shot down two more Bf 110s. IV./NJG1, under Lt Heinz-Wolfgang Schnaufer, took off from Leeuwarden airfield in what was to be their first, and last, Zahme Sau operation whilst navigating on the Y-system. However, soon after take-off, Schnaufer and Ofw Scherfling both had to break off the operation, as they suffered engine failures. Schnaufer proceeded to make an emergency landing at Wittmundhafen in north-west Germany, but on coming in to land, he was shot at by the flak defences. Although he made a safe landing, it was a bad omen for what was to come for the crews of IV./NJG1.

This left only two Bf 110s, flown by Fw Heinz Vinke and Uffz George 'Schorsch' Kraft, who pressed on to intercept what they thought were RAF heavies. When they had arrived north of Schiermonnikoog around 2300 hours, Uffz Kraft was bounced by Bob Braham and his Bf 110, G9+EZ (Wrk Nr 5469), was shot down in flames. His radar operator, Uffz Rudolf Dunger, baled out into the sea and was rescued two hours later by a German flak trawler but Kraft's body was washed ashore four weeks later on the Danish coast near Heidesande (Esbjerg), where he was interred. Until his death, twenty-two-year-old Kraft had shot down fourteen Allied bombers in a period of only seven months.

Immediately after Braham had shot down Kraft's Bf 110, he got on to the tail of the second machine of IV./NJG1. This was Bf 110 G-4 G9+BY (Wrk Nr 4874) flown by Fw Heinz Vinke, a night fighter ace with over twenty victories. Uffz Johann Gaa, the gunner, spotted the attacker, and Vinke immediately turned away sharply. The German crew had already assumed that they had shaken off the Beaufighter, yet only moments later Braham's attack from below and behind caught the German crew completely by surprise. Vinke's control column was shot out of his hands and the burning aircraft plunged down out of control with a severely injured gunner. Vinke baled out safely, and although Fw Karl Schödl, his radar and radio operator, was injured, he also managed to bale out. Once he had landed in the North Sea, Vinke inflated his one-man dinghy, and while he floated under the star-lit expanse of the night sky, he was appalled to hear the desperate calls for help from his friend Schödl. This continued for quite some time, but Vinke was unable to do anything to rescue his friend, who drowned. The bodies of both Gaa and Schödl were never recovered and they remain missing.

Next day, a ship sailed past quite close to Vinke's dinghy, but the vessel's crew did not notice him bobbing around on the high seas. Only eighteen hours after he was shot down by Braham's Beaufighter, he was picked up by a Dornier Do 18 floatplane of the German ASR Service. After losing his pilot on this night, Rudi Dunger crewed up with Fw Vinke and with their gunner, Uffz Walter, they became a most successful team. After scoring twenty-seven night kills, Vinke was awarded the Ritterkreuz on 19 September 1943; the Oak Leaves followed in April 1944. These were awarded posthumously, however, because on 26 February 1944 Vinke was shot down during an ASR oper-ation fifteen kilometres north-west of Dunkirk by RAF Spitfires. By the time of their deaths in action on 26 February, the crew of Ofw Vinke, Uffz Dunger and Uffz Walter had scored fifty-four victories in around 150 sorties.

The third Bf 110 lost on 17/18 August was a Bf 110 of III./NJG1, flown by Hptm Wilhelm Dormann, a pre-war Lufthansa pilot, with radar operator, Ofw Friedrich Schmalscheidt, which was later credited to Harry White and Mike Allen. Schmalscheidt was killed when his para-chute did not fully open. Dormann also baled out and suffered severe head injuries and burns. He never flew operationally again. Lt Gerhard Dittmann, a twenty-year-old pilot, and his radar operator, Uffz Theophil Bundschu, also twenty years of age, were scrambled from Leeuwarden in Bf 110 G9+FZ (Wrk Nr 5479) of 12./NJG1. Shortly after midnight, they were intercepted by White and Allen. After raking G9+FZ with gun fire it plunged down steeply, and although Dittmann may have tried to crash-land his aircraft on the Friesian coast, this did not happen and the Bf 110 exploded near Marrum at 0015 hours, killing both crew members. Although Dittmann had not claimed any night kills during the short time he had been with 12./NJG1, he had already shot down two B-17s by day, on 25 and 26 July 1943. He was one of those promising night fighter pilots who had joined the night fighter force early in 1943 but was killed in action before reaching his full potential. For once, the tables had been turned on NJG1. It had been a very black night for the night fighters from Leeuwarden.

On flying back to the General Staff HQ in East Prussia on 20 August 1943, Generalleutnant Josef 'Beppo' Schmid learned that the Chief of Staff, Generaloberst Hans Jeschonnek, had died overnight (he had committed suicide by shooting himself because Hitler and Göring clearly held him responsible for the deterioration of the Luftwaffe). Schmid therefore approached Göring direct with his proposals that the conduct of the entire defence of the Reich both by day and night should be placed in one pair of hands, and that France, the territory of Luftflotte 3, should be incorporated into the defence of the Reich. He seems also to have convinced Göring that he was the man for the task. Kammhuber was in disfavour anyway because his night fighting system showed few signs of success. Göring gave Schmid command of Fliegerkorps XII from 15 September, and Kammhuber remained General der Nachtjagd for two months longer before departing to command Luftflotte 5 in Norway.

With Kammhuber's departure the title of General der Nachtjagd was dropped, the relevant functions being taken over by a newly instituted 'Inspekteur der Nachtjagd', subordinated to the General der Jagdflieger. This was a great blow to the prestige of night fighting and resulted, according to General Schmid, in considerable neglect of night fighting interests. The change in the night fighter command had immediate repercussions. Schmid described the Divisional Operations Rooms as they were when he took over command as 'Richard Wagner theatres'. They were, he said, 'Oversized, overstaffed, over-equipped and utilising every device of electrical engineering, optics and cartography for the sole purpose of fixing the position of the enemy and one friendly night fighter on large-scale maps, they were built almost as an end to themselves. They ceased completely to function when the British tactics of flying in a narrow stream deprived the Himmelbett system of its effectiveness.' Schmid reduced the personnel of each division by seventy-five officers, fourteen officials, 3,290 NCOs and men, and 2,630 female employees. On 1 October, an extensive re-organisation was effected, in which Fliegerkorps XII was split up into three separate commands: Jagdkorps I, II and 7. (This was the end of unified night fighter control and the adverse effect on night fighter efficiency was so great that Schmid, in command of Jagdkorps I, had no difficulty in obtaining the re-subordination to himself of 7 Jagddivision on 1 February 1944. Much of his remaining time in office was spent in an only partly successful effort to reconstitute under himself the full and effective night fighting powers enjoyed from the outset by Kammhuber.)

Since the introduction of Window, few GCI patrols were flown. The twin-engined German night fighters thus released from GCI activity were employed at first on target interception. Control was carried out by the Jagddivision, all the aircraft of a Geschwader operating as a unit, with no limitation of the area of activity. High-power light beacons and radio beacons were set up and used as assembly and waiting points. At the same time single-engined night fighters were also employed in fairly small numbers on Objektnachtjagd (target area night fighting).

The simultaneous operation of several bomber streams, the jamming of the Lichtenstein AI and the Mosquito screening of the bomber formations resulted in the splitting up of German night fighter forces and reduced to a minimum the chances of success of individual Zahme Sau tactics. Indeed, owing to the inability to overcome RAF jamming, the Zahme Sau technique never reached its full development, but it was used to great effect during the Battle of Berlin and remained the main night attack tactic until the end of the war. General Schmid thought that had the Jagdschloss Panorama ground radar set been perfected early enough, events might have taken a different course. Schmid concluded that in view of the high standard of RAF Bomber Command tactics, the Germans acted correctly in not depending on one method of night fighting alone, but in employing the different methods singly and in combination in accordance with the situation, i.e. Zahme Sau against the massed bomber stream, Himmelbett against loose formations or single aircraft, Objektnachtjagd in the case of surprise attacks and against Mosquito formations.

An example of Objektnachtjagd, and the others that follow, can be seen through the methods and tactics of Jagdkorps I. For example, Objektnachtjagd was employed by the Jagdkorps on the night of 23/24 September 1943, when 628 RAF bombers were engaged in an attack against Mannheim. Air Chief Marshal Harris was in the midst of a campaign of area bombing German cities at night. Three heavy bombing raids in ten days by RAF Bomber Command on Berlin during August had resulted in the loss of 137 aircraft and great loss of life to Berliners in the Siemensstadt and Mariendorf districts and also in Lichterfelde. It was but a prelude to the Battle of Berlin, which would open with all ferocity in November, but for the time being Harris was obliged to abandon raids on the Reich capital and instead turn his attention to targets at Mannheim (5/6 and 23/24 September), Hannover (four raids in September and October), Kassel (3/4 and 22/23 October) and Düsseldorf.

First indication of the RAF attack on Mannheim on 23/24 September came from 1900 hours onwards. Long-range radar picked up the bomber formations leaving England and an attack on southern Germany was anticipated. The RAF approach was made in a concentrated bomber stream with no H2S bearings, and heavy Windowing. German radar sets and the fighter R/T service were jammed only in two cases. Meanwhile, the bomber formation was plotted, inaccurately, by radar and by the Aircraft Reporting Service but an alteration in their course in the area of Halmedy–Trier was recognised. Target indicators (Kaskaden) and the beginning of the RAF attack was reported by shadowing Fühlungshalter aircraft at 2210 hours. Five minutes later a message of beginning of attack was cancelled and the continuation of the flight in an easterly direction was reported simultaneously. Area Controller Darmstadt reported many RAF aircraft circling in the areas east of Mannheim.

Fifteen minutes later, reconnaissance aircraft and Flakartillerie reported TIs over Nürnberg and the beginning of an attack. It was supposed that a Mosquito formation flew ahead of the main stream to Nürnberg, where flares were dropped and an attack made. Nürnberg was therefore assumed to be the main target of attack and the German fighter controllers directed their target area night fighters there. The Mosquito spoof had done the trick, for the time being. The strong and persistent engine noises in the area west of Nürnberg came only from the night fighters assembled there. The main stream was deduced as concentrating east of Mannheim and the town was attacked from the east. The bulk of night fighters of I, II, and III JD saw the target indicators and the incendiary effects at Mannheim and therefore flew there without awaiting orders to do so. The fighters assembled at Nürnberg arrived late over the target.

At 2235 hours the beginning of a heavy attack on Mannheim was confirmed by the local flak artillery and the Area Controller Darmstadt, who had judged the situation correctly. Altogether, Jagdkorps I sent up 153 Bf 110s, seventeen Ju 88s and sixteen Do 217s from Jagddivision 3 in Holland, 2 JD from north-west Germany, and 1 JD from central Germany, while 7 JD (not subordinated to Jagdkorps I) came from southern Germany. Target Area Night Fighting was mainly employed, while an attempt at Zahme Sau by 3 JD with four Me 410s, two He 219s and one Ju 88 with SN-2 equipment to switch into the bomber stream over Trier brought no results. Himmelbett operations occupying the strip Bonn–Metz with twenty-four aircraft during the RAF withdrawal resulted in only one aircraft brought down, the German fighters being impeded by strong Window jamming. Overall German results though were good, Jagdkorps I claiming thirty aircraft (the actual RAF losses were thirty-two) for the loss of just seven aircraft. Four were shot down by RAF long-range night fighters, while one was brought down by return fire from a four-engined bomber and two were lost due to engine fires.

Night fighting was a precarious profession and during this period some of the Nachtjagdgeschwader's premier Experten were killed. On 27 September Major Hans-Dieter Frank, Kommandeur of I./NJG1, with fifty-five night victories, died when his He 219A-0 collided with a Bf 110 near Celle during landing. Two nights later Hptm August Geiger, Staffelkapitän of 7./NJG1, who had scored fifty-four victories, was lost to W/C Braham of 141 Squadron over the Zuider Zee. On 3 October Hptm Rudolf Sigmund, Kommandeur of III./NJG3, was killed when he was hit by flak over Kassel. He had amassed twenty-eight victories. On 13 October, Lt Heinz Grimm of Stab IV./NJG1 was lost having scored twenty-seven victories when he also fell victim to his own flak, over Bremen.

Another example of involvement by Jagdkorps I in Target Area Night Fighting occurred on the night of 22/23 October 1943 when 569 aircraft of RAF Bomber Command attacked Kassel and thirty-six bombed Frankfurt. The main force began crossing the enemy coast between Katwijk and the Scheldt estuary at 1905. Their course towards south-east was plotted by radar as far as the area north of Bonn and confirmed by isolated H2S bearings. Mosquitos continued a south-east course to Frankfurt, where flares and the beginning of their attack was reported at 2030 hours. Despite their efforts the deception failed. The turning point for the four-engined bomber stream was marked by flares south of Bonn and a further course in the direction of the north-east was reported by a German reconnaissance aircraft equipped with Naxos. Strong Window jamming of radar stations in the areas affected was carried out and so too was jamming of the German night fighter frequency and fighter R/T traffic. Fake orders put out by the first use of 'ghost voice' (Corona) by the RAF were recognised because of their faulty German pronunciation.

Despite all the counter-measures, the RAF lost forty-two aircraft this night, thirty-nine of them to the twin-engined night fighters (the other three were destroyed by Wilde Sau single-seat fighters and flak). More losses could have been incurred had it not been for the failure of the Himmelbetten on the return flight. 1JD put up seventy-two Bf 110s and twenty-four Ju 88s; 2 JD, the same; and 3 JD, twenty-nine Me 110s and two Ju 88s. The Luftwaffe lost just two aircraft to enemy action. Three more were lost in accidents and a fourth was reported missing. (Over Kassel, flak artillery fired strongly at German night fighters. The limitation of flak fire to 16,500ft was asked for but not granted by Befehlshaber Mitte.)

RAF Bomber Command continued the offensive against German cities, making four raids on Hannover in September and October, and then, on the night of 3/4 November, Düsseldorf was raided in strength by RAF Bomber Command. On the night of 4/5 November 1943 the RAF carried out mining of the western Baltic, with a small Mosquito spoof towards the Ruhr. It is another good example of Himmelbett operations. At 1819 hours German radar picked up fifty to sixty RAF aircraft between Cap Griz Nez and the Westerschelde river at 23,000 to 30,000 feet. Their further course was south-east into the southern Ruhr area. As their speed at first was only about 250mph they were taken to be four-engined bombers, but later, taking headwinds into consideration, the defences identified them as Mosquitos. Several aircraft of 1 JD for Himmelbett night fighting in the area of the western Ruhr were ordered to take off but the operation was abandoned after the approaching aircraft were identified as Mosquitos. Meanwhile, at 1802 to 1840 hours thirty to fifty aircraft at heights varying between 3,300ft and 5,000ft flying at 200mph were picked up by German radar approaching the northern part of west Jutland. 2 JD occupying two night fighter boxes in Jutland were scrambled to take on the heavies. They engaged sixteen bombers and shot down four minelaying Stirlings without loss.

An RAF attack on Berlin on the night of 26/27 November 1943 was met by a combined operation of target area and Himmelbett night fighting, under difficult weather conditions. Some 450 bombers were engaged in an operation against Berlin and 178 against Stuttgart. The first wave were picked up by radar over the mouth of the River Somme flying a south-westerly course and were identified as Mosquitos. The second wave of 'several hundred four-engined bombers', Windowing strongly, were plotted by H2S bearings from the mouth of the Somme to Frankfurt. From this bomber stream a formation of Mosquitos (identified by air speed and flying without H2S) branched off into the southern Ruhr. From Frankfurt some H2S bearings continued as far as the Nürnberg area, Kitzingen and Stuttgart. Flares over these cities were reported by Fühlungshalter aircraft and Frankfurt was regarded as the main target of attack. From there, the first withdrawals, too, began. After a reporting break of about half an hour there was a Fluko message from Gotha that strong enemy formations were flying over the city in a north-easterly direction. Soon afterwards there arrived the first radar reports from the southern stations of 1 JD plotting the course from the Leipzig area to Berlin. As there were no radar stations between Frankfurt and Gotha the gap in reporting found its explanation, for the Aircraft Reporting Service had failed and the 'Y' Battalion in Holland could not take H2S bearings beyond Frankfurt. The results of the H2S bearings of Befehlshaber Mitte reached the Gen. Kommando in the course of the twenty-seventh only. Whilst the four-engined bombers were continuing their course from Frankfurt to Berlin, an approach of Mosquitos from the Zuider Zee was ascertained with direct course to Berlin. (The Mosquitos' spoof attack on Frankfurt was a complete success, but the one on the Ruhr failed.)

Meanwhile, a weak minelayer formation penetrating as far as the Heligoland Bight was picked up in time by radar at the time of first crossings of the mouth of the Somme by the main force. The Himmelbett operation against the minelayers and aircraft on their return from Berlin failed owing to a combination of events. The complete failure of the seventy-three aircraft engaged in the night fighter boxes was due to the bad weather and Windowing by the RAF aircraft, but faulty organisation was just as much to blame. Crews operating in boxes other than their own caused much confusion and, furthermore, the crews, after four months' operation in target area night fighting, had taken to Zahme Sau flying and were therefore out of practice in the Himmelbett procedure.

The bad weather conditions had resulted in only the best German crews being ordered to take off. Even so, eighty-four fighters engaged the RAF formations: 3 JD took off and headed for the bombers via radio beacon Bonn to Frankfurt, while 2 JD flew directly to Frankfurt radio beacon; 7 JD flew partly to radio beacon Frankfurt and beacon Nürnberg. 1 JD, meanwhile, at first did not engage. They were held back because of the bad weather conditions and its units were not given the alarm until the receipt of Fluko messages from Gotha. They were first ordered to radio beacon Leipzig and then directed to Berlin. (The units

118

of 3 JD, the bulk of 2 JD and 7 JD, could not be directed to Berlin as they would have arrived late. They landed, refuelled and occupied boxes for fighting on the return of the RAF bombers.) 1 JD downed most of the twenty-eight main force bombers that failed to return to Britain. A further six aircraft were lost from the subsidiary force. Only two German night fighter aircraft were lost.

On 16/17 December 1943 the RAF made a night attack on Berlin and they were met with a combination of Pursuit (Zahme Sau), Target Area, and (in the Schleswig-Holstein and Jutland areas) Himmelbett night fighting tactics. German radar began picking up J beams from 1800 hours and the assembly of the RAF formations, their leaving England and approach, were all plotted correctly by H2S bearings. Mosquito spoof attacks on Kassel and Hannover were clearly recognised as such. Large-scale jamming of German radio and radar was carried out. Korps VHF was jammed by bell sounds, R/T traffic was rendered almost impossible, and Korps HF was jammed by quotations from Hitler's speeches. Korps alternate frequency and Division frequencies also were strongly jammed and there was a very sudden jamming of the Soldatenrundfunksender (Forces Broadcasting Station) 'Anne Marie' by continuous sound from a strong British jamming station.

Widespread mist and fog at 150 to 300 feet in the north German plains reduced the overall effectiveness of the fighter defence (twenty-three aircraft, mostly Bf 110s with short endurance, had to abandon their missions prematurely as there was no possibility for landing in the Berlin area owing to ground mists) and only crack night fighter crews were sent aloft to intercept the bombers. The thirty night fighters engaged in Objektnachtjagd (Target Area Night Fighting), twenty-eight for Zahme Sau, and thirty-four for Himmelbett (over Jutland), succeeded in shooting down eighteen bombers. Another seven were brought down by Wilde Sau night fighters and flak. Heinz-Wolfgang Schnaufer, Staffelkapitän of 12./NJG1, shot down four Lancasters to take his tally to forty victories. Only three German aircraft were lost.

After a certain initial success, Objektnachtjagd proved to have weaknesses easily exploitable by Bomber Command, and it was not until the twin-engined night fighters were used for route interception that the Luftwaffe began to inflict heavy losses again. This technique was subsequently improved to such an extent that deep raids into Germany could only be carried out at a heavy price in bombers. However, Bomber Command's new tactics of multiple raids and

119

shallow raids on invasion targets in France combined to offset the development of route interception.

100 Group (Special Duties, later Bomber Support) had been formed on 23 November 1943 to consolidate the various squadrons and units that were fighting the secret ELINT and RCM war against the German night fighter air and defence system. In tandem with this electronic wizardry, 100 Group also accepted 'spoofing' as a large part of its offensive armoury and it also controlled squadrons of Mosquitos engaged purely on Intruder missions over Germany. It would need to hone and refine all of these techniques if it were to be of any value against the German night fighter defences.

On 1/2 January 1944 when Bomber Command went to Berlin with a force of 421 Lancasters, twenty-eight bombers failed to return. The next night 383 Lancasters went to Berlin again and twenty-seven bombers were shot down. On 5/6 January, 358 bombers raided Stettin with the loss of sixteen heavies, and on 14/15 January when 498 bombers hit Brunswick, some thirty-eight bombers failed to return. On the night of 20/21 January thirty-five bombers were shot down by the German defences, which operated the Zahme Sau tactics to excellent advantage and who seemed to have rendered Window counter-productive. On 21/22 January, when 648 bombers attacked Magdeburg, the German night fighter defences destroyed fifty-seven bombers. Major Prinz Heinrich zu Sayn-Wittgenstein, Kommodore of NJG2, who had seventy-eight victories (twenty-three of them on the Eastern Front), shot down five more bombers flying Ju 88C-6 Wrk Nr 750467 R4+XM before he too was shot down and killed. The only fighter claim that night was made by a rear gunner of a Lancaster. Hptm Manfred Meurer, CO of I./NJG1, who had sixty-five victories to his name, was one of the three other night fighter crews lost this night. His He 219 'Owl' was hit by debris from his second 'Viermot' victim this night, and Meurer crashed to his death twenty kilometres east of Magdeburg together with his bordfunker, Ofw Scheibe, who had been the first AI operator in Nachtjagd to be decorated with the coveted Ritterkreuz just over one month previously.

On 30/31 January 1944 Berlin was attacked again, this time by a force of 534 aircraft. Thirty-three bombers were shot down. It was clear that new British tactics and new counter-measures would be necessary before a resumption of raids deep into Germany, and the Reich defences too were in need of an overhaul.

CHAPTER 6

NIGHT FIGHTER WAR: 1944

O n 30 January 1944 the first move to effect closer liaison between Luftwaffenbefehlshaber Mitte and the operational side of the Air Defence of the Reich saw the creation of Luftflotte Reich. Generaloberst Weise was relieved from his flak command of Air Defence of the Reich and replaced by Generaloberst Hans-Jürgen Stumpff. Stumpff had previously commanded Luftflotte 5 in Norway and Finland. His new command was now responsible for all day and night fighter aircraft and all anti-aircraft regiments. These changes were part of a belated attempt to reverse the decline of the defence of the Reich, which, after the situation created at the end of 1943 by the Bomber Commands of the RAF and USAAF, could no longer be ignored. Göring had opposed improvement but the Allied air forces had forced a number of changes to be adopted. Fliegerkorps XII was deprived of Jagddivision 4 (Metz) and became Jagdkorps I to which Jagddivisionen I, II and III were subordinated. Owing to increasing pressure on the industrial areas of the Vienna basin and Upper Silesia, the Jagdfliegerführer Ostmark and Oberschlesien, and a little later Ostpreusen, were established. In south Germany, Jagddivision VII (envisaged as Jagdkorps III) at first remained independent but later, deprived of Jafü Mittelrhein to whom the defence of the Frankfurt basin was given, was also subordinated to Jagdkorps I. The Jagddivision 30 (single-engined fighters) was dissolved and the personnel distributed among the remaining Jagddivisionen.

Changes too were made in the flak units and the Aircraft Reporting Service, the former being considerably strengthened by increasing armament and bigger batteries. The entire direction of Air Defence rested, as far as command was concerned, with Luftflotte Kommando Reich. At the beginning of April 1944 the staff of Luftflotten-Kommando moved to Berlin–Wannsee to the newly extended Battle Headquarters (formerly the Reichsluftschutzschule). Jagdkorps I directed the operations of day and night fighter formations, as well as the establishment and training of fighter units and their technical

121

equipment. The night fighter control was improved by the extension of the 'Y' system. The day fighter formations were appreciably strengthened numerically and improved types of aircraft were introduced.

On 19/20 February 1944 Allied counter-measures gained new impetus when a 'spoof' attack was carried out over the North Sea by an OTU force while 816 bombers attacked Leipzig. The main disadvantage of this type was that the aircraft had to turn back before reaching the enemy coast, thus reducing the period during which they appeared a threat to the enemy. (On 23 July the addition of a small force of special Window aircraft, which flew with the OTU aircraft but carried on when the Spoof Force turned back, removed the main weakness of the plain OTU spoof force.) The spoof raids that night met with limited success, while the Germans reported that about '100' (RAF figures are nineteen!) Intruder attacks on airfields at Gilze Rijen, Deelen and Venlo, caused only minor damage. A Mosquito spoof attack on Berlin kept German fighters back there but another Mosquito spoof, on Dresden, failed.

Pursuit Night Fighting procedure by SN2 was an essential factor in the heavy losses meted out by Jagdkorps I this night. They were also helped significantly by plotting accurately the H2S bearings, and gauging correctly the significance of a turn in the sea area north-west of Terschelling by the main force while the minelayers continued the original course.

3 JD assembled over radio beacon Osnabruck and was merged in by radio beacon Bremen. 2 JD assembled over radio beacon Heligoland and radio beacon Hamburg and was switched in by radar stations north-west of Wilhelmshaven and north of Bremen. (For fighting the minelayers some night fighter boxes in the northern part of 2 JD were occupied in Himmelbett night fighting). 1 JD, southern part, assembled over radio beacon Harz and was merged in by radar station Salzwedel. The northern part was led to the encounter of the RAF bomber stream via radio beacon Müritzsee and switched in in the area east of Hamburg. Single-engined units from Oldenburg, Bonn, Rheine and Stendal, as well as illuminators from Münster/Westphalia, were at first assembled over radio beacon Berlin and later diverted to Leipzig. Altogether, 294 twin-engined and single-engined fighters were sent against the bomber stream. Some seventy-eight bombers were shot down for the loss of just seventeen fighters.

An outstandingly successful RAF Bomber Command attack on Stuttgart on 20 February 1944 (four bombers only were lost) drew attention to the inefficiency of the 7 JD night fighter control, and Major Ruppel, one of the first night fighter controllers to be trained, was given the task of reorganising it. (Ruppel was in control of nine Himmelbett boxes in the Leeuwarden area (Raum 101) from August 1941 to February 1944, during which period Raum 101 accounted for 782 bombers. He was closely associated with II./NJG2, renamed IV./NJG1 on 1 October 1942, the ace night fighter unit based at Leeuwarden airfield.) It was the night fighter controllers upon whom depended more than anything else the success of night operations. A very special type of mentality was required to cope with their tasks, and lack of this mentality disqualified many otherwise diligent and gifted officers from being able to assess the air situation correctly. Owing to the rapid march of events during night raids and the multiplicity of incoming reports, both true and false, highly strung men were just as unsuited to the task as phlegmatic people. Ruppel reorganised 7 JD night fighter control to such good effect that shortly afterwards Bomber Command was brought to comment upon the change. He later took over Jafü Mittelrhein, thus controlling the key sector through which passed most of the heavy raids. Ruppel expressed keen admiration for General Kammhuber, his preceptor and former C-in-C, and strongly deprecated the general abandoning of the Himmelbett system.

Night fighting was favoured by conditions of good visibility and the night of 30/31 March 1944 seemed to offer the Luftwaffe ideal conditions for attacks. The weather over Belgium and eastern France was 0/10ths to 4/10ths thin cloud while Holland and the Ruhr was cloudless. At Nürnberg, destination of 795 RAF heavy bombers and thirty-eight Mosquitos, there was 10/10ths cloud, at 1,600 to 12,000ft, but the cloud veiled at 16,000ft with generally good altitude visibility. Jamming was carried out on a large scale but Mosquito spoof attacks on Cologne, Frankfurt and Kassel were identified for what they were because to the German defences they were apparently flying without H2S. The heavies on the other hand could quite clearly be followed on radar by their H2S bearings.

John Chadderton DFC, of 44 Squadron, had a feeling of unease, not helped by the fact that he was flying the Squadron's spare Lancaster, *E-Easy*, instead of his beloved *Y-Yorker*, which was having an engine changed after 'collecting some heavy metal' over Berlin six nights previously.

This trip was definitely not normal. Conditions were all wrong! For the last five months we had spent night after night clawing our way through varying densities of cloud to attack the major cities of Germany, including eight to the Big City itself. Despite the constant anxiety of icing and flak, this damp cloak of darkness was just what we burglars needed to enable us to creep in and creep out again, without being apprehended by the vigilant night fighters. But tonight it was all different, although at briefing we had been promised cloud on the outward route, here we were in bright moonlight, feeling very conspicuous and flying a long straight leg, 270 miles long in fact, with none of the jinks and deviations that might cause the night fighter controllers to make the wrong decisions about our destination.

I was about to make a routine intercom check on the crew when suddenly the mid-upper gunner came on. Bill Campion, an eighteen-year-old Canadian of an excitable nature, but possessing the sharpest eyes on the Squadron, bless him: 'Hey, Skip! Are the engines OK? There seems to be smoke coming from them!'

The rear gunner, a phlegmatic Glaswegian and the perfect foil to the eager Canadian, said, 'Wheesht yer bletherin' Champ – they're contrails!'

Contrails! How did he know? We had never made them before, although we had often admired the pretty patterns left by the USAAF on their daylight raids 10,000ft above us. Everyone craned their necks to look behind them through side blisters and astrodome but without much success, when Ken nudged my right arm and pointed down, where a thousand feet below another Lanc was leaving four long white fingers which were twisted into a cloudy rope by the slipstream – a perfect invitation to the night fighters. I decided to climb out of the layer of humidity, but *Easy* was very reluctant, and Ken had to put the revs up to 2,750, the throttles being already fully open. However, by now we had used about a third of our seven and a half tons of fuel, so with much mushing she was able to heave herself up another few hundred feet, as the clutching fingers of fog snapped on and off a few times and finally disappeared. While Ken was synchronising his propellers again I called the nav. 'Pilot to navigator, how much longer on this leg, Jack?'

As usual, his calculations were right up to date and he immediately replied, 'I've just got a fix on Giessen. We are about two thirds of the way along, about twenty minutes if you can manage to stay on course.'

I grinned to myself, which was a mistake as the slight wrinkling of the oxygen mask allowed some icy condensation to trickle down my chin – after all it was minus thirty-five outside and the cockpit heating of *Easy* was on a par with the rest of her. The wry smile was a tribute to all

124

navigators, sitting there behind their curtains, at a vibrating plotting table where just hanging on to pencils and protractors was a work of art, precise mathematicians, who couldn't really understand why ham-handed pilots were not able to hold a course to one degree. Our crews appreciated that we had got one of the best.

We were on our twenty-third Op and after some early mistakes and a great deal of luck, had developed into a competent crew, able to rely totally on each other. Some time ago, with our accumulated experience and Jack's navigational skill, we had been made the Squadron's 'windfinder' and PFF supporter. I relished this job of windfinder. It meant that we took off alone about half an hour before the rest of the Squadron came queueing up along the perimeter track with radiators and tempers overheating, and we then flew along in a relatively uncluttered sky to join the first wave of the Pathfinders in order to give them support against the searching German radar by thickening the shower of metal foil called Window. Using Gee until it was jammed at the Dutch coast, and H2S, Jack worked swiftly to calculate winds which were then transmitted back to Group by the WOP, Jock Michie, who had to risk breaking the radio silence that all bombers observed. At Group the winds from all sources were averaged out and re-transmitted back to the bomber stream in the half hourly 'group broadcast'. The windfinders complained that Group were far too conservative and always played safe with the averages.

Jack was still disgruntled about the last Berlin raid when he had found winds of well over one hundred knots due to freak weather conditions (since known as 'jetstream'). Group would not accept them, which badly upset the planned time over the target. The intercom crackled again: 'Nav to pilot. Group has done it again, Johnny. They are still using the forecast winds which will put everybody north of track.'

Unwelcome proof of this came from both gunners who had been reporting unusually large numbers of 'scarecrow flares', mostly off to the port quarter and quite a way behind. 'Scarecrow flares' had been first mentioned at briefing some weeks earlier with the explanation that the Germans were sending this impressive firework up to 20,000ft to look like exploding aircraft and lower our morale. We hardened cynics were pretty sure that they *were* exploding aircraft, but knowing nothing of the night fighters using upward-firing tracerless cannon we could not understand why there were not the usual exchange of tracer in the normal 'curve of pursuit'. What the gunners were reporting were the deaths of over fifty bombers. This was the night that the German controllers got their calcula-tions right and ignored a spoof attack in north Germany, deciding that the bomber stream would use a favourite flak gap just south of Cologne to penetrate into the hinterland and maybe turn left to Leipzig or Berlin. Me 110 and Ju 88 squadrons had been pulled in from the north and south to orbit fighter beacons 'Ida' and 'Otto' near Bonn and Frankfurt. They could hardly believe it when they found the bomber stream flying en masse between the two beacons and into their waiting arms, like the gentlemen guns in a partridge shoot waiting for the coveys to sweep over them. The resulting slaughter was much the same.

As the bomber stream was clearly recognised from the start, it was attempted to switch in night fighters as far west as possible. All units of 3 JD were switched in over radio beacon Bonn. 2 JD was brought near via radio beacons Bonn and Osnabruck and switched in by radio beacons Bonn and Frankfurt respectively. 1 JD was brought near via radio beacons Bonn and Harz and switched in by radar station north of Frankfurt, as was 7 JD. Single-engined units from Oldenburg, Rheine and Bonn were directed via radio beacon Frankfurt to radio beacon Nürnberg. Night fighter units from Ludgwigslust, Zerbst, Jüterborg and Wiesbaden were led directly to radio beacon Nürnberg. Altogether, some 246 night fighters, including single-engined night fighters, were engaged. In spite of the British jamming, the first switching in into the bomber stream in the area south of Bonn succeeded well. From there onwards the bomber stream was marked by crashes. The majority of crashes did not lie round the target, but in the area Giessen–Fulda–Bamberg.

F/Lt R G 'Tim' Woodman, a Mosquito pilot in 169 Squadron (Bomber Support) and his radar operator, Pat Kemmis, noted: 'Instead of the bomber stream being five miles wide it was more like fifty. Some had already been shot down and before I reached to the far side of the stream they were being shot down on my left. Masses of Window were being tossed out of the bombers which also jammed our radar. We tried three times but each time came up below a bomber, the rear gunner spotting us the third time, his tracer coming uncomfortably close whilst his pilot did a corkscrew. It was hopeless, we were doing more harm than good. Ahead the bombers were being shot down one after another, some going all the way down in flames, some blowing up in the air, the rest blowing up as they hit the ground. I counted forty-four shot down on this leg to Nürnberg. What was happening behind I could only guess . . . I was inwardly raging at the incompetence of the top brass at Bomber Command.'

Sgt Leslie Cromarty DFM, flying as rear gunner in Lancaster LL777 *Royal Pontoon* of 61 Squadron, recalls that

On the Nürnberg raid I think we lost three aircraft but our squadron had taken a battering. We were on the Berlin raid less than a week before when Bomber Command lost over seventy aircraft and so we only had about a dozen crews left this night. We were the most experienced crew. Next came S/L Moss who was killed this night. We had an outstanding navigator, Sid Jennings, and also the best aircraft in the Squadron. *Royal Pontoon* was a Canadian-built Lanc with R-R Packard engines with paddle-bladed props. It could climb much higher than most other Lancasters. We never did find out just how high it could go because at 30,000ft the contrails would begin and we would drop below that height for obvious reasons. We were flying as 'windfinders' as usual. As we flew south of Cologne at about 26,000ft, Len Whitehead, the mid-upper gunner, and I began reporting aircraft going down. Sid got a bit fed up with logging them after a while and told us that as there were so many they must be 'scarecrows'. As we began approaching the target area a Lancaster flew close alongside us. It was upside down and blazing like a comet. I asked Sid to come and look at this 'scarecrow'. We tried to turn away from it but it seemed to follow us. Then it slowly dipped and exploded.

As we approached Nürnberg we were horrified to see the great spread of the target area. Most aircraft were turning and bombing too soon. We saw the last of the PFF aircraft going down with TIs pouring out of it. I think it was JB722, F/L Evans of 8 Group. We continued turning on to the target but by the time we arrived all the markers had gone out. We began to circle. Sandy Lyons, the bomb aimer, thought he saw either a railway station or yard and so we bombed that and left the target area. We continued to log aircraft going down as we flew along the 'Long Leg'.

John Chadderton DFC, meanwhile, headed for his bomb run at Nürnberg.

In the perfect conditions it was easy to follow the bomber stream and the aces among them managed to shoot down six or seven apiece [Hptm Martin Becker, Staffelkapitän 2./NJG6, shot down seven for his twentieth to twenty-sixth 'Abschüsse', which earned him the Ritterkreuz] before they had to break off and refuel. We, the lucky ones at the front end, had managed to slip through the deadly gap before the wolves gathered, and we ploughed on towards turning point C where we made a right-handed turn almost due south towards Nürnberg seventy-six miles away. Normally, a steep turn like this would throw off many fighters, but conditions tonight so favoured them that they were able to follow round the corner and shoot down another thirty bombers.

Scotty, the bomb aimer, now came into his own. He increased his Windowing rate to the maximum number of bundles per minute and about halfway through the twenty-minute run to the target he handed the job over to Ken with obvious relief, and took up a prone position by the bombsight. But now another adverse factor was bedevilling the raid. The Met men who had promised us high cloud to hide in on the long leg, had also predicted that Nürnberg would be clear of cloud for the attack. The marking force of Pathfinders were therefore stocked up with near-ground bursting TIs which couldn't be seen through cloud, and so when they opened the attack five minutes before zero hour these fell useless and unseen. Some of the markers carried a few 'skymarkers', a parachute flare released above cloud so that the bomb aimers could direct their bombs through a theoretical spot in the sky resulting in a fall on the target. Unfortunately, to be accurate, the flare release and bombing runs must be downwind, and here we had a crosswind of seventy-five knots, so that when two very lonely red flares appeared dripping yellow blobs, Scotty gave me a stream of 'left, lefts' in an attempt to follow them.

This was no way to do a bombing run and I consulted the nav who agreed that the town on his H2S screen was drifting away to the right. I had to make a quick decision. 'Right Jack, we'll drop them "on the box"! Scotty, abandon bombing run. I'm turning onto 270°M.'

We headed back to Nürnberg and although the centre of towns gave a mushy picture, Jack was able to pick up the river and gave Scotty the 'now' to drop the load which fell without trace through the cloud. I felt the exhilarating 'twang' under my feet as the straining floor reasserted to normality and *Easy* surged upwards like a tired hunter taking the last fence after a muddy chase. I held the course for thirty seconds for the obligatory photo flash and camera run, both useless tonight, but which one day would earn the crew an aiming point photograph and forty-eight-hour pass. In the middle of a normal raid this always seemed the longest half minute of my life with searchlights and flak all around and a hideous inferno below, but here at Nürnberg it was quite unreal: a bit of flak about, the odd skymarker still drifting on a reciprocal underneath us, and the occasional bump of a slip-stream passing at ninety degrees to us. The latter reminded me that it was a bit dicey on a different course to everybody else, so I hastily turned on to 201°M for the thirty-one miles out of Nürnberg to position D where

Above: Lancasters 'M' and 'Q' of 15 Squadron, the latter flown by Geoff Claydon and crew, pictured in 1944. *(via M. J. Peto)*

Right: Sgt Leslie Cromarty DFM, Lancaster tail gunner, LL777 *Royal Pontoon* of 61 Squadron September 1944–April 1944, who flew a second tour on Lancasters in 189 Squadron, September 1944–2/3 February 1945. *(Leslie Cromarty)*

Below: Lancaster JO-J of 463 Squadron. *(Jack Hamilton)*

Ju 88 R-2 of II./NJG2 at Venlo airfield, Holland in May 1944, with FuG 220 Lichtenstein SN-2 radar. *(Coll. Roba, via Pütz)*

Oblt Heinz-Wolfgang Schnauffer of 12./NJG1 at Leeuwarden, points out his forty-seventh Abschüsse – he scored his forty-fifth to forty-seventh kills on 15/16 February 1944 during a Bomber Command raid on Berlin (forty-three aircraft lost). *(Coll. Hans Bredewold, via Ab A. Jansen)*

A Halifax pictured at Shipdham, a USAAF Liberator base in Norfolk and home of the 44th BG, after putting down in emergency following a raid on Germany. Heinz-Wolfgang Schnauffer, the leading night fighter ace in World War Two, revealed that a corkscrewing Halifax was an easier target than a corkscrewing Lancaster. *(Bill Cameron)*

B-17F 41-24490 *Jack The Ripper*, of the 324th Squadron, 91st Bomb Group, MIA, 22 February 1944 when it was flown by 1/Lt James I. Considine and crew. It was the last original 91st BG Fortress to be lost. *(USAF)*

The Hall crew at Casper ΛΛB, Wyoming about March 1944, prior to flying to England to join the 566th Squadron, 389th BG at Hethel, Norfolk. *Front row L–R:* 1/Lt Arthur G. Smith, navigator; 1/Lt Duane A. Hall, pilot; Lt Nick Hattel, co-pilot; 2/Lt Robert Dahleim (replaced by Lt Charles R. O'Leary), bombardier. *Back row L–R:* S/Sgt Charles Devlin, nose gunner; S/Sgt Joseph Dufau, tail gunner; T/Sgt Dan I. Raymond, flight engineer/left waist; S/Sgt Robert H. Sherwood, top turret gunner; S/Sgt Alexander Novich, right waist gunner; T/Sgt John W. Lindquist, radio operator. Hall's crew won 'Crew of the Week', best over 100 crews in final combat (phase) training and a prize of dinner in town. *(USAF)*

P-47Cs 43-25515 'T' *Ann K* and 43-25585 'V' *Pat* of the 63rd Fighter Squadron, 56th Fighter Group pictured in the summer of 1944 with their D-Day stripes freshly painted over. *(Bill Cameron)*

Below: 'The other Fw 190s attacked. *The Little Gramper Jr*'s left rudder and vertical stabiliser disappeared. The left wheel fairing blew off . . . No.1 engine took a solid hit and came to a strangled halt . . . No.2 engine was set on fire . . . The gas from the chordal gash in the wing was whipped and atomised by the slipstream . . . "We'll blow any second! I won't even make it," thought Sherwood. It was time to leave.' *(USAF)*

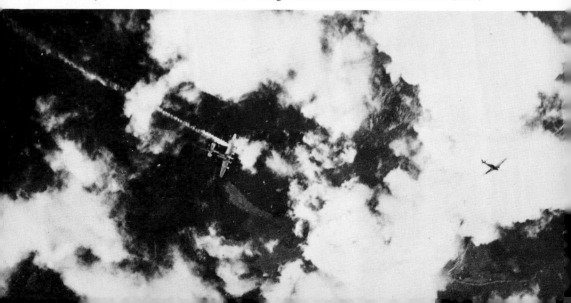

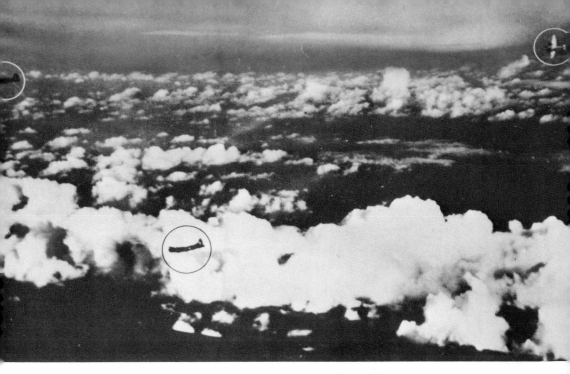

'The B-17 grows larger very rapidly. Their gunners already fire at us, we can spot the small white puffs from the guns in front of us. And already we are within their range – 800 metres – 600 metres – fire – and already pull up over too. I have not been able to see the effect of my gun fire. Today, I have experienced my first such attack.' *(USAF)*

'When they came out of the far side of the cloud bank Bob was sobered, and saddened, by the pitiful sight all around him. There was one ship with a rudder gone. Two more had feathered props, and were trailing smoke. God! There was another. The crew were coming out. They've opened their chutes too soon. He felt tears in his eyes. Oh the poor bastards. He counted only four chutes. The bomber was spinning now. There would be no more chutes.' *(USAF)*

A B-24 Liberator is set on fire after taking a direct hit. *(Sgt Clifford Stocking)*

Right: 6 August 1944; 42-51258, a 492nd BG B-24J-1-DT Liberator, leaves the target, the Schulau oil refinery near Hamburg, which can be seen burning in the distance. This was the unlucky 492nd BG's penultimate mission. *(USAF)*

In the summer of 1944 the 8th sought oil-producing centres in Germany. On 20 June, for instance, oil refineries at Politz were bombed. *(USAF)*

Approximately 75,000 Luftwaffenhelfer (schoolboys) from age 16 who entered the flak school in their neighbourhood, helped man flak batteries. In addition, about 15,00 women and girls, 45,000 volunteer Russian PoWs, and 12,000 Croatian soldiers, were drafted into the air defence of the Reich. This photograph shows 'Opi' Dahms *(left)*, Friedrich Kowalke *(centre)* and A. Prüfer *(right)*. *(Friedrich Kowalke via Robert Foose)*

Below: Flak tower set amongst the ruins of a defeated Germany. *(via Pat Everson)*

we thankfully took up a westerly heading that would take us home.

The gunners reported that the target had livened up a bit after we left, but not very much, and after several minutes they called our attention to another target away over to our right which seemed to be cloud free and with a lot of action. Tongue in cheek I asked Jack if he was sure we had bombed Nürnberg and received the expected forceful reply, with added information that the burning town was probably Schweinfurt (we learned later that about one third of the force went there by mistake.)

Les Cromarty and the rest of the crew of *Royal Pontoon* flew on home too.

Just north of Paris we saw a number of searchlights round a town. We had all been very quiet up to that point and I think B Fitch, the skipper, must have thought we were all dozing off because he dived among the search-lights and Len and I had a ten-minute shoot-out with them. By the time we began approaching Coningsby we were about half an hour late. We thought that they would be worrying about us thinking we were lost. Our callsign was 'Starlight' and we used to land on the number system. When we called up we expected to get at least fifteen or sixteen and be 'stacked', but instead we got, 'Number one, pancake'. We just could not believe it and so we called again, but got the same reply. We were in fact the first to land, shortly after an aircraft from 619 Squadron crashed off the end of the runway. [Fourteen bombers crashed in England]. One or two more aircraft landed but I think most of the others landed at other airfields.

When I returned from the Nürnberg fiasco the ground crew told me that my friend Harold Pronger, mid-upper gunner in an Australian crew, and his WOP/AG had baled out over the North Sea. I wanted to go out on a search right away but the ASR section told me that because the water temperature was so low no one could survive for more than an hour. I think the worst thing about those raids was losing one's friends. After a while you just became hardened to it but eventually you just stopped making close friends with anyone outside your own crew.

Altogether, ninety-four bombers had been shot down, although the Luftwaffe claimed 107, for the loss of just five night fighters. One of those who made it back was *Q-Queenie*, as John Chadderton concludes: 'At last over the sea we put the nose down a fraction to gain speed without caning the engines or spoiling Ken's proud fuel record of over one air mile per gallon. With these tactics and a bit of navigator's log cooking in our beloved *Y-Yorker* we could normally rely on being the first back (our ground crew had a considerable bet on it), but *Easy* lacked an aerodynamic finesse and when at last I called for landing instructions at Dunholme Lodge I was a bit narked to hear my mate, Australian Roy Manning in *Q-Queenie*, got 'No. 1 to land'. And so to interrogation – just a normal sort of trip – 1,500 miles, seven and a half hours and the Squadron lost two aircraft.'

The Nürnberg raid brought, for a brief period, the virtual cessation of heavy attacks. In the spring of 1944, with big advances made in the de-jamming of the radar sets by the Nachtjagd and SN-2 fully operational, the Germans were once again in a strong position to parry the blows of RAF Bomber Command, which for some time were almost completely limited to the continual Mosquito attacks. German night fighter crews developed more than a healthy respect for the twin-engined British fighter. (As a result of large-scale use of the Mosquito in both 2nd TAF and 100 Group late in 1944, the German night fighter crews developed what became known as 'Moskitopanik' and night fighter crews flew very low, or at 'Ritterkreuz Height', as if they flew higher they would never survive to receive the decoration. This caused many accidents and German night fighters often flew into the ground.)

Survival was of course uppermost in the minds of RAF bomber crews too and, once intercepted, they would often try to lose their attackers by using the 'corkscrew' manoeuvre. Heinz-Wolfgang Schnaufer, the leading night fighter ace in World War Two with 121 'Nachtabschüsse' of which 114 were 'Viermots', revealed during inter-rogation just after the end of the war: 'All pilots considered the corkscrew a most effective evasive manoeuvre but a corkscrewing Halifax was an easier target than the Lancaster, although the Lancaster caught fire, when hit, more easily.' Their idea of the Halifax was a robust but slower aircraft than the Lancaster, less manoeuvrable and with a poorer search. The pilots could not distinguish between different types of corkscrews, and usually followed the target aircraft through one complete movement of the corkscrew, which enabled them to anticipate change of direction. They invariably attacked on the change of direction at the top. If the bomber was not shot down at this stage the experienced pilots would break away altogether, or sit off for a time as they thought that to attempt a second attack on the aircraft straight away would be suicidal. Pilots did not hold off from a corkscrewing bomber and fire on the change of direction, as they considered it was too difficult to antic-ipate the position of these changes. The more violent corkscrew starting with a really steep dive and turn, was usually most successful as the night fighters hadn't the speed to follow. He had never lost a corkscrewing bomber, but he thought that the less experienced pilots may do so. The majority of bombers tended to corkscrew to port. Schnaufer preferred to attack on the starboard side and break away to starboard as he thought there was less chance of a collision with the bomber.

One of the young men who joined the German night fighter force and whose story gives a vivid impression of the conditions, often desperate, in which the Luftwaffe night fighter crews had to combat the RAF night bombing offensive in 1944, was Josef Scholten, an officer radar operator.

On 1 November 1941 I was called up to join the Air Signal School at Liegnitz in Schlesien. Already, on the second day we were gathered in the auditorium and our Company Leutnant, who also was the political educational officer, entered and distributed to everyone a form with the request that we should read it through and he impressed us to sign it. The form stated: 'I voluntarily join the flying personnel.' The Leutnant added that it was an honour for us that we were allowed to devote ourselves to the Führer, the People and the Fatherland. All but eight men signed the form. These eight were sent to the armoury where each received a rifle and were sent to the barracks' square. At this spot, the Leutnant broke the will of these poor men by marching: all signed the form afterwards.

After finishing the recruit training, we went, in mid-1942, to Pockling to the wireless operator training centre. There, we flew in the Ju 86, with diesel engines, and the Caudron C445. Thereafter, from July to October 1943, I successfully passed through the Blind-Flying school at Belgrade/Semlin. We had three Ju 52s and three He 111s on strength. At daytime we usually flew for five hours, at night two and a half to three hours. One day, when we applied full power to the engines for take-off, the engines started to cough. We had to abort take-off. On inspection, we found that the Partisans had rendered the fuel unusable – we received our fuel from the petroleum fields in Romania. We were unable to fly for eight days. On another occasion, one of our He 111s had come down at night somewhere in the countryside but the crew did not report to us. Our aircraft searched for the missing plane for two days but it was not found. A search party of infantrymen shortly after found the machine in almost impassable terrain. The six men (two instructors and four pupils) all had their throats cut. We as non-operational crews did not carry arms, but after this incident, the aircraft were equipped with carbines.

In the final phase of training I attended the Night Fighter School at Manching/Ingolstadt, from October 1943 to early April 1944. Here, we usually flew in the Ju 88, but also in the Ju 52. Most of the time we practised in the GCI type of night fighting, but when we became operational, we did not fly this type of operation (we then flew freelance night fighting sorties). In the GCI night fighting, success or failure was mostly determined by the expertise of the officer in charge on the ground, and some of these men were not good enough to lead us to the bombers.

Since early April 1944 Scholten had been an SN-2 radar operator in 3./NJG3 based at Vechta: 'During one operational sortie, which led us from Vechta into the Ruhr area, we kept clear and to the left of the flak zone, flying at a height of 6,000 metres, when we received a message over the R/T that enemy aircraft were expected to penetrate over the Loewen area of Belgium. We had no option but to fly straight over the Ruhr area near Düsseldorf, and to make sure that we were not hit by our own flak, we climbed to a height of 6,400 metres. The flak batteries in this area fired to a height of 6,000 metres. I was busy on the AI set, when the air gunner, who was sitting with his back towards me, pointed to the right and I could also see the exploding flak shells. These quickly crept closer and my pilot, Hauptmann Buinschein, gave orders to fire off the colours of the day. This had no positive result, and the flak kept firing at us. Then the Hauptmann said he had been hit by shrapnel in his leg and he was going to dive down to a safer height. When we had come down to 2,500 metres, we plunged into a solid layer of clouds, out of sight of the flak batteries. We landed safely, and on inspection of our aircraft, we discovered eleven shrapnel holes. Fortunately, the piece of shrapnel which had hit the leg of our pilot had bounced off the zip fastener of his flying suit and into his fur-lined boots.'

Early in June, Scholten's unit was transferred to Le Culot, south of Brussels.

On or around 15 June we flew down to Ath near the Belgian-French border on an operational detachment. That night, we were immediately scrambled as the second machine of our flight. We had just gained a little height when a bright flash illuminated the sky and the air gunner screamed that the flare path at Ath was extinguished. It turned out that the Resistance had blown up the electricity supply works, so no more aircraft could take off. Still, on this night we claimed our first aircraft shot down, near Orleans. It was a Lancaster. I successfully led the pilot to the bomber by SN-2 radar.

Around 25 June we flew a sortie towards the mouth of the River Scheldt. We were well on our way, when suddenly we were informed that enemy

132

bombers were approaching Amiens. We headed in the direction of Amiens and from a long distance we could see the sky illuminated by many search-lights. However, we couldn't see any flak shells exploding. We were cruising at a height of 6,000 metres, when an aircraft was caught in the beam of a searchlight at a height of some 4,500 metres. The Hauptmann descended steeply to carry out an attack. While approaching the illumi-nated aircraft, we flew straight through a formation of four-engined aircraft. When we got closer to our target, we saw that it was a twin-engined machine. Because the Hauptmann had his doubts about the identity of the aircraft – it might very well have been one of ours – he closed in and flew in formation with this plane. We observed the twin-engined aircraft closely and saw that it had a tail gunner, and I clearly saw three white stripes, both on its wings and fuselage. We decided it was hostile and went into the attack. First, the tail gunner's turret was shot away. We then fired a burst into the right engine and wing. Then all of a sudden, we were caught in the beam of a searchlight and had to break off the chase. Only after firing the colours of the day twice did they let us go.

A few days later, we were returning to Le Culot from a mission when during landing the left undercarriage cracked and we slithered along over the concrete with our left wing, which resulted in a long trail of sparks. I immediately jettisoned the canopy and the plane came to a halt to the left of the runway on the edge of the grass field. I fired off a red flare, as we did not know if the canopy had landed on the runway. Thereupon we had to pull the pilot out of his cabin, as he had failed to jettison his canopy which now jammed. We only succeeded in opening the side window of his canopy and pulled him out this way.

One night we were returning from a sortie over France when I got a contact on the SN-2 at a distance of some 4,000 metres. I gave the pilot a course to intercept. We closed in to a distance of 2,000 metres, but the Lancaster was weaving violently. I assumed that this machine was equipped with a night fighter warning device. Anyway, the pilot was able to outmanoeuvre us quite well. We were unable to get in closer than 800 metres. Through gaps in the layer of clouds we then saw that we were flying over the sea, which forced us to break off the chase. (We were ordered not to fly out over the sea and not to fly over the invasion area.) Hauptmann Buinschein told me that we were getting low on fuel through all the tossing and turning and I should get a QDM. I got through to the radio station and received a bearing, but because I had forgotten to give the station the prefix 'NF', I couldn't make out anything of the ciphers. The bearing I had received was meant for our bomber units.

The Hauptmann then said he was going to jettison the empty auxiliary tanks to gain a bit more speed, and ordered me to try and get another bearing. We descended all the time and when we broke through the clouds the Hauptmann said he recognised the sign of the searchlights of Brussels. We were now able to touch down safely a short time later, but for the next fourteen days or so we had to fly on operations without auxiliary tanks.

The brief respite the German defences had enjoyed in the spring of 1944 was curtailed in June when 'long' Window made its appearance on 23 July, and SN-2, previously unsusceptible to Window, was now effectively jammed. To meet the threat posed by the Allied invasion, twenty day fighter Gruppen and one night fighter Geschwader were withdrawn from the defence of the Reich, together with fifty light flak-batteries and 140 heavy batteries, which included the bulk of the railway flak; 3,500 medium and light guns had already been moved from the Reich to the Channel coast. On the other hand, the first weeks of the invasion brought a noticeable respite in RAF and USAAF heavy bomber activity against the Reich territory.

In mid-July Josef Scholten's pilot was promoted CO of the Staffel and his crew was posted to 9 Staffel of NJG3 at Jagel near Schleswig. Scholten continues:

This unit flew the Ju 88 and our crew for the time being still consisted of three men. Because of the fact that our radar equipment was jammed by the ever-increasing use of Düppel by the enemy, our unit was only able to gain a very few night kills.

At this time we received orders from the 'powers that be' to the effect that those crews who had gained none or only one kill were to be given three more operational sorties during which they had to shoot down one or more bombers. If not, the pilots would be transferred to the day fighter arm, and their crews to the Army Division 'Hermann Göring'. As a result, our losses rose rapidly, as we flew until the tanks showed empty, in a desperate attempt to gain a kill.

From Jagel we took off for a sortie in the Kiel area. Over Kiel, dozens of searchlights were waving about and flak shells were exploding. Although I had dozens of contacts on my SN-2 set, the blips jumped up and down and did not keep steady. I was forced to report to my pilot that the radar set was u/s. We broke off the sortie and touched down at Jagel. After landing, the SN-2 operators were called up to go to the Operations Room. Here, we were met by the radar operator of the Kommodore Obstlt

Lent [Ofw Walter Kubisch, Ritterkreuzträger, KIA in a flying accident 5 October 1944, eighty-nine victories, of which eighty-one were at night in Lent's crew. He was the second radar operator in the Luftwaffe night fighter force to be awarded the Knight's Cross.] He debriefed us on our experiences. He then told us that the jamming of the SN-2 sets was caused by overwhelming quantities of Düppel which resulted in the fact that neither the flak nor the night fighter arm had succeeded in claiming any kills. [The introduction of electronic jamming both of ground and airborne radar was to prove even more effective than Window. It nullified the entire efforts of the original German HF research. The ground jamming of German radar and the beginning of large-scale diversionary attacks by 100 Group (RAF) in the summer of 1944 had also created new problems for the defence of the Reich.]

One night, we were transferred on a detachment to Plantlünne. From this 'drome, we also flew an operational sortie. We took off, but on lifting off from the runway the flaps did not retract and the air gunner had to pump them in by hand. All this wasted a lot of time and while we were struggling with the flaps, a raid took place on Hamburg. We arrived over the target too late, and the city was already burning. Hauptmann Buinschein now said that he intended to land at Stade, and I must get in touch with this base. As I was fully occupied with the radio set, I could not hear if the pilot told the air gunner that he should pump out the undercarriage. When floating in for a landing, our plane suddenly dipped to the left and crashed. I tried to jettison the canopy, but I did not succeed. The left engine was already on fire. I shouted to the other members of the crew to assist me in opening the roof of the canopy, but they could not, as they sat in their seats shocked and unable to move. I then kneeled on my seat and succeeded in pushing open the canopy. While I struggled with the canopy, my Mae West must have got entangled with the machine-gun, which was attached to the roof of the canopy – as a result I was dragged out of the side of the cockpit together with the roof of the canopy and got stuck under it, so that I could not move any more.

One of my crew climbed out of the plane. I shouted over to him that he must help me and he bent over me to lift off the roof of the canopy. At first I could not recognise him, as his face was covered with blood. All he said was that the flight engineer was still in the machine and I should go and get him out. The engineer was still laying stunned in his seat. I dragged him out. The pilot's seat was already on fire too. We were not yet fifty metres away from the wreck when the ammo went up. A medic soon arrived at the spot, and he drove us to the sick quarters. The flight engineer was taken to hospital; he had severe concussion and never returned to our unit. The pilot was taken off operations for eight days, as he too had concussion.

On a sortie from Jagel we claimed our third kill. We were directed to fly to the Heligoland area when we received a message that enemy bombers were approaching Braunschweig. We now had a four-man crew in the 88. Over Braunschweig there was a lot of activity with searchlights and flak fire. We were some five kilometres away from the target, when the enemy aircraft carpet-bombed the city. From a height of 6,000 metres it was a horrible sight. Soon after, the searchlights caught a machine in their beams and we went into the attack. First, we fired at the right inner engine, but the tail gunner replied to our fire and we only just succeeded in evading his tracer. Our next burst went into the right wing again and we already could observe a trail of smoke. Then, all of a sudden, the searchlights went out and we lost visual contact. So suddenly, I couldn't find the target on my SN-2 set either but, shortly after, around 2,000 metres behind us we saw an explosion, which surely was the end of our Lancaster.

Shortly after we were transferred to Düsseldorf, where once more we flew on an operational sortie to Hamburg. We were ordered to proceed to the radio beacon at Hamburg and orbit there until further orders. At first, nothing much happened here so our formation leaders were already getting restless and asked ground control where the Mobelwagen ('furniture vans') [RAF heavies] were. In answer to our queries we were told to wait further. Then suddenly, we were instructed to return straight to base. We later found out that over the North Sea, a few Mosquitos had approached in line abreast, at the speed of four-engined bombers, and throwing out quantities of Düppel all the time. Our ground control had interpreted this as an enormous formation of four-engined bombers. When the Mosquitos had approached the coast, they applied full power and were finally recognised as such.

Werner Zell, a twenty-year-old pilot from the Saarland, was another among thousands of young men trained in the mid-war years to fly and fight in the air defence of the Reich. Zell had gone through recruit training and Flying Training School AB112 at Nellingen near Stuttgart in 1943 and the first half of 1944. Although he needed all the thirty dual training flights before going solo on the Buecker 131 and 181 and Klemm 35, he made it and in July 1944 was the proud recipient of his pilot's wings. Whilst at AB112 Zell had his first taste of war, in the spring of 1944: 'One fine day, when we were just being instructed, all of a sudden several P-47 Thunderbolts made their appearance and from zero feet strafed our aircraft which were dispersed on the airfield. A Ju 88 which was parked on the south-eastern edge of the field, and a Fw 58 Weihe at the northern edge of the field were set on fire by the fighters and destroyed. Also, the Flight Control and maintenance hangar, which was well stuffed with aircraft which were being repaired and overhauled, were on fire. Yet, this only caused minor damage. We were very lucky that they did not attack our personnel barracks, as they would certainly have inflicted casualties. The spectre lasted about ten minutes and was our first taste of the ever-increasing air superiority of the Americans. Another danger was the Mosquito long-distance night fighter, which had been chasing a Ju 88 until after it had touched down and then shot it up. A number of the crew were injured in the attack. We were now instructed to fly our training aircraft to the alternate field at Hechingen in Hohenzollernburg, as soon as the air raid warning sounded.'

After receiving his pilot's wings, Zell was required to be selected as flying instructor instead of a posting to an OTU and then an operational fighter Wing. He was posted to the Flying Instructor School in Brandenburg for advanced training on the Arado 96. Zell went to IV./JG102 based at Eggebeck in Schleswig-Holstein, a Training Fighter Wing where they were not left undisturbed either. Apart from many fatal training accidents, the ever-mounting Allied air superiority caused casualties here too: 'Unfortunately, a Feldwebel, a former bomber pilot who had been decorated with the German Cross in Gold and the Frontflugspange, lost his young life. A Mosquito which suddenly turned up over the airfield shot his aircraft on fire, whereupon it crashed through the roof of a farmhouse in which the station commander had his quarters and set the house on fire. He was the first pilot of our group who was killed in the Fighter Pilots Training Course. Shortly after this incident a Mosquito which attacked the drome at night was shot down with the very first burst of 3.7cm flak which was fired at the intruder, and the aircraft was burnt, together with its crew.'

On his final operational sortie, on 26 August, Josef Scholten and crew took off from Düsseldorf and headed towards Frankfurt am Main. Scholten recalls:

We had only just arrived at our operational height when the radio equip-ment went u/s and the SN-2 set fell out. Since we had been the first aircraft to take off, we couldn't land while there were still aircraft taking off, so we proceeded towards Frankfurt. When we got there, the raid had already

137

ended and as we were not able to chase the bombers, we decided to head back to base. We flew at a height of some 5,000 metres and beneath us there was 8/10ths cloud. Since we were looking for an airfield which should switch on its flare path, we fired the colours of the day and a red flare. We did this a couple of times, and then suddenly, probably a Mosquito fired a burst to the right of me into the engine. Hauptmann Buinschein immediately took evasive action, but when our aircraft once again flew straight and level, two more bursts of fire struck the engine on my right side. The engine burst into flames and at 3,500 metres we had to bale out. I landed in a pine wood; my parachute was caught by the branches of the trees first. Then I suddenly fell down on to the ground. I felt a sharp pain in my left foot and was unable to get up. Fortunately, I later found out that the other members of the crew were unharmed. I then fired off all the rounds in my pistol. I didn't fire off any Very lights for fear of a fire in the wood. The place of the crash was near Morsbach in the Westerwald. I was found by some men who took me to the nearest village and I was then transported to hospital at Morsbach. After a spell I was transferred to the hospital at Wissen-Sieg. In early September 9./NJG3 was transferred from Düsseldorf to Uetersen. I remained in hospital until Christmas Eve 1944 and did not return to my unit.

CHAPTER 7
THE LITTLE GRAMPER'S TOUR

At the start of 1944 Germany had realised the urgency for increasing its day fighter forces to combat the ever-growing American attacks by day. During the winter and spring of 1944 the German aircraft industry was the chief target of the USAAF raids. On 11 January over 570 heavies attacked industrial targets in the Reich. Large formations of fighters, estimated at 500-plus, attacked and shot down fifty-eight bombers, including four B-24 Pathfinder aircraft which were being used for the first time. Fw 190s of I. and II./JG26 claimed eleven B-17s this day. JG1 and JG11 claimed thirty-seven B-17s, plus 'Herausschüsse' of another four Flying Fortresses. JG54 was also involved in the combats on this day, claiming a few kills as well. One of the young fighter pilots to gain his first kill during the big air battles on 11 January was Fw Friedrich 'Fritz' Ungar. He had been a flying instructor during 1942/43 and was thus a very experienced pilot before he was posted to 9./JG54 'Grünherz' in August 1943. On 11 January, Fritz was to fly his fifth 'Feindflug' from Ludwigslust (150 kilometres north-west of Berlin) where III./JG54 was stationed at that time:

'Alarmstart' [Scramble!] a voice is droning through the loudspeaker. What follows is routine. All pilots walk from the airfield barracks to their aircraft which are lined up and ready to take off. They are accompanied by the technician ground crews, who assist their pilots with getting strapped in and starting the engines. Already the first machine is taxiing forward to the take-off spot. Every Staffel is formating into a line, and every pilot knows his position. Immediately 7 Staffel takes off; as soon as they are in the air the 8th follow and then the 9th. It is 1045 hours.

From the loudspeaker we had heard that several bomber boxes were entering the Reichs area at great heights and they were coming in over Holland. The target of the over 600 bombers, which are intruding in our airspace on an easterly heading: the aircraft factories in the Braunschweig–Magdeburg area.

Today, 11 January 1944, is the first day of the year with a little better weather. In the meantime we have formed up and whilst still climbing we fly on a westerly course. Our Jägerleitoffizier in the ground control station is guiding us towards the bomber formation in such a way that we can attack exactly from head-on and at the same height. The height and course on which to fly are constantly passed on to us over the R/T. Every pilot is kept busy keeping station in the Gruppe and all the time, we glance ahead. Are we already approaching our target? Can one already see them? The engine is droning his song evenly. Our thoughts go ahead, to the fight which is awaiting us.

A few months previously, one could still attack the bombers from behind. Now they come in at daytime in big 'Pulks' of around twenty aircraft each. When attacking them from behind we would be in their defensive fire for too long and with the additional fighter escort, we therefore have only one option left – attack from head-on.

Things now get moving. Our Gruppenkommandeur has spotted the formation and corrects our course with five degrees to the right. We have been guided very precisely and approach the 'Pulk' exactly from head-on. I switch on my guns while in the meantime I look for my adversary who is flying in my direction and considering my position inside the Gruppe.

The B-17 grows larger very rapidly. Their gunners already fire at us, we can spot the small white puffs from the guns in front of us. And already we are within their range – 800 metres to 600 metres – fire – and already pull up and over too. I have not been able to see the effect of my gunfire. Today, I have experienced my first such attack. These seconds run down more mechanical, in the way we have been trained. I suspect that I have not secured any hits or only caused little damage. However, we are now in the middle of the box formation and have to race to the back and out of it! There are a lot of gunners with their double machine-guns who are waiting to get a shot at us. They have the best chances of hitting us if we fly straight and level, and therefore, we tear up sideways and gather together during the next few minutes a long way behind the 'Pulk'. There, we are also out of range of the escorting fighters. But what is that? Before I have found my comrades again, I see a lone B-17 flying on a southerly course! Quite obviously, it has sheered from the formation to the right. It is not on fire, doesn't trail any smoke. I can't see any signs of damage. I could shout with joy! I have a feeling as if one has presented me, the novice, with a B-17 to practise with. And what's more, I can't see any escorting fighters in the area.

Immediately, I place myself behind it, some 300 metres higher and push the throttle through the gate, so I can get at it a bit faster. At a distance of 600 metres I dive down to the same height as the bomber. I am even faster now and at 400 metres I fire a burst at the right outer engine. Almost at the same instant I see two men bale out on their parachutes. A bright flame erupts from the right wing, which means I have hit a fuel tank. I see no defensive fire from the B-17 and fly over it quite closely and away. When I am some 100 metres in front of it, I lay my next attack from behind. Once more, I fire at the right outer engine and whilst doing this I see at least four more men baling out. The crew has obviously given up on their aircraft. But what I couldn't see at that time: the bombs were jettisoned into empty countryside.

During the next few moments the B-17 proceeds steadily on course, then slowly her nose goes down, the angle increases and then in a steep dive plunges down and towards the ground. At 1130 hours I watch how she crashes at the edge of a wood to the west of the village Ockensen, forty kilometres south of Hannover. A large fire erupts and a giant cloud of smoke billows up – they mark my first Abschüsse.

In high spirits, I circle the area a few times and waggle my wings, see two parachutes landing and at 1145 hours I land at Hannover to top up my fuel tanks. In the control tower, where the take-off and landing times are registered, a Feldwebel sits behind a writing table. He has the same rank as me. In my enthusiasm I can't slow down and tell him about my first kill. He congratulates me and really is delighted. It is not an everyday experience for him too to hear about such an event. He promises me to phone to Ockersen and ask around for any eye witnesses who should then send me a report. This comes in handy for me, as it will help me to get official confirmation of this Abschüsse. Indeed, after a few days have gone by, I receive two handwritten eye witness reports. They state that all ten crew members have landed on their parachutes and no one was injured.

Fw Fritz Ungar went on to claim two more American Abschüsse with JG54 and JG26 and survived the war unharmed.

Two weeks later, on 21 January, the Tagjagdgruppen turned their venom on the Liberator formations. Thick cloud caused 401 bombers to abort, leaving twelve objectives in France intact and 390 heavies bombed V-1 rocket sites. Both the 44th BG's 'milk runs' to Escalles-sur-Buchy (66th and 68th Squadrons) and Agathe D'Aliermont (67th and 506th Squadrons) in the Pas de Calais turned sour, and six Liberators were shot down. *Liberty Belle*, flown by Capt Keith Cookus in the 67th Squadron, was shot down by flak returning from Agathe D'Aliermont. The other five were all shot down by the fifteen Fw 190s of I./JG26, led by Hptm Karl Borris, which bounced the 66th and 68th Squadrons over the French coast on the return leg. In the 66th Squadron, *Queen Marlene*, piloted by 2/Lt Martin E Spelts and 2/Lt William L Smith, was downed at 1514 hours while making a go around on the target. The other four losses came from the 68th Squadron, flying the tail-end Charlie position. Borris's pilots attacked from the rear and in a succession of attacks sent *RAM IT-DAM IT*, *Victory Ship*, and two other B-24s down in quick succession. Four fighters were claimed shot down but JG26 escaped unscathed.

The size, power and penetration of the American attacks increased. All-out raids by the US Strategic Air Forces, 20–25 February 1944, which came to be known as 'Big Week', cost 226 bombers. During March US heavies made the first American raids on Berlin and in April the 15th Air Force in Italy began its oil campaign in the Balkans. From May onwards, the German synthetic oil plants were attacked one after another. Losses were heavy but replacements continued to pour into the ever-expanding 8th Air Force in East Anglia. At Hethel, Norfolk in May 1944, Lt Duane A Hall's nine-man crew arrived at the 389th Bombardment Group (Heavy) base just outside Norwich and were directed to a barracks in the 566th Squadron. The four officers – Hall and Lieutenants Nick Hattel, co-pilot, Arthur G Smith, navigator, and Charles R O'Leary, bombardier – went one way and the enlisted men another. T/Sgt John W Lindquist was radio operator, T/Sgt Dan I Raymond was flight engineer and left waist, S/Sgt Alexander Novich, right waist gunner, S/Sgt Charles Devlin, nose gunner, and S/Sgt Joseph Dufau, tail gunner. S/Sgt Robert H Sherwood, the top turret gunner, was appalled at the barracks. It was an uninsulated tar paper hut with only one entrance door. This led to a small four-foot-long vestibule with a second door. The wooden structure, one of many huts, was falling apart. Inside were cots for the gunners of five crews – thirty men. There were a few double-decked bunks as extra beds. The hut was full except for six empty cots. The crew quickly claimed their spaces and were widely separated from each other. Bob Sherwood was not prepared for the sinister silence which greeted them. No one yelled the usual, 'I see they've lowered the standards again.' Not a soul announced, 'Here comes the fresh meat!' No one made a sound or looked at them. Looking around the hut Bob was disturbed to see an old and torn die-cut sign which proclaimed, 'Merry Christmas'. In May?

He looked closely at the men in the cots. He wasn't prepared for the green-tinged faces, the tired, listless eyes. His crew looked out of place, in their best uniforms and bright expectant faces. Strangely dressed reclining figures, one more outrageous than the next, allowed themselves to be scrutinised and took no notice. They wore rumpled fatigues, assorted parts of summer and winter uniforms. Some had hats on, the knitted infantry wool cap, fatigue hats with the brims snapped up, fleece-lined leather caps. My God! There was one guy wearing a steel flak helmet.

The whole picture was disturbing. The rest of the crew got it. He could see them tip-toeing around trying not to upset anybody. It was difficult moving around the narrow cots in the three-foot space between each bed. Bob Sherwood felt his confidence slowly ooze away. What a bunch to live with – all in each other's laps. These men were all insane.

The afternoon wore on. The new crew unpacked and stowed their gear as best they could on pipe racks above the cots and in the blessed foot lockers. Much of the gear went under the bed. At evening chow, the men drifted out of the hut singly and returned to their cots quietly within a half hour. Hall's crew did what everybody else did. They tried to blend in and be invisible until they could get the lay of the land.

At six p.m., the double doors burst open. Bob Sherwood raised himself up to see a tall angry man dressed in a field jacket, spotted fatigues, and no hat, or insignia. Every pure white hair in his head stood straight up in the air. He began to shout. 'All right you fish eaters, you better come to mass! I want to see all you fish eaters at confession and Sunday services! Are you a Catholic son? No. That's all right, I'll talk to you anyway. God is going to take care of you and I'm going to help him! The guys all call me "White Flak". I don't care what you call me – just come to services. Come to confession and get rid of that load of sin I know you're carrying around. I know you boys, you've got lots of sin. If you'll come to confession you'll shoot straighter and kill more Krauts. That's what the Lord wants. Me too!'

The room was still silent. 'White Flak' continued, still shouting: 'No Catholics at all? OK, OK. You know none of you are going to heaven unless you see me first. Anyone who wants to get converted can find me any time.' With that he exited, slamming doors hard enough to shake the whole hut. A voice in the cot next to him said, 'Don't pay any attention to "White Flak". He does that performance for all new crews. He's crazy but he's a good guy.

'Listen Bob, you and your crew are lucky. You are with one of the good groups. The 389th holds the 8th Air Force gunnery record for confirmed fighter kills. The Krauts pass us up, more often than not and hit some other group. They know our tail markings. They leave us alone.

143

Of course, if you lose an engine or two, and can't keep up with the bomber stream, then the fighters will gang up on you. They look for the crates with feathered props. They look for smoke and a lot of oil on the vertical stabilisers. If you're on fire they're right there to make it burn a little brighter.' A small shiver went down Bob's back. He'd had enough of fires in the old war-weary Liberators they had flown in phase training.

'Listen, don't worry. You guys look pretty sharp to me. You'll make it. I'm the instructor gunner for the Squadron and I'm going to take care of you. I'm going to be on your tail for a while and see that you know what you're doing. I'll see you off on your first mission. This game is twenty-five per cent luck and seventy-five per cent skill. You gotta bear down on that seventy-five per cent. Forget about luck. Edge the bet in your favour.' The instructor gunner looked Bob square in the eye. 'Don't sweat it. One third of your missions are going to be easy. One third are going to be tough. One third are going to be impossible. It's this last third you've got to avoid. The best of British luck.'

Next day Duane Hall's crew were assigned to a B-24H, in good condition, called *The Little Gramper Jr*. She had finished up one crew, a good sign there, thought Bob Sherwood. He spent the next three hours crawling around the turrets, inspecting the bomb racks. He visually checked the exposed wiring, tracing the two, fist-sized bilateral wire bundles. These were arranged overhead on each side of the fuselage. Bob checked the 1,200-round ammo feed tracks on each waist gun. He poked around the hydraulic systems of the tail and ball turrets, searching for leaks. He came to the conclusion that the Liberator was an unusually good bomber, well maintained by the ground crew. He could read the signs. Not a speck of dirt, no sign of leaks in the hydraulics. Even the bomb bay catwalk was cleaned. The ground crew cared. You could tell.

The balance of May was spent flying practice missions. No bombs were dropped. The Hall crew never left the coast of England. Each member of the hut contributed a one-pound note to a pool. The winner would correctly date D-Day. Bob Sherwood had drawn 29 May, a date that came and soon passed by. Someone else would collect the £120. The 389th were flying mostly tactical missions to targets in France, airfields, coastal defences, rail centres. On 3 June all leaves were cancelled and the base sealed. No one was allowed on or off. The men told each other, 'This is it.'

Duane Hall's crew were alerted to fly, 6 June. The night before, the men of the hut listened alternately to the BBC and the enemy propaganda station. Both came in loud and clear. Lord Haw Haw, the traitor William Joyce, was in great form. 'Shove it sideways,' someone yelled.

The target for 6 June was St Lo, France. The Liberators were to hit the rail yards, prevent the enemy from moving in troops and supplies that could be used against the invasion force. Take off 1555. Bob Sherwood translated that to 3.55 p.m. He never could get used to military time.

The gunnery instructor met him at the plane, as he had promised. He moved along with Bob, joining him in the inspection of all the turrets, the gun sights, the bomb fuses and bomb rack release boxes. Occasionally, he would offer a suggestion. 'Straighten the cotter pins safeties in the nose and the tail fuses before you take off. That way you won't have any trouble getting them out while you're climbing to altitude. You won't have enough light in the bomb bays with the doors closed and the racks full. The dim bulkhead lights aren't enough. Always carry a flashlight.

'Check the bomb shackles for chewed-up ears on the release levers. If necessary, get the shackle changed before take-off. Wipe the oil off the guns. Otherwise the bolt will freeze. You'll get a big temperature drop after 10,000ft. If the chamber is empty and the guns freeze, you'll have no guns for the whole mission. You won't be able to charge them. The gun heaters won't thaw them. Take off with a round in the chamber. When you test fire over the Channel, that first round will blow the bolt free and the ammo will feed. First three rounds will be slow and then the guns will take off at their regular rate of fire, 1,000 rounds per minute. And don't forget to go to the tail turret and reach your hand up into the discharge chute. Sometimes a spent cartridge case will fall crossways in there. More cases will pile up on top of the jam. It will eventually stop the guns from firing. You won't be able to clear the stoppage in the air.'

The take-off and climb to altitude went smoothly. They found their proper position in the formation. An hour and a half later they were leaving the coast and flying above the overcast Channel. As they neared the French coast they could see the intense activity opposite the landing beaches. Even at this day's operational altitude of 17,000ft, and despite the drifting cloud cover, they could see the approaches to the beaches crammed with ships. There were ship convoys strung out all the way back to England. It looked like you could walk back.

Every Allied plane that could fly was up this day. They converged on the landing area from every point of the compass. Some singly, some in

145

ragged 'vics' of three. Occasionally, Bob would see proud, tight formations of thirty to fifty Spitfires or P-47s, flashing their way in from the sea, going to unknown targets. Over 8,500 Allied planes were aloft. No German aircraft were seen. They dropped their load on St Lo and exultantly turned for home, shedding altitude rapidly. A short mission, they landed in just five and a half hours. They had slammed all twelve of the 500lb super demo bombs right into the rail junction. The RDX explosive was great stuff, more bang per ton than TNT. What a great mission. God bless that Canadian scientist for creating RDX. Bob realised that he was now sweating. The plane was making its careful way along the perimeter track going to its hardstand. 'Damn, I forgot to turn off my heated suit,' he said. He found out later that no one had encountered much flak. No fighters were seen by the Group. The whole 8th Air Force had only lost three planes, only two of which were bombers. They were not virgins any more and they had done well. 'This whole thing is going to be a snap. Damn those lying Stateside instructors,' thought Sherwood.

There was a let-down after the thrill of D-Day. The 389th was alerted to fly every day after 6 June. Every day Hall's crew were slated to fly, each day there was a stand down. The weather was impossible. Fog and rain. Anything that was not paved turned into brown mud. The crews stayed in their damp, dark huts. They dashed out only to get meals. The humid mess hall smelled of powdered eggs, stale grease, and wet wool.

Finally, on 11 June they hit a fighter base at Cormilles-en-Vexin, twenty five miles north-west of Paris. Next day they went to Conches, forty-five miles north of Paris and ripped up another fighter base. On 14 June they attacked Ju 88s and Bf 109s at Châteaudun airfield, forty-five miles west of Paris. As on previous missions, the flak was meagre. One low burst did throw the tail of *The Little Gramper Jr* up in the air. It hung there, nose down for a brief and tortured moment. Neither *Gramper* nor the crew suffered damage. The heavy plane waddled her way back to normal altitude. Next day took them forty miles north-west of Tours, the Le Porte Boulet bridge over the Loire. On the way in, over Le Havre, flak beat up the wing and vertical stabiliser de-icer boots. There was a hit on the bombardier's tunnel just under the pilots' feet.

These few missions were not bad at all. Three hours' preparation, five to six hours of flying. The crew were confident now. They were hurting the enemy and protecting the invasion troops by wrecking the Luftwaffe on the ground. They all agreed that, so far, the war was not bad at all.

On 18 June they flew again. It was Father's Day. In the mess hall

146

everyone on Hall's crew started to call each other 'Dad'. They pantomimed passing out cigars. Some even went as far as to cough on imaginary smoke. To underline the play, they produced wallets and pretended to show pictures of the latest baby. Other crews moved away from them with grumpy growls: 'It's one o'clock in the morning for Chrissakes.' 'You'll eat flak soon enough. That'll shut you up.' 'Raunchiest crew I ever saw.'

The briefing told them they were going to Hamburg to hit an airfield. The alternate target, in case the weather locked them out, would be the docks. The flak was going to be moderate but accurate. They would carry twelve 500lb bombs and drop them from 20,000ft. The gas load was 2,300 gallons. The Tokyo tanks would be empty. They would use only the main tanks. Bob was thrilled to be going to Germany at last. He had been trying to get there for two years.

They took off and formed up at operational altitude. They started their fifty-mile circle around the radio beacon some place in the Cambridge area. After twenty minutes of slow turning, they were suddenly confronted with the thing they dreaded most – collision. 'Top to pilot!' Bob yelled. 'Aircraft at nine o'clock, level and closing fast.'

'I have it top,' said Hall evenly. He hauled *Gramper* up with a heart-stopping wrench, slamming on emergency power at the same time. The threatening bomber passed below them on a diagonal course and disappeared into the darkness. They had missed each other by only fifty feet. The battle of 'Buncher Six' had almost claimed another victim. The 8th lost one aircraft for every thousand aircraft flown in collisions.

'Skipper, this is top. Good save. Must be one of those Horsham St Faith jockeys. I'm pretty sure it wasn't one of our group.'

'Roger top.' The interphone was silent except for the usual popping static. *The Little Gramper Jr* flew on in silence. Each man had his private thoughts. The airfield they were supposed to bomb was clouded over. Sherwood could see the Elbe. It would lead them right to the docks at Hamburg.

'Pilot to crew. It's two minutes to target. We're going to bomb. Bomb bay doors coming open. Thank you. Let's get rid of the weight.'

'Bombs away!'

'Pilot to crew. There's some high cloud ahead. We're going to go through it.'

They entered the unusually high cloud bank and it was dark as a cellar. No sooner had they got inside when every flak gun in Germany, it seemed, opened up on the bombers in a planned box barrage. Big ugly blotches from exploding shells were just outside Bob Sherwood's turret. He could hear the flak dust swishing against *Gramper*'s skin. There was an occasional 'wang' as a spinning, larger piece, cut lethal holes in *Gramper*'s body and clanged around inside seemingly searching for something to kill. Bob hunched down in the turret trying to make his body small. You don't want to do that, thought Bob. If you do get hit the damn thing will go through all of you. He forced himself to look at the bursts. That's better, he thought. See, their aim is off. The bursts are getting further away. They're stopping now. We're out of range. Hot momma! We're still alive. Keep goin' *Gramper*, I'll give you all the gas you can drink.

When they came out of the far side of the cloud bank Bob was sobered, and saddened, by the pitiful sight all around him. There was one ship with a rudder gone. Two more had feathered props, and were trailing smoke. God! There was another. The crew were coming out. They've opened their chutes too soon. He felt tears in his eyes. Oh the poor bastards. He counted only four chutes. The bomber was spinning now. There would be no more chutes.

'Pilot to crew. Fighters reported in the area. Look sharp. Do what you can without power. Try to move the guns so they won't think we're dead in here.' *The Little Gramper Jr* made it back but she was going to need new engines and a lot of loving care. Jesus! 300,000 parts in a B-24 – 20,000 careful man hours to build her and one screw missing could cause the loss of a plane.

The nineteenth of June was *The Little Gramper Jr* crew's lucky seventh mission. They were gong to Amiens to hit the V-1 rocket launching platforms in the woods near the town. The bomb load was forty 100lb demolition bombs with tail fuse only. At briefing the crews were given the details on the V-1s and V-2s. Bob and Arthur Goodwin, the tail turret gunner, sat rigidly, shocked by the revelations of Hitler's secret weapon. 'Key-riced,' said Goodwin. 'I thought old Hitler was lying about his secret weapons.'

They bombed the woods near Amiens. They saw their bombs produce neat, black mushrooms of smoke in the dense green canopy of trees. There was no satisfying secondary explosion from alcohol and oxygen tanks. No fuel dumps flew skyward. No flames. No nothing.

On 21 June the 389th went after a power plant at St Martin L'Hotier, eighteen miles from Dieppe. It was another quick mission. Two and a half hours to get ready, four hours' flying, and half an hour to debrief. They dumped their twelve 500-pounders from 21,000ft. They did not see the results. The lead Pathfinder was using Oboe and bombing through the clouds. *Little Gramper Jr* turned for home with the group, and landed at 2100 hours. With British Double Summer Time, there was still plenty of daylight. They made their elephantine way along the perimeter track to the hardstand. Looking out the side of the turret Bob could see a gaggle of Lancasters against the pink clouds on the horizon. They were going out to the enemy in ragged stream at low altitude. Bob Sherwood shook his head in wonder. They do everything differently. Neither of us would change places.

The Group had been split up, some of the 389th going to Berlin. They did not do so well. The formation was hit at the IP. When they turned on to the bomb run twenty Me 210s worked them over. At the target, fifty Me 210s chewed on them. Coming back out from the target Bf 109s made head-on attacks and then swung around and came in on the tail. Bob heard that they had lost six bombers from the 389th. They had lost six at Politz the day before too. Things were getting serious. The Luftwaffe were getting closer.

Bob Sherwood was in the hut when the men from operations came in to pick up the clothes and belongings of the other crew. They were last seen on fire and spinning in over Berlin. No chutes were seen. Bob felt sad. He had not had a chance to get to know them. It disturbed him to see the silent work detail, bundle clothes, pictures of wives and sweethearts, letters, into foot lockers. The men were fast but the time went slowly. He hated the gunners who dashed in a little later, guys he did not know. They were looking for stuff to take. Sure, there was a supply problem. They were short of everything, but the attempted raid on the dead men's possessions upset him. It was hard on the men in the hut. They dealt with it in silence.

On 23 June Hall's crew went to Juvincourt, north-east of Reims. They carried fragmentation bombs, six clusters of thirty bombs. The clusters opened up and scattered the 20lb frag bombs over a wide area. They were after the Ju 88s on the ground. The frag bombs would rip up the planes, set them on fire. They had fifteen minutes of flak in the target area, mostly inaccurate. They landed at 2300 hours, coming in as the last of the daylight faded from the horizon. Bob Sherwood had been apprehensive about Ju 88s following them back and taking *The Little Gramper Jr* and the rest of the group when they were most vulnerable.

The crew changed clothes after debriefing. They were dismayed to find themselves alerted for tomorrow's mission, starting at 0100 hours on 24 June. When they got to briefing they found they were one of

149

sixteen 389th ships going to Paris; actually Bretigny, ten miles outside of Paris. Another airfield. The crew knew that targets in the Paris area were bad. The Germans had 10,000 flak guns in a big circle around the city. Berlin had 6,000. All the rail lines went through Paris. Bob and all the crew agreed that they would rather be going to Berlin. Bob Sherwood did not feel good about the mission. He thought they had been lucky so far. Going to Paris today was asking for it. The odds were too short.

At the IP, beginning an eighteen-minute straight and level run into the target, the flak came up in a thick concentration. The aim was erratic. For some reason they broke off the attack midway down the bomb run. The 389th turned to a different heading. They started a bomb run on a new target. The flak followed right along. Now they were taking occasional hits. Nothing serious. They broke off the attack again. Closed the bomb bay doors and took off on another course. The flak followed right along, the bursts persistent and nagging. Bob Sherwood felt the rush of air in his turret as the bomb bay doors opened for a third time. Suddenly, the bomb bay doors shut again. They were in a steep bank, clawing their way around to a reciprocal heading. The German gunners were getting better. They were serving rounds faster; 155mm bursts were mixed in with 88mm. They were getting hit now, over and over again. In the middle of the steep banked turn, there it was, the Eiffel Tower! There was something wrong with it. It was leaning over at a forty-five-degree angle! There was a blotched overlay of flak bursts in front of it. Keep turning Hall, I never want to see Paris again.

'Pilot to crew. We're going home. No bombs today. We jettison in the Channel.'

Even though the bombs went out with the arming wires still in the fuses the bombs went off on impact. Good old sensitive RDX, thought Bob Sherwood, that stuff is never safe.

After leave in London it was back to the war on 28 June. At 0427 hours they and thirty-two others took off from Hethel for Saarbrucken. Fighter support was unusually good and close to the bomber formations. Bob Sherwood watched the fighters weaving overhead at 23,000 to 28,000ft. Sometimes they would reveal their position by the momentary contrails that formed briefly at the wingtips when the fighters changed direction. It got cold in the turret. Getting antsy Bob called up the guns. One by one they came in on the interphone. He pictured the men in the waist, standing throughout the mission with their 37lb of flak armour and their big pot-shaped flak helmets crushing their heads into their necks. Looking out the open waist windows, being careful not to get into the slipstream that crept around the wind deflectors. A few seconds in that minus sixty-seven blast and they would wind up in hospital with frostbite.

The fighters did not come. He looked for contrails and sun flashes. Anything that came in closer than 800 yards was fired upon.

'Nose to crew. Flak dead ahead, level.' Right outside the top turret a fresh pattern of flak appeared. The Germans had got their number, thought Bob. The men in the waist threw out small handfuls of Chaff to confuse the gun-laying radar. Mingled with the black were bursts of blue and white. He recognised this as a signal for the German fighters to attack. He scanned the sky, looking for signs of the attackers. He forced himself to look into the white hot ball of the sun, the most likely place the little dots would appear. None of the crew saw anything. The interphone was silent. *Gramper Jr* flew on, tightly tucked in her place in the Squadron box.

Again the flak started up! Instead of 88s they had run into 105s. The big bursts were off to the left. The ground gunners rapidly corrected their aim. He could hear the explosions now. They sounded like water-filled paper bags being crushed in a hand clap. Flak smoke sucked into the bomb bays and leaked through the flight deck hatch. He could hear the pinging and the whine of pieces of flak, thumb-sized jobs, ricocheting off the vertical armour plate in the waist. He could hear it slicing through frames and longerons in the bomb bays. Partially spent pieces 'wanged' their way amongst the racks, then they took a solid hit on the right wing. No. 3 engine was hanging out of the wing at a forty-five-degree angle! Abruptly, the right wing started to vibrate. Progressively stronger vibrations were growing in the wing and transmitting themselves to the fuselage. Looking out at the right wingtip, Bob estimated the amplitude at the tip to be eight inches, and growing. The period was two to three beats per second. He compared it to the left wingtip and found it stiff and unyielding. Now the vibrations were distributed throughout the plane. The tail was shaking now, and the vertical stabilisers and the rudders were showing a periodic shudder around *Gramper*'s longitudinal axis. His turret was vibrating now. Beat frequencies were appearing in the right wing. The vast skin of flush riveted duralumin was selectively oil canning. Wing panels were dimpling in and out. Although the engine had ceased to function, the prop was windmilling. That prop would come off if the engine's crankshaft broke. It would probably slice right through the fuselage, take out the pilots, the radio operator, and Bob Sherwood. He watched critically, as twenty-two gallons of engine oil sprayed out, flew back in the

151

slipstream and stained the tailplane. With No. 3 out, we'll have no hydraulic power for the landing gear and brakes. We'll have to come in on the putt-putt. He pressed one earphone against the gun receiver in order to suppress the racket of the wrenching, screaming wing and fuselage. The three working engines were bellowing under their increased power loading. The dead engine was going to kill them all. *Gramper* was shaking herself to pieces. She was groaning like a wounded animal. Then the nacelle and engine tore itself free from the tortured wing. It fell away clean, downward and outboard. Immediately, the destructive vibrations in the wing stopped. The fuselage ceased shrieking. Flight was smooth again.

With the engine gone and with it the black oil fog, they might be able to hide their condition from the fighters. They were keeping station in formation. The rudder trim tabs had corrected for the loss of power on the right side. The remaining engines were taking up the strain, coaxed into synchronisation with careful adjustment to throttle and pitch.

'Right waist to crew. Fighters coming up fast. Now at three o'clock low. Two funny looking fighters, coming straight up. They ain't ours and they're after us. Hey! They're Me 163 "Komets"; the rocket plane!'

'Top to ball. They are coming up at four o'clock. They're almost level.' He watched the little wicked toys slow-roll and waver in direction. Just as the Komets reached an altitude of 1,000 yards above them the white plumes of rockets choked off. The planes continued to climb on momentum but soon wavered and stalled out on one wing. They flipped over and began a screaming dive towards them. They had let too much time go by to make a good attack. They fell earthwards.

At the IP a mile-wide black smudge 1,500ft high cloud of flak smoke appeared in the distance. The Germans were putting up a box barrage. They plunged into the black cloud. *Gramper* was flying nice and steady. The formation was packed in extra tight. Looking above him Bob could see into the bomb bays of two aircraft. God forbid, they should slide over the top at the moment the group released its bombs. The bombs went out without mishap. Then the fighters hit them. Eleven Fw 190s came in from six o'clock low. They soon noticed that *Gramper* had only three engines. The tail and then the ball turret opened up. A Fw suddenly reared up and stalled out. A thin streak of smoke trailed from its fuselage. In a hammerhead stall, now, the fighter fell off from the line of the attack. It was slicing away towards three o'clock low. The rest of the attackers broke away to either side of the tail and went for the deck.

The Group returned to base in good order, landing at 1047 hours. The

152

389th had had a good day. Only two bombers and their crews were lost, one of them, Lt Saari, was last seen heading for Switzerland. After noon chow, Hall's crew discovered they were alerted to fly next day. They would be up again at 1.00 a.m.

The 8th AF flew to Kothen, ten miles from Dessau, on 29 June. They were briefed to destroy the Junkers Jumo factory. On the way in the flak was intense. Near the target every crossroad seemed to have its flak battery of four to twelve 88mm guns. *Gramper* took hits in the left wing. It did not seem to bother her. She passed the IP and started the run in on the target. The formation lumbered on to the bomb release point, dropping their loads into smoke which the Germans had created to obscure the plant. No results were seen. The massive Fairchild aerial camera in the waist of each bomber was triggered off at the moment of bomb release. Each plane would make sixty negatives, 5 x 7s of a three-mile circle of white smoke. The bomber stream would produce 6,000 pictures of failure. Bob Sherwood was depressed; 2,800 tons of bombs from the 1,000 planes would burn impotently in the fields. When they got back it was learned that the 389th had lost six planes and their crews.

Crews were stood down because of bad weather. For the first two days crews slept twelve to fifteen hours a day. They felt restored and optimistic again. Inactivity began to hurt them. They longed to return to their dangerous trade. On the fifth day of no flying the crews busied themselves with housekeeping. They did the things they normally did not have to do, like sweeping and mopping floors. After standing down for six days, a mission to anywhere was a pleasure. They went to the rocket sites again on 6 July, to Humières. There were no losses.

The next mission, on 7 July, was a maximum effort deep into Germany: 350 B-17s would bomb Gotha, 650 B-24s would strike Halle. As the briefing ended the gunners aboard *Gramper* drew themselves wearily to attention. There were mumbles of 'a real bitch', 'a ball buster for sure' and 'a gut cracker'. S/Sgt Arthur C 'Red' Goodwin now replaced Joe Dufau as tail gunner. 'Red' was an ex-paratrooper and ex-juvenile circus trapeze artist. Bob Sherwood noticed with affection and amusement that 'White Flak' was in his usual place near the end of the runway. Standing erect in his jeep, with both arms outstretched, he was blessing the departing Liberators. Bob liked that. It made him kin to the ships and sailors of the past, who left port for high adventure with the benediction of the priests.

The Little Gramper Jr was 'tail end Charlie' in 'Purple Heart Corner': the lowest and last aircraft of the group formation. Duane Hall's and

153

Nick Hattel's job was made more difficult by being last in the formation. All the small changes of speed and direction made by the aircraft up ahead were amplified in their position.

At the IP a red shell burst appeared at three o'clock, level. It was followed by several powder blue explosions. That meant fighters. Nine Fw 190s came in at three o'clock level a mile out, heading straight for *The Little Gramper Jr.* The interphone came to life: 'Waist here. I can see them for a change.'

'Tail sees them. They're going into a big curve in line astern. Hey! They're forming up. There are four in line abreast followed by three and then two. They're doing some nifty flying back here. Make no mistake, they're coming at us. I'm opening fire at 1,000 yards.'

'Pilot to nose. You ready to toggle on the lead ship?'

'Yes, I'm ready.'

'Top to ball. You still got them?'

'Yeah, top! I got them framed and ready for hanging. They're coming in nice.'

Gramper shuddered slightly as the bombs left the bay. Bob Sherwood was grateful when Hall shut the doors and stopped the eddies of disconcerting air on the flight deck. He was tracking the middle two fighters in the first rank. The flak was still coming up. The fighters did not seem to care. 'These guys are aggressive as hell,' he noted professionally. He was dead calm now and time stretched out. Everything was moving in slow motion. *Gramper* seemed happy to be fighting instead of taking punishment. She was dishing it out. The four Fw 190s broke off the attack and flashed below the tail. 'Red' had certainly saved their collective lives by holding down the triggers of his tail guns and pouring 400 armour-piercing incendiary bullets into a Fw 190 at about seventy-five yards. The 190 blew up first! (Red got all the way home to Idaho. Two weeks later he drove a sixteen-wheeler over a cliff and was killed.) As he looked over his shoulder at two o'clock high he saw the element lead take a direct hit on the tanks. The flames were plumes of yellow-orange. The injured plane lost airspeed radically. Duane Hall chopped his throttles in response. The bomber fell away on the right and began to spiral down. Four men jumped out of the waist hatch. The gear was dropping. Someone came out of the nose wheel doors. No one else appeared. The engines were still turning. Bob Sherwood raced to the conclusion that her pilots were dead or dying. At that moment, the B-24 stopped flying and fell like a stone. 'Tail to crew. I counted five chutes. Confirm.'

'Roger tail, me too. Top out.' God! It was hard to talk.

The original nine Fw 190s returned to make a beam attack. 'Top to crew. The whole bunch are back again. Coming in at three o'clock level. They're going to hit us again.' The tactics this time were different. The Fw 190s came in on a wide curve, in single file. The waist opened up, quickly followed by the tail. The last Fw broke off and went for the sun to come in from right overhead. Bob Sherwood forced himself to look into the sun. 'He's up there some place. Come out you bastard!' As if in answer, the enemy fighter, 1,000 yards almost overhead, slow-rolled and split-essed out into a lazy dive. The outline of the fighter was a dull blur against the white hot ball of the sun. Eighty-five degrees was as high as Sherwood could go. His first twenty rounds from each gun found their mark. The fighter was firing now. He broke off at four o'clock. He was wallowing, out of control. The German jettisoned his canopy. Dan Raymond pumped slugs into him and wisps of smoke were curling out of the cowl of the massive BMW radial engine. The pilot was half in and half out of the narrow cockpit. Sherwood could see his black leather flying clothes and helmet. He'd almost made it out of the cockpit, then got tossed inside again as the fighter swung back and forth in a 100ft arc. Flames appeared in the cockpit. The pilot redoubled his efforts to get out and finally made it. Then he made a fatal mistake. He opened his parachute. It did not catch on the tail surfaces but as the chute snapped open the aircraft exploded and the flames burned the crown of the parachute. A tiny ring of fire danced around the top and ate a hole in the canopy.

The other Fw 190s attacked. *The Little Gramper Jr*'s left rudder and vertical stabiliser disappeared. The left wheel fairing blew off. The left main gear fell on the wing and hung there like a broken leg. No. 1 engine took a solid hit and came to a strangled halt; 20mm rounds now started in on the left wing. The obscene holes walked across the wing towards the top turret, opening up crown-shaped petals of metal. No. 2 engine was set on fire. It breached the left wing tank, directly behind the flaming engine. It cut the upper flange, and web, out of the main wing spar, right down to the lower flange. The gas from the chordal gash in the wing was whipped and atomised by the slipstream. The flames and the vaporised gas cloud came together at the wing's trailing edge. 'We'll blow any second! I won't even make it,' thought Sherwood. It was time to leave.

'Pilot to crew. Stand by to bale out. Do it now. Bale out! Bale out!'

The flight deck bell urged Sherwood into action. They all got ready to jump. Bob Sherwood was already in the bomb bay and he would have been first to go when the fire in the engine suddenly went out. Hall turned off the bale-out bell and said he thought they could make it. The left main spar was almost through and was flying the load on the three auxiliary spars. It was just enough to keep the wing on if the pilots did not roll *Gramper* or if they ran into rough air. Luckily, ten P-38 Lightnings turned up and drove off the Fw 190s towards Halle. Incredibly, Hall and Hattel got the wreck to the Dutch coast and then the 120 miles across the North Sea to East Anglia. To save the engines they slowly lost altitude. Crossing the English coast at Lowestoft they dropped down to 300ft. Then they bellied in at Hethel. Halfway along the runway the crew could feel the left wing dropping. Hall jerked it up several times and then there was insufficient speed to maintain aileron control. The brakes squealed and the wheels juddered in complaint. *Gramper* went off the runway and sank into the grass turf. The good landing gear buried itself into the earth and they came to a stop after half a ground loop. There was a grinding of metal as the wingtip tore free and the props on Nos. 1 and 2 engines suddenly turned into pretzels. Incredibly there was no fire and no one was hurt.

When they got to the briefing the crew were so exhausted they could hardly talk to the intelligence officer de-briefing them. Even the 'booze' did not free their lips. They were the only survivors of the three bombers attacked and separated from the bomber stream. The 389th had lost five planes, including *Sack Warmer* and two others from the 566th Squadron. One crew had twenty-seven missions in. No chutes were reported. 'Damn,' thought Sherwood. 'They were a quiet bunch, played cards every waking minute, didn't bother anybody.' Their stuff was gone and so was Hall's crew too because they had been reported going down near Halle. They brought it back during the night when the news of their survival came in.

After chow the next day Bob Sherwood wandered down to the flight line. It seemed strange to him not to find *Gramper* on the dispersal point. He walked to the next hardstand where he saw the ground crew working on the engines of another B-24. He smiled at the sight of the well-developed blonde reclining on the nose. He thought that she was a little too raunchy, not nice like *The Little Gramper Jr*. There was a hole in the B-24's nose. The bombsight window was broken, the nose turret cocked out of line. What really aroused his curiosity was the sight of a water truck drawn up in front of the nose. A hose leading from the truck up through the broken window disappeared inside. What were they doing? The ground crew chief was standing to one side of the plane looking lost. What's going on, Sherwood enquired? The crew chief turned his white and confused face towards him. 'They're washing the bombardier's brains out of the Norden. He got hit by flak on the bomb run. Go look in the waist. Go on, look. Come back and tell me what you see.'

Bob Sherwood went to the waist and boosted himself inside. Standing erect he saw the full horror. The walls of the fuselage were hanging with three- to four-inch chunks of grey meat. They looked like hacked up chunks of a large fish, bloodless and grey. Sherwood took the ground crew chief away and fixed him up with a coffee in the ground crew's shack before walking back to *Gramper*'s hardstand. He wouldn't trade places with the chief for anything. There was no mission the next day and then Hall's crew went on a much needed and well earned pass to London.

Once he got back to the 389th, Bob Sherwood tried to forget London and its softening influences. He had to bear down and become a soldier again. There was still a lot of war to fight. Nothing had changed. In a way, he was glad to be back on the treadmill, for each mission that went by made going home seem that much closer. The only trouble was the crew had so far to go. How could they possibly make it? The only vague grey area in his mind was how would they all take the mental punishment. Would they break, one by one? Some of the crews were beginning to fall apart. You could tell when they became quiet, withdrawn, and interested in nothing. Some were given to unreasonable outbursts of temper over little things. Some started to drink heavily. Occasionally, a whole crew would just mechanically withdraw. The trick was to hold your mind together. Somehow you had to drag your body along and get the job done. If death came it would probably be quick. Stabbed by a bullet, or a piece of flak. Snuffed out by fire or crushed in a crash. Might just as well forget about it. The best way to fight back was to think that you were already dead.

Because they had done such a good job beating off the Luftwaffe at Halle, Hall's crew were chosen to fly two missions with Lt Col Jimmy Stewart. On 16 July they went to Saarbrucken in N+. The briefing officer said that Stewart would be flying deputy lead. A gunner next to Bob Sherwood said, 'He's the movie actor, isn't he?' Sherwood's heart sank but he cheered up again when the gunner on the other side of him said, 'Yeah, that's right, the actor. He's good though, a hot pilot, on the ball ... Everybody says he's great. He takes care of the men under him. He's a good Joe.' The mission was without loss. For the mission to Belfort on 17 July, Hall's crew had *Gramper* back again. On 18 July Major Jack Dieterle, the 566th Squadron CO, was shot down on the mission to Hubert–Folie.

157

On 19 July, Hall's crew were one of eleven 389th crews that went to the Me 262 factory at Laupheim, fifty miles north of Lake Constance. The briefing officer told them that the jet was going to be difficult to deal with. It had an unheard of speed of over 500mph at sea level and as much as 550mph at altitude. It was to be armed with 30mm cannon. It was suggested that gunners would not be able to track the 262 and shoot at it effectively. The turrets couldn't move fast enough. Bob Sherwood had a hunch that their equipment would work if the 262s would stay out beyond 400 yards. Damn it all! The Luftwaffe's latest tactic was to come in close, as little as seventy-five yards. Some maniacs were coming even closer, trying to get right in the bomber with the crew. If the briefing officer was right they'd have to give up 'position firing' and go back to the ABC method.

They took off at 0515 hours and climbed to altitude in the false light of the pre-dawn. Sherwood was pleased to see that they were buried within the Squadron box. No more 'tail end Charlie' in 'Purple Heart Corner' for Hall's crew. The penetration of the enemy coast was without incident and the groups made their way across Belgium and moved on into Germany on a south-easterly heading. Nearing the target area the Group tightened up the formation. Sherwood could feel Hall on the controls working for smoothness, resisting over-control. The bomb bay doors were open and they had started a good run in on the target. Sherwood's mental clock told him that it was just a matter of twenty seconds to bombs away. He looked out ahead in the direction of flight but no smoke appeared. Then he heard the bomb bay doors close. He checked the planes ahead. Yes, they were closing their doors too. What the hell was going on?

A short time later the doors opened. He recognised the secondary below them. It was a satellite factory and airfield. He turned his turret aft. Not a damn thing back there. He was getting more tense, waiting for the first bursts of flak, the appearance of the first fighters. Working the turret around in a circle, he was startled to see the bomber stream out ahead, where they should be, but they were leaving his group behind. My God, we're eleven planes out here alone! The doors are still open. He longed to call Duane Hall to get some explanation but he didn't dare break his concentration at this critical time. The rest of the crew was silent. They must be wondering too. Then the flak started. The small band of eleven bombers flew on with their bomb bay doors open, ready to drop their bombs. Oh God, this is murder! We're low today, only 17,500ft. Sherwood was talking to himself. His neck was getting raw from the abrasion of his clothing on his skin in the cold air. The seat was killing him and his parachute buckles were biting him in the butt. The Squadron continued on in.

What was going on up ahead? The lead ship was exchanging its position for another bomber. They must have some mechanical problems. Maybe the bombsight fell apart? When was this nonsense going to end? A bunch of experienced men, stooging all over the sky. At last they dropped their loads. After a bit 'Red' Goodwin said, 'Our Squadron pickle barrel expert made us drop everything into the woods. We didn't earn our pay, this time. Maybe, the Germans will give us a medal for saving their spa. I don't know about you guys but I feel like hell, I'm going to get drunk tonight.'

When they got back the crew was too exhausted and frustrated to try to find out what went wrong. Indeed, in the days that followed, the mission was never discussed. There was a complete blackout on the happenings of the day. The worst thing was that the bombardier in the lead ship, after bombs away, had closed the bomb bay doors without hitting the rack salvo lever. He did not know it but he had one hung bomb in the racks. He'd closed the doors and then hit the salvo lever. The hung bomb came off and took one of the bomb bay doors with it. The door flew back in the prop wash and hit *Naughty Norma* in the 566th Squadron, flown by David Deeter. It hit the No. 3 engine and he was last heard from saying he was heading for Switzerland.

On 20 July the Group went to Gotha and the Me 110 plant. When they got there the target was badly overcast and they bombed marshalling yards at Friedburg. There were no losses. Next day they were out again, this time to Munich, but bad weather intervened and the bombers hit Saarbrucken instead. In the process of flying all over Germany the formations were exposed to over an hour of flak. One 565th Bomb Squadron Liberator was lost and Ray K Caldwell's *Ginnie Gal*, a 565th BS B-24, crashed in Switzerland.

A mission to Laon Chambry on 23 July was unopposed and the flak minor. On the next day, 24 July, the 8th Air Force went to St Lo. Crews were forced to dump their bombs in the sea because the target, just in front of the Allied armies, was obscured by cloud. Flak bracketed the 389th formation and a B-24 in the group behind the 389th blew up after a direct hit. Bob Sherwood recalls, 'There were no flames, no warning. All that was left was just a big, black, ugly ball of smoke.'

The twenty-fifth of July looked a better day, at least it did at three o'clock in the morning. The mist was thin and would probably burn off some time after take-off. The briefing was short. It was back to St Lo again. *Gramper* was hit in the bomb bay by flak at the target. There was a hole in the wing between No. 2 and No. 3 engines. They missed the fuel tanks so it was not critical but the whole formation was busted open. As they dodged around the sky flying a constantly changing course *Gramper* groaned like an old horse. Two B-24s, both from the 567th Squadron, were shot down. Sherwood saw one of them, a B-24 above them, catch fire and pull up into a stall. The torching aircraft steepened her dive and slow-rolled to the right, just missing *Gramper*.

'Top to right waist. Top to tail, count the chutes.'

Four men came out of the bomb bay and waist hatch. Then there was a pause. The next man jumped but opened his chute too soon. The blow torch flame kissed the nylon canopy for an instant and the parachute collapsed. The airman went into a clawing frenzy, his arms and legs thrashing, trying to gain purchase in the thin air. The plane stalled again and spun towards France. No one got out after that. Bob Sherwood closed his eyes and beat his mask against the gun sight. He smashed one gloved fist down on his thigh. The pain of it did nothing for him.

In all, eighteen men parachuted out of the two Liberators. It seems that the 389th hit the target perfectly but groups that followed had to drop on the smoke and dust of the first groups over the target.

After a three-day leave the crew of *Gramper* went to Bremen on 29 July. On take-off Hall could see less than a third of the way down the 6,000ft runway at Hethel because of heavy rain. As soon as they reached the black overcast the ship was plunged into sudden darkness. The effect on the crew was depressing. Bob could only see four feet beyond the nose turret and could barely see the tail. If they hit another plane neither crew would know a thing about what had happened. As soon as possible Bob made his way into the bomb bays and pulled the pins on the forty-eight bombs. He felt weary, very weary as he performed his task. When he was able to see the altimeter he was not surprised. They were at 14,000ft. It was still dark outside. There was no break in the dense over-cast. They broke out finally, to an area of three-mile visibility. There was no sun. It was hidden by towering cumulus cloud columns that rose out of the grey-black overcast. Lightning displays appeared below.

As the planes approached the IP Hall said: 'Listen guys, it looks bad up ahead. There's a big box barrage right on our course. We'll reach it in about three minutes. Get your flak armour on. 'Bob Sherwood forced himself to look at the black wall of smoke. It was about 1,000ft high and they were slated to pass through the middle of it. Once in it bursts

P-51D Mustangs operated over the Reich with increasing regularity late in 1944/early 1945 and pilots racked up numerous victories against the depleted Luftwaffe. *(via Mike Bailey)*

The 56th FG was unique in the 8th Air Force in that it retained its P-47 Thunderbolts and used them operationally until the end of the war in Europe, long after every other group had converted to the P-51D. The P-47D pictured is 42-26628 LM-C *Miss Fire Rozzie Geth II* (his girlfriend was Rosamond Gethro) flown by Capt Fred Christensen, who finished the war with twenty-one victories. *(Bill Cameron)*

B-24M-10-FO 44-50838 in the 714th Squadron, 448th BG, flown by 1/Lt Robert L. Mains and 1/Lt John E. Riviere, was the third B-24 from the Group which was shot down by Me 262s on 4 April. T/Sgt Charles E. Cupp Jr, the radio operator, was the only survivor. *(USAF via Patricia Everson)*

1/Lt Robert L. Mains' crew just prior to going to England. *Front row:* Lt John Johnson, bombardier; Robert Mains (KIA 4 April 1945); Lt John Hankin, co-pilot; 1/Lt Allan Lake, navigator (KIA 4 April 1945). *Back row:* Sgt Charles Daman, waist gunner (KIA 4 April 1945); T/Sgt Charles A. Cupp, radio operator/gunner (PoW 4 April 1945); Sgt Anthony Villari, waist gunner (KIA 4 April 1945); T/Sgt Frank Merkovitch, engineer/top turret gunner (KIA 4 April 1945); Sgt Anthony Munoz, ball gunner; S/Sgt Harry Allen, nose gunner (KIA 4 April 1945). *(via Ed Chu)*

On 4 April 1945 Captain John M. Ray's ship, B-24H-30-FO 42-95298 *Trouble 'N Mind* in the 713th Squadron, was one of two 448th BG B-24s shot down by Me 262s during the mission to Parchim airfield and was abandoned near Kyritz. All the crew are believed to have baled out before the aircraft entered a spin but three were murdered by hostile civilians. Ray and five other crew were taken prisoner. *(via Mike Bailey)*

Left: Major Walter Nowotny whose Me 262 fighter unit, 'Erprobungkommando Nowotny', became operational in October 1944 and during the first month of operations shot down twenty-two American bombers. Nowotny was KIA on 8.11.44 after gaining his 258th Abschüsse. *(Bundesarchiv)*

B-24 *Frisco Frisky*, captained by 1/Lt Edward Anderson, which survived the 3 March 1945 onslaught by Me 262s during a raid on Dresden. Two other 448th BG Liberators were shot down by the German jets. *(via Mike Bailey)*

B-17 Flying Fortresses dropping bombs over Germany. By February 1945 saturation daylight bombing had reached such an extent that desperate measures were called for on the part of the Luftwaffe and training for ramming attacks on B-17s and B-24s was begun. *(USAF)*

Above: Oberst Günther Lützow *(middle)* calling up volunteers in JG104 for Training Command Elbe in February 1945. *(Dr Fritz Marktscheffel)*

Above: Major Otto Köhnke, organiser of Rammkommando Elbe. *(Coll. Werner Zell)*

Below: Oberst Lützow *(left)* shaking hands with Major Reinhard Seiler, Commodore JG104, on the day volunteers are called up for Training Command Elbe. During World War Two, Lützow scored 105 victories, Seiler, 100. Lützow went missing on 24 April 1945 when flying an Me 262 in Galland's JV44, in the area of Donauwörth. *(Dr Fritz Marktscheffel)*

Uffz Werner Zell of Training Command Elbe.
(Coll. Werner Zell)

Uffz Klaus Hahn, a Jagdflieger who had just turned twenty, was one among 2,000 who volunteered for Training Command Elbe. *(Coll. Werner Zell)*

Lt Walter Konantz, 338th Squadron, 55th Fighter Group. *(Walter J. Konantz)*

Still frame from the camera gun film shot by Lt Walter Konantz on 11 September 1944, when he came into contact with enemy fighters for the first time. *(Walter J. Konantz)*

Above: Oberleutnant Walter Schuck, who flew a Me 262 in 3./JG7 on 7 April 1945. During about 500 operational sorties Schuck accumulated 206 victories, mainly over the Eastern Front with the 'Eismeerjäger' of JG5. He became Staffelkapitän of 3./JG7 on Me 262s on 24 March 1945, aged twenty-four claiming eight jet victories before the end of the war. *(Coll. Werner Zell)*

Above: Ogfr Hans-Dieter Eitle in his Bf 109G M-13 at Klecan airfield on 7 April 1945. Eitle did not take off on the ramming mission as shortly before he was due to go, the twenty or so remaining Bf 109s of his group were ordered to abandon the mission.
(Coll. Hans-Dieter Eitle)

Right: Lt Brökelschen, a Rammkommando Elbe pilot, pictured in his Bf 109G of JG102 in 1944 when he was serving as an instructor. On 7 April 1945 Brökelschen rammed a B-17 and survived.
(Coll. Brökelschen via Werner Girbig)

Ogfr Herfried Breinl, pilot, Rammkommando Elbe, who survived the 7 April 1945 ramming mission. *(Coll. Werner Zell)*

B-17 44-38514 J which was rammed on 7 April 1945, most probably by Uffz Werner Zell, but returned to England. *(Coll. Werner Zell)*

The fallen eagles, an abandoned Fw 190A somewhere in Germany, 1945. *(via Steve Adams)*

appeared on all sides. Sherwood increased his oxygen flow to hold down his rising fear. His legs were chilled. He increased the heat. One good thing, he thought, there would not be fighters inside of a box barrage this dense. Hell, they'd run into each other trying to make an attack. It's so dark in here I'm going to have to turn down the brilliance of the gunsight reticle. The image is too bright.

'Pilot to crew. Everything OK? Everybody all right?' The crew checked in rapidly. It calmed their nerves. It took their minds off the sound of explosions of the shells. The bomb bay doors opened and let in an appreciable amount of flak smoke. It was immediately sucked into the Martin dome. Bob reached up to make sure the three-inch butterfly ventilator in the top was fully closed. His eyes were watering from the acrid smoke. His cheeks were prickling from the acid colloids. There was sweat between his shoulder blades. It was trickling down his back. Shut down the heat, his brain told him. Do it now before you get any wetter.

After six and a half minutes in the black barrage they burst out on the far side. The misty daylight, even though it was weak, was still an abrupt shock. He pushed his flying goggles up on top of his helmet. They had helped to control the effects of the smoke in his eyes. He restored his Raybans. Almost immediately he saw the enemy.

'Top turret to crew. I see three Me 210s or Me 410s at six o'clock. They may have rockets. Look around guys. There must be more of them.' The wing span for the 210 or 410 was fifty-five feet. The range to the fighters was 1,500 yards. He took the opportunity, while the enemy planes were still out of range, to slew the turret in a circle, checking the whole bowl of the sky. There was nothing up there.

'Tail to crew, they are beginning an attack on us. They're starting out nice and slow. Hey! There's a single P-51 up above them. He's attacking. I don't think they know he's there – top to tail, open fire. Maybe we can scare them, get them to break off early. I make the range 1,000 yards. Open fire now!'

As the attacking twin-engined aircraft splayed out from line astern to an echelon of three they discharged a flight of rockets. They corkscrewed towards them and wandered away. The Zerstörer's noses were lit with flashes from the 20mm cannon. Bob Sherwood hunched his shoulders and gritted his teeth waiting for the first hits. The enemy was in close now – 400 yards. He fired longer bursts. No sense in saving his guns or the ammo. 'Slam 'em! Jam 'em! Kill them!' Abruptly, the attackers broke away to the four winds. The P-51 was chewing on the tail of the last plane, with his six .50s. He was following every twisting turn

161

with ease. The swirl of fighters dropped from sight. At that moment the bombs left their racks. 'Top to pilot. That's the end of the attack. No enemy in sight. We didn't get hit anywhere. I think we must have hit them some.'

On the way home across the Channel the rain acted up again and the planes had trouble letting down over England. *Gramper* made a good approach but at the last minute when they were committed on the final glide path, two bombers cut them out and they had to pull up and go around again. It was a dangerous time when they could run into some other bomber also staggering around the pattern. At last they were able to commit for a landing. Hall made a steeper than usual approach in order to get out of danger faster. Bob Sherwood was 'overjoyed' when the Liberator touched down and rolled to the end of the runway. Hall pulled off quickly to the perimeter track leading back to the hardstands. The rain was an uninterrupted deluge. Christ, with weather like this, you could run into somebody on the perimeter track! They reached the safety of the hardstand. The ground crew were there in ponchos and raincoats to guide them through the turnaround. They looked like drowned rats. How long had they been out there waiting for them to appear through the storm? A wave of affection swept over Bob. For the moment, these faithful men summed up the idea of home and safety. With five more missions to go was he too tired, too damaged to go on?

Their twenty-fifth mission, on 31 July, was to Ludwigshafen on the west bank of the Rhine, opposite the city of Mannheim, to attack the IG Farben works, and specifically, the methanol alcohol plant. The 389th got hit by flak ten minutes to the target. Bob Sherwood forced himself to look at the flak. Fine dust hit them. It sounded like a wire brush on snare drums. It meant larger pieces would hit them any time. He listened to the engines and was cheered by their synchronous roar.

'Pilot to crew. The deputy pathfinder has been hit! He's pulling out to one o'clock high. Count the chutes. There should be thirteen. Pathfinders carry a big crew. Out.'

The PFF plane (a 564th Squadron ship flown by Captain Lamb and carrying Major Andy Low, the 453rd BG Operations Officer and air commander) was in trouble all right. Fire was blooming from her right wing. She was holding her altitude but the plane's course was weaving. Sherwood thought with anguish that the crew must be down on the floor, hauling themselves forward with the great strength borne of terror. He was yelling on to his mask: 'Come on you pilots! Get out of that coffin. Put the ship on auto-pilot and get out!' Good! Some were

162

coming out of the forward bomb bay. He counted only four men escaping. There were no more. The bomber began a long right-hand slip away from the formation, losing height rapidly and disappeared.

'Nose to pilot. Bombs away!' It looked like the groups ahead had really done it. The whole damned plant was coming up in the air! Debris was at an estimated 18,000ft and it was still coming up. My God what a sight!

The return flight proved uneventful. They knew they were low coming in for a landing. When the Liberator broke out of the overcast, the resident horses and cows on the little farms were looking up at them. They did that, hardened as they were to the thundering aircraft. Those animals were worried. Hell, so was he.

Next day the crew finished the work of pre-flight and had enough time to stand around talking to Jesse Johnson, the crew chief. It was 11.30 in the morning. Take-off would be 1215 hours. 'If you can,' Jesse said, 'burn up the engines today so I can get new ones. When *Gramper* was rebuilt after the Halle mission and the crash they used engines from the hangar queens. They had plenty of time on them, near 1,000 hours. I'm tired of working on them. I want to get some new engines, or rebuilds. By the way, I was told that if you can get to the target today without an abort for mechanical reasons, then this plane will have set up a group record. She's done twenty-five missions with you guys, four with the crew that finished before you. Today would make thirty. I'm supposed to get a medal, a Bronze Star. It'll mean a lot to my gang if you can do it. Now for Christ's sake, don't do anything stupid. If you have to come back, do it! The hell with the medal.'

The 389th went sixty-five miles south-east of Paris to hit a railway bridge at Nogent-sur-Seine. Half an hour from the target, attention was suddenly riveted to the No. 1 engine, which was vibrating badly. Hall feathered it. Then he had to reduce power and leave the formation. He dropped the nose to keep from stalling. Without warning it went into a left-hand spin. Finally, Hall and Hattel corrected it. From some place the two pilots had found the strength to exert enough right rudder. They had cut back the power on 3 and 4 and let No. 2 pull them to the right. The bomber steadied up to straight flight and the pilots began a cautious attempt to pull the nose up to the horizon. For a moment it achieved level flight, then she fell over on the right wing and began a vicious side slip to the right. They shed over a mile of vertical height before the right wing began to come up. Again they came to level flight. They held it this time and dropped their bombs but they had to jettison everything, including

163

guns and ammunition, to get home. The thought that they had won the Bronze Star for Jesse Johnson cheered them.

The next mission was back to Nogent-sur-Seine again but the formation received a recall signal and they came home. On 13 August they went to St Malo. They bombed the close, adjacent island of Iles de Cezembra. Just two groups dropped 144 tons on the 150 by 300 yard rock from 15,600ft. The bombs took off the top of the granite island, obliterating the eight flak guns which threatened the American troops in the Brest Peninsula. There was no opposition of any kind. After bombs away the bombers flew in a wide circle over the gutted towns of St Lo and Caen. There was no sign of human activity down below. Next day was another stand down. They were up at three a.m. the following day to fly to Fismes Anizy-le-Château, forty miles from Paris. The crew vowed never to go to Paris after the war. They never wanted to see the city again. Flak was heavy. A piece penetrated the fuselage and went out the other side. Another piece hit the back rest on the flight deck bunk and filled the flight deck and the cockpit with short strings of cushion stuffing. An oxygen tank was hit and the torch-like flame melted a three-foot cut in the fuselage. The bucket wheel on the supercharger on No. 1 engine was smashed. The engine continued to run but supplied no real power, starved as it was of manifold pressure. Their target, a bridge, was well hit. Going home the crew were unusually silent, each man reflecting on how near death had come.

The suspense of the thirtieth and final mission was made worse by more stand-downs. Finally, on 18 August they went after Metz, near the German border. The target, aircraft in their dispersal areas, was plastered. As *The Little Gramper Jr* turned away she was hit from below by well-aimed cannon fire from a Ju 88. A single 88mm projectile passed through the flight deck, narrowly missing both pilots, the radio operator and the top turret. The round failed to explode. When he finally pulled himself out of the aircraft and got down on the ground, the wet smell of the grass and the caress of the soft wind overwhelmed Bob Sherwood. He walked away from the B-24 and sat down on the warm earth. With his chin in his hands he sat looking at *Gramper Jr*. With a pang he realised that he would probably never fly in her again. She would be some other crew's passport to life. She was a magic dragon.

CHAPTER 8

THE BATTLES OF MAGDEBURG

A s can be seen from the previous chapter, flak and fighters constituted a considerable force to be reckoned with in the skies over
the Reich in the summer of 1944 when the 8th sought oil-
producing centres in Germany. In the defence against daylight
high-altitude attacks, the co-operation of flak and fighters and the
operation of the Grossbatterien proved successful. In spite of
the continual loss of young personnel to the fronts, Germany found it
possible to double the numbers of personnel, principally by decreasing
the personnel per battery and using the Reichsarbeitsdienst and approximately 75,000 Luftwaffenhelfer (schoolboys) from higher schools. All
schoolboys in Germany at age sixteen had to enter the flak school in their
neighbourhood. This decision had been taken after the German disaster
at Stalingrad when thousands of soldiers within the borders of the
Fatherland were needed for frontline duties. In addition, approximately
15,000 women and girls, 45,000 volunteer Russian PoWs, and 12,000
Croatian soldiers, were drafted in to the air defence of the Reich.
Extensive use was made of smoke screens during daylight and improved
decoy fires and flare rockets.

One of the Luftwaffenhelfer in mid-1944 who manned one of the thirteen batteries in the old Hanse town of Magdeburg was Friedrich J
Kowalke. Magdeburg, situated on the Elbe in eastern Germany, was
protected by thirteen flak batteries comprising six, later eight, 88 or
105mm guns, and two railway-mounted flak batteries comprising four
105mm guns. In the mid-fourteenth century Magdeburg had been a
leading member of the Hanseatic League, a commercial association of
towns in north Germany formed to protect and control trade, and the
local Magdeburg laws were adopted by many European cities. By
the outbreak of World War Two, Magdeburg had become a large industrial city with much-needed industries essential to the Third Reich. The
Brabag synthetic oil plant, built in 1936, the Junkers aero-engine factory
at Magdeburg/Neustadt, the Krupp tank works at Buckau, and an
ordnance depot at Friedrichsstadt were among the main producers of war

165

materials for Hitler's Germany. Friedrich Kowalke's early youth (he was born in 1927) was marked by an increasing interest in the aircraft industry and he soon gained the ability to identify each type of aircraft, either in the air or on the ground. On reaching his sixteenth birthday in February 1943, Kowalke too had joined the flak school:

On the one hand the Luftwaffenhelfer had the same duties as soldiers; on the other hand our teachers had to continue our education as well as possible. Problems arose and one consequence was that all the boys of my school, the Wilhelm-Raabe Schule, had to be concentrated at one flak battery. Furthermore, this battery must be located near the city and reachable by tramway without a large footpath. Finally, our teachers' demands led to us being based on a route from battery Sohlen in the south, over battery Pechau to battery Lemsdorf. Sohlen and Pechau covered the year 1943 mainly. This was the time of RAF night flybys to Berlin and, sometimes, the Leipzig area. Both batteries had modern equipment and changed their gun calibre from 8.8 to 10.5cm during summer 1944. Lemsdorf was ill-fated with captured Russian guns of 8.5cm calibre, drilled to 8.8cm calibre to use German ammunition. This caused some implosions in the barrels. FuMG radar, coupled with an effective ballistic director (KdG 40) was the best fire control unit at that time. We must handle an auxiliary ballistic director (KdG Hi. or 'Malsi').

Lemsdorf was a so-called 'Heimatflakbatterie', which means the larger amount of personnel comprised 'Luftwaffenhelfer' and 'Flakwehrmänner' [day workers of the nearby industry who manned the guns at night]. Generally, the leading officers were aged First World War veterans. They had problems making decisions, especially in identifying enemy aircraft. In such a situation the job of a so-called 'Flugmelder' [observer] was of importance.

Now this was my hour due to my ability to see and know the geometric differences between friend and foe aircraft. My instrument was a moveable telescope mounted, supported by the four-metre base optical rangefinder, part of the ballistic director. Only this job of an observer had given me the chance to concentrate myself on all the events, which happened during Allied air operations in the Magdeburg area, especially those of the 8th Air Force carried out in daylight.

The following typical daylight scenario was repeated so often during 1944. Detection of large air movements over East Anglia by 'Würzburg-Riesen' [long-range radar]. Our time was between seven and eight o'clock in the morning when we received this initial 'Luftlagemeldung'. First bomber formations are overflying the Dutch coast. Now 'Alarmstufe I' (alert) was given to all flak batteries in our area. Positions had to be occupied. When the first bomber formations were approaching the Münster–Osnabruck area the civil population was warned. Corresponding to that penetration the command of 'Luftflotte Reich' normally gave the order that aircraft of Fighter Division 1 had to assemble over Magdeburg. Furthermore, the activity of smoke pots began on the ground to generate smoke screens over potential targets.

Often, the next sequence was either a flyby to the Berlin area, (north of Magdeburg) or a flyby to the Leipzig area (mostly south of Magdeburg). German fighters received their next order and disappeared to meet the spearhead of the bomber stream. Sometimes we saw dense condensation trails or heard the continuous deep roaring of bomber formations in the distance, interrupted by the high singing noise of escort fighters. Also, P-51s were seen hunting German fighters (Me 109s) on the deck. Further 'Luftlagemeldungen' arrived. Now the bombed areas were named; less special targets. Also, air battles were mentioned by our special broadcasting system.

Withdrawal saw similar flyby conditions. Bomber boxes were seen gleaming in the sun, seeming to be in a parade condition. Sometimes we saw stragglers and in one case a B-17 made a belly landing near Magdeburg. Single-engined German fighters (Fw 190s) made emergency landings on a nearby airfield. Warning time for the civil population was over. A short time after this the same took place for the flak and we left our positions. Normally, our time was about two o'clock, depending on the season.

Normally, my location was battery Lemsdorf to the north of the city. On 11 January 1944 I was in town when the daylight alarm was given. Suddenly Magdeburg flak opened fire against a small formation of so-called four-engined bombers, heading to the west. They were Me 110s [that] took the fire because they seemed to be four-motors due to their outboard fuel tanks mounted outside of the engine nacelles. On the night of 21/22 January I was outside of Magdeburg when a large-scale night attack by the RAF took place. Fortunately, the illumination cascades of the Pathfinders had drifted away due to strong westerly winds when the following bomber stream arrived. What happened was a field saturation bombing [to] the east of the town (but one year later, 16/17 January 1945, the RAF made no error).

On 20 February 1944, the first day of 'Big Week', due to the frosty weather, we heard the bomb detonations, and felt the resulting ground shocks of the Bernburg raid, twenty-four miles south of Magdeburg. Two days later there occurred the first daylight raid on Magdeburg. We heard the Oschersleben flak at clockwise direction 8 when the bombers were attacked by fighters. AGO Oschersleben, one of the Fw 190 production lines, was an important 8th Air Force target. I detected a single B-17 group (fifteen aircraft) with my telescope, flying in a northern direction. Obviously having missed their primary target due to overcast, the group turned to the east, looking for a target of opportunity within the Magdeburg area. The suburb of Cracau in the east suffered some bomb damage from these aircraft. They may have belonged to the 94th Bombardment Wing.

This was the first time we had seen B-17s and heard their typical formation noise. Due to their flight path they took AA fire more from the southern batteries. About 5/10ths overcast did not allow optical tracking, thus it had to be done by radar. The typical scenario at our position: 'FuMG Ziel aufgefasst', data being electrically transferred by voice to the ballistic director to prepare the same for the guns; battery commander [chief] gives 'Feuer frei' then he or a next in charge handled the fire bell, positioned at each of the six guns. Normally this procedure was accompanied by the call, 'Gruppenfeuer . . . Gruppe', which meant that salvos were required in a three-second sequence if possible. This depended very much on the fitness of the loading soldier at each gun, who really had to do a hard job. [This job was forbidden for the 'Luftwaffenhelfer'].

'Bomb row at two o'clock' was the next call. We saw the fountains, running from right to left, looking like an avenue of poplars. At the same time we heard the jet-like noise of the falling bombs and some time later the rumble of their detonations. The B-17s disappeared to the north-west, taking flak from the other batteries now.

On the Berlin penetration of 8 March we had the opportunity to track many B-17 boxes within a bomber stream. They were clearly visible against high cirrus overcast, flying outside of our flak battery range [tracking was performed by the four-metre-base optical rangefinder]. Our time was far after twelve o'clock. The most northern flak batteries of Magdeburg had fired all their ammunition against the bomber stream. Thus it was clear geographically that the bomber stream's penetration leg ran along the Midland Channel from west to east. One B-17 was seen making interrupted loops, thereby shooting some salvos of flares, and spinning down at last. I have learned that this was the fate of *Holy Terror III*, a B-17 of the 100th Bombardment Group. [Lt Norman Chapman and his crew, who had been hit earlier by fighters but had stayed in formation and dropped their bombs on Berlin, left the formation after the target and all the crew baled out. They were made PoW.]

When looking towards Berlin with our rangefinder about one hour after our first penetration observations, we discovered a large bomber stream approaching, which meant that it was on its withdrawal leg, moving from east to west. At first many B-17 boxes were seen. Later on, B-24 boxes appeared too, making up the rear. This armada avoided the flak zone of Magdeburg to some degree, flying a west-north-west course, well timed by repeated placing of marker bombs or corresponding flares. Some Me 109s were seen making head-on attacks on one of the B-17 boxes. The last observation I made that day was a single B-17 circling to the ground defended by a P-38. One or more Me 109s were in the neighbourhood. Then dusk came . . .

On 8 May there was a Berlin flyby of B-17s about twenty-two miles north of Magdeburg. The time might have been eleven o'clock. Suddenly, there happened a mid-air explosion within the bomber stream. Later we observed combat boxes gleaming in the sun in an east-north-east direction from us. The B-17s were on a south easterly course now.

The 8th Air Force was resolute enough to continue the 'oil campaign' and on 28 May, Sunday of Pentecost, we had a daylight alarm. Brabag at Magdeburg/Rothensee in the north of the city was one of the most often bombed synthetic oil targets and took its first raid that day. Another target that day was a military depot at Köningsborn, a village located ten to fifteen miles east-south-east of Magdeburg. Observations from AA batteries in the south were difficult due to activity of smoke pots on the ground. This meant it was not possible to plot the bomb runs on the chart. Later on, fires were visible in the north. There was some secrecy of German authorities, probably due to the good bombing results.

At one of the Pentecost days we had a party within the battery, organised by Lt 'Duke' Hartmann, our first younger battery chief at that time. We called him 'Duke' in relation to band leader Duke Ellington, because he was a fan of him too. We had much fun with this young officer. There was an event, typical for us teenagers on the one hand, and Duke's youth (he might have been twenty-one) on the other. A Klemm 35, open cockpit light aircraft started a strafing exercise on our battery. We had to defend with carbine rifles, loaded with blank cartridges. 'Missing' any results for a long time we finally took clods of earth from a ploughed field nearby and tried to hit the propeller disc of the aircraft. And Duke tolerated this action. Later, there was a pilot's protest transferred to our higher flak command.

On 20 June 1944 again Brabag at Magdeburg/Rothensee and the military depot at Köningsborn were on the 'menu'. The fifty-two B-17s of the Köningsborn force were overflying our Lemsdorf battery from west to

169

east, bomb bay doors open. The air was vibrating due to the deep roaring of that formation, interrupted by our flak fire. The same formation took a similar route for withdrawal [east to west] but was divided into two groups now, flying independently from each other. After repeated AA fire some parachutes belonging to the first group were seen in the west.

Kenneth P Garwood, radio operator aboard Lt DeBrandes's B-17, was one of those over Magdeburg who was fighting for his very existence: 'We started our bomb run to the target through very heavy flak and about that time, the fighters hit us. We dropped our bombs and the fighters came through their own flak to hit us. We were the last element in the group, and were therefore prime targets. All of our gunners were firing and the ship was filled with smoke. One Fw 190 flew up along our right side, and as I swung my gun around to shoot, a burst of 20mm flak came through the floor of the radio room, and small pieces hit my leg. I dropped the gun for a moment, and he was gone. He was so close I could see him clearly looking the damaged bomber over. By that time, our inboard engines were burning, and because of the location of the fuel tanks, that was an automatic bale-out signal. I reached for my chest pack which I always kept at the base of the radio transmitter, and when I picked it up, it was in shreds. The flak must have hit it when it came through the floor. I was prepared to jump while hanging on to one of the others, but my ball turret gunner located a spare chute near the tail, and snapped it on to my harness. Our tail gunner, Tommy Rogers, had been hit, and he was helped from his position into the waist where he baled out with the rest of us who were in the rear of the ship. We were all accounted for on the ground after we jumped, except for T/Sgt Lambrecht, our flight engineer, who was never found. When we hit the ground the German civilians were waiting for us, and I had a few bruises and a black eye for a few days. Our bombardier was also badly beaten, but none of us, except the tail gunner, who was wounded by the enemy planes, had to be sent to hospital.'

Friedrich Kowalke, meanwhile, watched the scene above the city.

A single B-17, very noisy due to its over-running engines, was coming back in a wide circle, taking much AA fire again. After having lost much altitude the ship made a belly landing near the village of Schleibnitz. As an observer, I had to make contact with the same, by bicycle. This activity was part of the eager procedure, to get the merit for our flak battery to have downed or co-downed an enemy aircraft. Searchlight soldiers, who

were first at the landing spot, told me that there were no crew members on board the ship. At that time we were not able to identify the unit of the US bomber.

The twenty-ninth of June 1944 was a beautiful, cloudless morning when we were at our positions. The primary target was the Junkers aero-engine plant at Magdeburg–Neustadt. 'Anton', 'Berta', 'Caesar', 'Dora', 'Emil' and 'Friedrich' (the names of our guns) were ready for action. It might have been about ten o'clock when I detected the eighty-one B-24s with my telescope, approaching from the south-south-west, squadron-wise in line astern. It was the first time we had a raid with B-24s of the 2nd Bomb Division. Their formation noise was not so deep compared to that of the B-17s. I am now able to say that the aircraft belonged to the 14th Bomb Wing, comprising the 44th, 392nd and 492nd Bomb Groups. The 44th BG were the leading group, having despatched thirty-six planes in three elements. From the 492nd BG twenty-one planes were over target (two elements). The rest of the twenty-four aircraft belonged to the 392nd BG, making up the middle two elements of that column.

They met an intense flak barrage over Magdeburg. No wonder. They passed a flak avenue that must take all the AA fire from south to north. Furthermore, our tracking was optical; that means it was not disturbed. There was no co-ordinated flak strategy at that time. In case of optical tracking generally the lead plane of the leading element was fixed by the rangefinder. Had the same aircraft gone out of range of a battery there was no rule what had to be fixed as the next one. From this point of view, the leading element of the 44th BG must have taken the bulk of AA fire. One B-24 was hit, thereby having a collision with a second one and both aircraft went down.

Both Liberators belonged to the 506th Squadron. After being hit by flak *Cape Cod Special*, flown by 1/Lt Howard K Landahl, went into a slip to the right, and when attempting to pull out of formation, its right wing made contact near the top turret of *My Ever Lovin' Gal*, flown by 1/Lt Gerald S Westcott. Sgt Frank Rinaldo, the tail gunner aboard *Cape Cod Special*, wrote later: 'We were getting hit by flak all the way on the bomb run. I had my flak suit over all my body. When the bombardier said 'Bombs away', I looked up at my window and it was all shattered. That was enough for me. I said, 'Let's get the hell outa here!' That's when we got the first direct hit. It knocked me over, and when I started to get up, we were hit again. I was knocked out for a few moments and when I came to, all I could see was open space where the bomb bay had

171

been! Luckily, I had a back type chute on. I dived out and our two waist gunners baled out on the bomb run. Both the pilot and co-pilot were blown out after the collision. The radio operator and bombardier had jumped out of the bomb bay just after the direct hit and before the collision.' 1/Lt Thomas C Conzoner, bombardier, adds: 'I parachuted down with no problems, and ended up in the same field with Frank Rinaldo and Walter Yount, the radio operator. We attempted to hide in a grain field, but within an hour we were rounded up by the Land Watch. Randolph Smith, my co-pilot, and Howard Landahl, my pilot, were both alive; however, Landahl was mortally wounded in his upper right thigh to lower abdomen, which was fairly wide open and he was in shock. I did what I could for him but Landahl died in my arms about twenty minutes later.'

There were only three survivors aboard *My Ever Lovin' Gal*. The other six were killed (there was no ball turret gunner aboard, Joe Gasky having been invited to London by Bebe Daniels). One of the survivors was S/Sgt Walter V Lawrence, the left waist gunner: 'Fred DuBose, the radio operator, who was closing the bomb bay doors after bombs away jumped before the explosion. The explosion threw me out and the heat was terrific. Luckily I was wearing my chute. I pulled the rip cord and somehow it did not catch fire nor was it hit by flying debris. On the way down I counted chutes and assumed we all got out. At this point, I did not know about the collision with Landahl's plane. My only injuries were a broken collar bone, pulled muscle in my left arm and a sprained ankle on landing. Fred and I went to help Lt Landahl. Both his legs were mutilated, broken in several places and he had evidently lost most of his blood during the descent. I put a tourniquet on for a bit, but after cutting his trouser leg to see what was wrong, I removed it. His wounds were not bleeding. Fred gave him another shot of morphine but he died shortly after.'

Friedrich Kowalke and his fellow battery gunners set off on bicycles to make contact. He recalls: 'The tail end of one of the B-24s had come down in the village of Gerwisch.' The 44th Bomb Group had twenty-six out of their thirty-six aircraft damaged on this raid. A 66th Squadron B-24, which was flying deputy lead in the 392nd BG formation, was hit by flak and lost the No. 2 engine. Charles B Handwright, the pilot, managed to reach England but was forced to crash-land, between Lowestoft and Southwold, when all four engines quit.

On 7 July 1944 Friedrich Kowalke recalls that:

The scenario was similar to that of 29 June. However, the Leipzig area received the visit of the 8th Air Force. Suddenly the silence was interrupted when our special broadcasting system was reporting about an air battle between Oschersleben and the Harz mountains. We searched at seven o'clock with our optical instruments and saw a macabre scene shortly afterwards. Some B-24s were in flames at the same time, others were surrounded again and again by flashing projectiles. What had happened? The 14th Bomb Wing had just departed from the Bernburg area when Sturmgruppe IV./JG3 of Cpt Moritz started a company front attack from six o'clock on the low-flying squadron of the 492nd Bomb Group with the result that all of the same were downed. This success was mentioned next day by the 'Wehrmachtsbericht', in particular, the first sortie of a 'Sturmgruppe' was named, which had shot down thirty, in reality, eleven (*sic*) [eleven B-24s in the Low Squadron, and one in the Lead Squadron, were shot down by fighters] four-engined bombers. Such events were often used by Nazi propaganda to keep up the morale of the nation as P-51s had gained air superiority.

July saw no raids on Magdeburg. Often we stayed at our positions, waiting and waiting. During such silence Lt 'Duke' Hartmann loved it now and then when we played an allied commander conference with distributed roles (Harris, Spaatz, Doolittle, etc.). Such pleasure was over, when he left Lemsdorf battery to take over the Pechau battery, the latter having changed its 8.8 guns to 10.5 at that time.

The fifth of August was a very impressive daylight attack since our Lemsdorf flak battery was located about one and a half miles away from the Magdeburg/Krupp tank plant which was attacked. The first combat Wing of the 3rd Bomb Division over the target area were ninety-three B-17s ordered to bomb the Junkers aero engine plant at Magdeburg–Neustadt. The force comprised the bomb groups of both the 4th and 92nd Bomb Wings, the latter now flying B-17s instead of B-24s. This force had approached from the north-east but was difficult to observe in time due to smoke pots on the ground. Also, the common image of tight formations was not recognisable, particularly after the force had left the target area. Was this the result of the very dense flak barrage they suffered on the bomb run? The bomb run passed the 'Grossbatterie' located to the east where concentrations of eighteen to twenty-four guns were predestined for box barrages. The damage to the target was 'fair' because at least two thirds of the bomb load fell in the built-up area near the plant.

A short time after the raid the other combat Wing, comprising B-17s, approached from the east in a good order, split into six or seven squadrons in line astern. Now our tracking was fully optical and the batteries in the south (8.8 and 10.5cm) performed intense tracking fire. With the setting of marker bombs we knew that Krupp was also on the 'menu'. The bombardment with explosives caused heavy damage and was described as 'very good'. One B-17 was hit by AA fire and rolled on to its back at an instant and spun down in flames. It must have been one of the two aircraft lost in the 100th Bomb Group, the only one in the 13th Bomb Wing which participated in the raid. [Kowalke is right – the first B-17, piloted by Ben Scott, went down in flames. Seven men were made PoW, the other two were killed. The second B-17, piloted by Anthony Gallagher, was hit by flak as the bombs were released. It disintegrated, killing all nine men aboard. As it blew up the blast sent Henry Woodhall's B-17 over on its back and straight down with pieces of Gallagher's Fortress. Incredibly, Woodhall managed to pull the B-17 out of the dive and they dive-bombed Brunswick!] The bulk of the Krupp force belonged to the 45th Bomb Wing.

Hank North, a tail gunner in the 452nd Bomb Group in the 45th Wing, recalls: 'I think the thing that scared me most was just scanning the sky and the flak was coming up. I just happened to turn my head to the right and the bomb bay doors were open. We were on the run. Apparently, this '17 caught a shot in the bomb bay door and that thing just became a gulf of flame in a matter of seconds; just like nothing was ever there. It just exploded and all I saw was a ball of fire, flak, smoke and a vacant spot.'

Friedrich Kowalke continues:

Black smoke was billowing from the target and 'chaff' was gleaming in the sun for a long time in front of that dark background. In the late afternoon we got the visit of the 7th PG (a Spitfire or Lightning). They were no match for our guns.

Early in the morning of 16 August, education had begun in our barracks by 'Benny' Hoppe, our teacher of mathematics. As repeated so often the scene was interrupted shortly afterwards, because 'schwere Möbelwagen' [codename for B-17s/B-24s] were on their way again. We took Benny with us to our position at the fire control centre. Eighty-seven B-17s and sixty-seven B-24s were ordered to bomb the target. The first combat Wing over the target area was the B-24 force, split into squadrons in line astern and heading from the west. However, the target was Polte [ordnance production], located at Magdeburg/Wilhelmstadt. The bombing with explosives mainly seemed to be inaccurate. A short time after this raid the other combat force appeared, also heading from the west. This was the Rothensee force. During its bomb run a mid-air explosion of a B-24 was observed, thereby leaving the burning wing of the aircraft as a whole piece (without the four engines) for a long time in the air.

On 24 August the weather was beautiful and clear again and we waited at our positions during the morning. 'Kampfverbände über der Lüneburger Heide' was one of the sources of information. Some time later I detected them at ten o'clock, flying a south-easterly course, about thirty miles away. They were silver B-24s with red-striped fins (96th Bomb Wing). Then we saw a typical IP scenario. All elements turned to the right in a wide circle, to start their bomb runs against targets at Brunswick, heading the same from an east-south-east direction. Still visible with our optical instruments the marker trails were over Brunswick, about fifty miles away.

All of the Magdeburg raids mentioned had been carried out in nearly or fully cloudless weather at the target areas. On 11 September however there was 10/10ths overcast over the southern part of Magdeburg. This was a large raid by the 2nd Bomb Division assigned the Brabag synthetic oil refinery, Rothensee and the ordnance depot at Magdeburg/Friedrichstadt. Participating units belonged to the 20th, 95th and 96th Bomb Wings. We heard the typical noise of bomber formations approaching from the south-west. Suddenly, marker bombs from a pathfinder were seen against the overcast, coming down near to our battery at Lemsdorf and at an instant the crashing of bombs and fountains of earth and smoke were around us while the AA fire was going on. Fortunately, there were no following 'Bombenteppiche' [carpet-bombing patterns]. Our hearts were in our boots. When we could arise again we looked to see what had happened. A Warrant Officer shouted himself hoarse. He wondered how our additional new guns 'Gustav' and 'Heinrich' were still in action although they had not been surrounded by protective walls yet. As a result we had counted more than forty craters in a nearby field, one of them located immediately near 'Gustav' – and nobody was hit! Other bomb patterns were seen or heard in the direction of the suburbs of Buckau and Friedrichstadt (Werder). That was our first impression of an H2X bombing suffered on 11 September.

Next day the overcast had disappeared and the 8th Air Force hit the Brabag refinery, Rothensee and the ordnance depot at Friedrichstadt again. This time the attacks were made by units of the 3rd Bomb Division; 144 B-17s were over Magdeburg/Rothensee belonging to 4th, 92nd and 93rd Bomb Wings probably. It has been reported as only 'fair' results, possibly due to an extensive smoke screen. The other force, comprising seventy-three B-17s, received our AA fire. They approached from east-south-east, heading for Friedrichstadt. I think that these aircraft belonged to the 45th Bomb Wing, the well-known fellows since 5 August. We had tracked them with our optical rangefinder, thereby seeing the instant when their bombs were released in salvos, rather sequentially. Bomb patterns were difficult to observe, due to the smoke pots.

On 17 September my activities as a 'Luftwaffenhelfer' ended. We had some private parties shortly afterwards, so far as Allied Air Command gave us. As usual our comrade 'Blacky' Schwartz was ordered to support these parties with nice girls. My next official duty was the 'Reichsarbeitsdienst', located in the Stendal area. But the Magdeburg raids went on. On 28 September, 445 aircraft of the 1st Air Division attacked. The 1st Bomb Wing had as their primary target the Brabag oil plant, the 40th Bomb Wing the Junkers factory, the 41st Bomb Wing the Polte ordnance factory and the 94th Bomb Wing, the Krupp tank works. The single bomb Wings met 10/10ths overcast at their target areas and the bulk of the bombing had to be performed by PFF means. Although I was no longer an eye witness my mother, who was living at Tangerhütte, a small town north of Magdeburg, near Stendal, at that time, had tried to arrive at Magdeburg by train immediately after the raid but she had to return to Rothensee because the marshalling yards had suffered very much. Large fires were seen in the direction of the suburbs at Neustadt and Wilhelmstadt between the Junkers aero-engine plant and the Friedrichstadt ordnance depot. Patterns of explosives and incendiaries had fallen here and there. One small incendiary had hit our family home but total damage had been prevented by a courageous man in the house.

After the collapse of the German front in France in the autumn of 1944 the Air Defence of the Reich was faced with an entirely new situation. Luftflotte III (formerly in Paris), which was left with only a few operational fighter and flak units, was withdrawn into the area of Luftflotten Reich and placed under Luftflottenkommando Reich in the beginning of 1945. At the same time, Luftflottenkommando III was dissolved and reorganised into LW Kdo West. By November 1944 the air defence of the Reich had reached its quantative peak. The first rocket plane equipped fighter units became operational on the front. In the west, at a slightly later date, Fliegerdivisionen 14, 15 and 16, were created out of Jagdkorps II and Jagddivision 5 to correspond with three army groups. All flying units operating in support of the army were placed under the control of the Fliegerdivisionen; Flakkorps IV had just been built up on the Saar front from units withdrawn from France

176

and batteries withdrawn from the Reich air defences.

On Christmas Day, the re-grouped American ground forces took the offensive in the Ardennes and the German troops were forced back towards the German frontier. German air defence was further weakened when the large-scale Russian offensive in January 1945 caused considerable transfer of flak and fighter power to the Eastern Front. Up to the end of February 1945, approximately four Jagdgeschwader and exactly 400 heavy and 100 light batteries were transferred to Luftflotte 6. The further advance of the Allied armies in the west forced another transfer of strong flak units from within the Reich, firstly for the protection of the Rhine bridges against aerial attack, and then for ground operation at the front to compensate for the Wehrmacht's great shortage of artillery.

By January 1945 Friedrich J Kowalke was staying at Tangerhütte for a short time:

> My family was living with my grandmother at the time. The fourteenth of January was a beautiful winter's day. When the alarm was given I knew the 8th Air Force was on the way. As a former 'observer' I did not like to stay in an air raid shelter. Some B-24s were approaching in line astern from the north, obviously heading for Magdeburg. Clearly visible was the 'chaff' activity of the waist gunners. Some escorting P-51s made up the rear of the column. A short time afterwards B-17 elements in line astern appeared from the east, flying on a north-westerly course. They were on their bomb run for the Derben oil storage works. Due to the frosty weather we heard the bomb detonations, which were accompanied by violent ground shocks. A Fw 190 was seen spinning fiercely to the ground, obviously a victim of some P-51s.
>
> We observed an RAF raid on 16/17 January from Tangerhütte too. When we saw the illuminating cascades in the south we knew that the city of Magdeburg was the target for a typical RAF saturation bombing raid. The 371 participating aircraft left a wasteland of ruins. During February and March 1945 and the rest of the war when I served in Denmark as a 'Heeresflak' soldier, raids on Magdeburg reached their climax, mainly carried out by the 2nd Air Division. How much the flak defences had been increased, I don't know. The Liberators participated in raids on 3, 6, 9, 14 and 15 February as well as 2 and 3 March. In every case the primary target was the Brabag synthetic oil refinery at Magdeburg/Rothensee but it seemed to be a rule in overcast that units pick up their secondaries by H2X, mainly the large marshalling yards between Brabag and the Junkers factory.

Quintin R Wedgeworth, flying in *Wabash Cannon Ball* in the 578th Squadron of the 392nd BG, recalls the 2 March raid on Magdeburg.

The briefing outlined the usual strategy for this target; the primary objective was the synthetic oil refinery north of the city, but it was stipulated that it must be a visual attack. Otherwise, the secondary was to be the marshalling yards in the centre of the city. Only two squadrons from the 392nd were being committed to the effort. Our squadron would fly high right off the 44th Bomb Group and the 576th would fly high right off the 491st Bomb Group. We made landfall on the coast of the Netherlands just north of Bergen aan Zee. In anticipation of some enemy reaction we discharged chaff for fourteen miles but the Dummer Lake defences were strangely quiet! Near the town of Celle, Lt Down's crew broke away from the formation and headed back, but apparently under control. (We learned later that they bombed a target of opportunity and then were subsequently hit by AA fire while attempting to leave the French coast near Calais. One of the waist gunners was injured and died before they could reach Manston.) Although unusual, the ascent did not terminate until we had reached the IP, where we finally levelled off at 24,000ft. The point lay over the village of Wittingen. The chaff screen was dispersed immediately and continued all the way into the target. We didn't have long to wait before the first bursts of flak began to appear; mostly below us. I pulled my helmet down (already had the vest on) around my chest and dragged the chute a little closer! Taylor was soon reporting that the lethal black puffs were climbing higher! Ahead of us, and uncomfortably close, it was sure enough bursting at our level. Suddenly it was on all sides. The whole ship shuddered and bounced. Inevitably a loud metallic 'clang' told us that we had been hit. The question was where? It wasn't visible from any of our stations. At 1037 hours I toggled the bombs loose in unison with the lead ship.

As we circled left to withdraw, we (unknowingly) came close to becoming involved in a major air battle. Anticipating an attack against their dwindling oil supplies, the Luftwaffe had assembled a large force of Me 109s and Fw 190s. However, the 353rd and 357th Fighter Groups intercepted them near Wittenburg. The Mustangs downed thirty of the enemy aircraft while losing eight of their own.

Even though by this time the Luftwaffe was plagued by a most severe lack of aviation fuel, the Reichsverteidigung succeeded in sending up some 200 fighters to combat the American bombers on 2 March. Among these units was JG301, which scrambled all serviceable Fw 190A-8s, A-9s, and long-nosed D-9s, as well as all available Bf 109G-10s. Within a few minutes, north of Magdeburg the Bf 109s of IV./JG301 were over-whelmed by the strong Mustang escorts and claimed a few B-17s shot down; they suffered dreadful losses. Around twenty Bf 109s of the Gruppe were lost, with eight pilots killed or missing, and a further five injured. I. and II./JG301 suffered further heavy losses on this day, losing nine Fw 190 pilots killed and one injured in air combat with the Mustangs. These losses in fact effectively meant the end for JG301 in the Reichsverteidigung. I./JG2, III./JG26, II., III. and IV./JG27 and II. and III./JG300 lost an additional sixteen pilots killed or missing and five injured – forty-three of the some 200 fighters had been lost during 2 March 1945, with only fifteen Abschüsse to compensate. The Reichsverteidigung was quickly bleeding to death in her last desperate efforts to stem the American 'Viermots' . . . Wedgeworth continues:

> The return trip was not the usual uneventful story either. As before, we commenced discharging a screen of chaff prior to reaching Dummer Lake. During this operation, someone accidentally fired their gun (or guns). Lt Blakeley's ship, raked with the heavy .50 calibre ammo at close range, tumbled down from the 576th formation and was last seen spiralling down with only two chutes being observed. The flight back across the Netherlands was a sombre one.
>
> Except for one squadron, the effectiveness of this day's effort was poor. Although the target was partially obscured by clouds, our squadron bombardier got a visual sighting and put seventy-four per cent within 2,000ft of the MPI at the oil refinery. The other element (including the 576th) bombed the marshalling yards and wound up with poor results from the H2X. Amazingly enough, our ship was the lone recipient of all that flak!
>
> The same oil refinery at Magdeburg was once again scheduled for attack on 3 March. Our crew had the day off. For the first time in the last seven strikes, the weather permitted all three squadrons to bomb visually. Even so the 576th made a poor drop; they were 3,800ft short. Our squadron was leading and although they didn't exactly put it right down the barrel, they managed to squeeze fifty-four per cent into the 2,000ft mark. Several close sightings of Me 262s probably interrupted their train of thought to some degree. The flak didn't help either. It was intense and moderately accurate, causing extensive damage to ten of the ships.

Friedrich J Kowalke concludes: 'Although embedded in the mythology of National Socialism there was no hate from our side against the 'Terrorflieger', as the bomber crews came to be called by the official German press at that time. Now and then there was some fascination for the largest air armada the world has ever seen. In particular, the steady ability to assemble up to 2,000 heavies, to give them effective fighter cover along the whole legs and to pick up and hit special targets, demands respect. The Luftwaffe did not possess such a comparable strategic instrument. On the other hand, I am still wondering that the RAF had seen strategic bombing with other eyes than the USAAF.'

CHAPTER 9

FIGHTER FORTISSIMO

L ate in July 1944 Walter J Konantz arrived at Wormingford to join the 338th Fighter Squadron, 55th Fighter Group, which just a few days before had changed from the Lockheed P-38H Lightning to the P-51D Mustang. The 55th had been the first to use the 'fork-tailed devil' in combat with the Luftwaffe, on 15 October 1943, and had been the first American group over Berlin, on 3 March 1944. Five years before, in 1939, Walter Konantz had soloed in a 40hp J-2 Cub. As a senior in high school in 1940 he owned his own plane, a 1929 60hp Monoprep open cockpit, high-wing monoplane made by the Monocoupe Co. He entered the USAAF as a cadet in February 1943 and was commissioned a 2/Lt in Class 44-B a year later, graduating to P-40s before being shipped to England.

The 55th Fighter Group at this time was engaged in daily escort missions for the B-17s and B-24 Liberators and strafing missions, in addition to the normal fighter pilot's role of aerial combat with Luftwaffe fighters in the air. On 8 August 1944 Walter Konantz flew his first mission, an escort for the Fortresses, to Romilly-sur-Seine airfield south of Paris. It proved 'uneventful' and he logged the time at four hours twenty-five minutes. Four days later, on 12 August, the mission proved very eventful with ground strafing and dive-bombing runs in the Verdun–Nancy area where fifteen railcars containing ammunition and a city water tower were destroyed. His aircraft was badly damaged by flying debris from the exploding cars but he made it back to base. Inspection revealed that the leading edges of the Mustang's wings and the tail were dented and the propeller spinner had been knocked off. Konantz noted in his log that Lt Gilmore was shot down by flak. Next day there was more dive-bombing and strafing south of Paris. This time Konantz hit a railway station with his two 500lb bombs and strafed a German staff car. On the morrow it was back to protecting the bombers again when the 55th Fighter Group escorted the B-17s to the Mannheim–Ludwigshafen area. Even so, he managed to shoot up two locomotives on the way home.

On 15 August Konantz joined the 55th Fighter Group escort to Venlo and Twente (Enschede) airfields in Holland, which were the target of the B-17s. He saw flak hit one of the B-17s, which exploded with his bomb load. In his log he noted: 'Saw only the four engines falling out of the fireball.' Missions followed almost daily. They were a mixture of escort and strafing/dive-bombing sorties. On 17 August the 55th FG dive-bombed and strafed east of Paris. Konantz damaged a string of boxcars and coaches and destroyed two oil tank cars before cutting the railway with his bombs. He had still not sighted an enemy aircraft but the next day, 18 August, during an escort for Liberators to Roye–Amy airfield in southern France, he spotted a 'bandit' and dropped his fuel tanks early in anticipation of combat. However, the Luftwaffe pilot escaped and Konantz landed with just five gallons of fuel remaining.

Seven days later, on 25 August, the 55th escorted Fortresses to the synthetic oil refinery at Politz, north-east of Berlin. He saw a B-17 go down in a vertical dive after being hit by flak over the target, but no enemy fighters ventured within range of the Mustangs. It was much the same pattern the following day but weather forced an early abort and he became separated from his squadron. He came back alone and landed at an RAF station in northern England. On 27 August Konantz flew as a spare into Holland but he was not needed and he returned to base. Two days later he went strafing just over the French border into Germany. As the second or third man on most of the train strafing he shot up three trains, one of which was a long troop train. Konantz wrote: 'Train was moving fast when I raked it from the rear to the front and saw soldiers jumping out the windows while it was still moving, thirty to forty mph. When it finally stopped, I saw fifty to sixty people lying in the fields and ditches near the tracks. Another train made it safely into a tunnel and would not come out. Lt Lanham shot down a Do 217 twin-engined bomber and I saw it crash.'

On 3 September Major Darrell Cramer shot down Hptm Emil Lang, Kommandeur of II./JG26. Lang was credited with 173 victories in 403 combat sorties before he met his end, when he was surprised by Cramer, during take-off from St Trond airfield in Belgium. More German aircraft were shot down on the 5 September escort mission for the B-17s to Stuttgart when the 343rd Squadron shot down fifteen biplane trainers. Walt Konantz saw some German planes on the ground but the flak was too intense and accurate to try a strafing attack. Two more escorts for the B-17s followed on 8 and 9 September. On the second of these missions, Walt Konantz saw a B-17 explode and men jumping out of it with their parachutes on fire. On his sixteenth mission, on 10 September, Konantz shot up two locomotives and damaged the entire string of boxcars behind on the way home from an escort mission for B-17s going to Nürnberg.

On 11 and 12 September 1944 Walt Konantz came into contact with enemy fighters for the first time, during escort missions for B-17s going to Ruhland on both days. He has written of the 11 and 12 September missions (his seventeenth and eighteenth):

This was the biggest air battle of the war for the 55th FG. We were scheduled to escort 3rd Air Division B-17s to Ruhland. Fifty-two Mustangs took off at 0937. Just before rendezvous with our bombers, we were climbing through 24,000ft and I had to get rid of my second cup of coffee. To use the relief tube in the P-51, it is necessary to undo the lap belt, unsnap the leg straps of the seat type parachute, then scoot well forward on the seat to use the tube which is a plastic cone attached to a rubber tube which vents overboard out the belly of the plane. It is stowed on a clip under the seat. I was completely unbuckled, sitting on the front edge of my seat when a voice came over the radio: '109s, here they come.' About fifty Me 109s had bounced our squadron of sixteen P-51s and about fifty more engaged our other two squadrons up ahead . . . Just a few seconds after the warning on the radio, a single Me 109 passed directly in front of me in a forty-five-degree dive. With a reflex action, I peeled off after him. He evidently saw me as he steepened his dive to the vertical. I firewalled the throttle and steepened my dive to match his. During this wide open vertical dive our speed increased to near compressibility; both airplanes were as skittish as a colt on a wooden bridge. As I was vertical and virtually weightless, the slightest movement on the stick would cause me to leave the seat and be stuck against the canopy. A very slight pull on the stick would put me back down in the seat. I felt like a basketball being dribbled down the court as I bounced back and forth between the canopy and the seat. Just before I started a careful pull out at about 8,000ft I saw the airspeed needle bumping 600mph, 95mph over the redlined airspeed of 505mph. Holding a steady 4-g pullout, I regained level flight at about 3,000ft. Meanwhile, the 109 was bouncing around and appeared pretty unstable and hard to control at that speed. He started to pull out of his dive about the same time I did but was not successful. His right wing buckled through the wheel well area and he spun into the ground with a fiery explosion. The pilot had no time to get out.

I claimed a 109 destroyed that day and what confirmed the claim was that after the massive twenty-minute dogfight, one of the 55th FG pilots reported that he counted thirty fires on the ground, which would account for the twenty-eight Me 109s claimed and the loss of two Mustangs. I never got close enough to the 109 to fire my guns and I was too excited to think to take camera gun pictures of the impact point. My plane had only a few popped rivets which speaks well for our beloved P-51 and its equally dependable Merlin engine. I would also compliment the sub-contractor who made the sturdy canopy.

On 12 September we were again on a bomber escort mission to central Germany. We had escorted our bombers to their target and were headed back towards England, cruising along at about 22,000ft, spread out in a comfortable formation. About the same time as they were called out on the radio I spotted two Me 109s headed north. Our entire squadron of sixteen Mustangs made a ninety-degree right turn and swung in behind the pair of 109s which were three or four miles ahead of us and at about the same altitude. As had been demonstrated in the past, the Mustang is a bit faster than the 109 and we slowly began to close on the two enemy planes.

I figured that when the Mustangs got in range and the bullets started flying, the 109s would break right or left and certainly would not continue to fly straight and level at full throttle. I thought I might put myself in a good position if one of them turned right so I moved far to the right of our main formation and waited. Sure enough, when the shooting started one broke to the left and one broke to the right and came my way. I was in a perfect position to cut inside his turn and catch him in short order. I moved up to perhaps 100 yards behind him and with the vibration of my first few rounds fired, my gunsight bulb burned out. Being only 100 yards behind him, I started moving up to point blank range where I could just use the centre of the windshield as a gunsight.

I was about ready to try another burst from about fifty yards when I saw some tracers come close over my wings from behind. I looked at the Me 109 ahead. This guy seemed very determined to get this victory hoping he would not hit me. His stream of bullets was coming uncomfortably close so I moved out of his line of fire to the right and was flying formation with the 109 about fifty feet off his right wing. I could see the pilot clearly, looking wildly behind as the bullets of the second Mustang began to pepper him. Then his canopy flew off and he stood up in the cockpit to bale out but the 280mph slipstream jerked him out of the cockpit and rolled him back down the top of the fuselage until he hit the vertical fin and rudder. He then bounced at least ten feet higher than his plane and fell away. I expected that he would have been killed or badly injured so I watched him fall and fall until I could no longer see his body, then watched the area he was aimed at to see if I could see a puff of dust or perhaps his chute spilling when he struck the ground. However, at an estimated 6 to 8,000ft above the ground his chute opened and he survived the encounter.

Walt Konantz's next seven missions were, on the whole, uneventful, apart from getting a 'big blast of flak' from the Belgian coast on 28 September, and suffering engine cut-out and missing problems at high altitude on the escort mission to Münster on 5 October. The next day, during an escort mission to Berlin, 100-plus Fw 190s were sighted but the Mustangs failed to catch up with them before they disappeared in the clouds. After another escort mission on 7 October, when he was forced to return early and alone after the failure of his oxygen supply, Walt Konantz flew a change of role on the fourteenth, when he completed a weather mission for the Third Scouting Force ahead of the bombers attacking Saarbrücken. By now he had a change of Mustang too. He had taken over Lt-Col John McGinn's *DA QUAKE*, a Mustang which McGinn flew on his last mission on 6 October. Konantz renamed the aircraft *Saturday Night*.

By September 1944 the continual raids on Germany's oil-producing plants had caused the Reich's oil reserves to fall to only 7,000 tons. Ironically, the Me 262 Jagdverband, which used low-grade petrol, which was still in abundance, were not greatly affected. During September Hitler had reconsidered the Me 262's role as a fighter rather than the fighter-bomber he had once envisaged. Forty were immediately formed into a fighter unit, commanded by the Austrian fighter ace, Major Walter Nowotny. 'Erprobungskommando Nowotny', as it was known, became operational in October 1944 and during the first month of operations shot down an estimated twenty-two American bombers.

Walt Konantz's thirtieth mission, on 2 November, when the Mustangs escorted the B-17s to the vast I.G. Farbenindustrie synthetic oil refinery at Leuna, three miles south of Merseberg, proved quite exciting, as his log testifies: '. . . saw twelve Fw 190s pass 3,000ft below us but no one else saw them. I was leading Blue Flight and told the others to watch me and I would lead the attack until the other flights saw them. I dropped my tanks and dived down towards them but forgot to switch to an internal tank and my engine quit while I was still about 1,000ft above them and 400 to 500 yards behind them. By the time I got my engine running again, I had lost the element of surprise as well as my excess speed over the 190s. The other three members of my flight

185

were nowhere to be seen either and since the 190s knew I was there by that time, I followed them for several miles, futilely calling for assistance until they eventually disappeared in the clouds. I was rather put out with the other three members of my flight, who claimed they never saw me leave the formation.'

On 5 November the Mustangs escorted the B-17s to Ludwigshafen. Walt Konantz shot up two trains on the way home and landed at RAF Coltishall, Norfolk, for the night after bad weather prevented him carrying on to Wormingford. Four largely uneventful missions followed by the end of November, and December too was rather quiet with the Luftwaffe conspicuous by its almost total absence during escort missions for the bombers. Death could always come when one least expected it though. On 30 December, during an escort for the B-17s to bomb Mannheim railway marshalling yards, Walt Konantz noted: 'Lost Lt Metcalf who went in out of control from 28,000ft. Probably was unconscious from oxygen system failure.'

The next mission, an escort for the B-17s on 31 December, was uneventful. On New Year's Day 1945 the Mustangs escorted the B-17s to Derben oil refinery near Stendal. It was quite notable, at least as far as Walt Konantz was concerned, as he explains: 'Lt Bodiford got hit by flak and baled out over France. He came back a few days later carrying his wadded-up parachute. My girlfriend made Bodiford and me an aviator's scarf out of it and a pair of panties for herself. On this mission we saw a couple of airfields with parked German planes but they laid a curtain of flak over them too thick to try to strafe.'

His forty-ninth mission the next day, to the German border as a spare, passed without him being needed and he returned to Wormingford after just two hours. However, his fiftieth mission, on 6 January, when the 55th escorted B-17s, was marked with a strafing attack on Giebelstadt on the way back out and the 338th Squadron claimed thirteen aircraft destroyed. Walt Konantz recalls: 'I got a Ju 88 which was slow catching fire but when I looked back it was starting to burn. Capt Buskirk was hit by flak from the airfield and baled out. Lt Ramm was badly damaged by flak but made it back to base. He had to belly in at 200mph as battle damage made his plane uncontrollable below this speed.'

On 13 January thirty-seven Mustangs of the 55th Fighter Group went looking for targets on a freelance support mission. A dozen P-51s of the 338th, having destroyed fourteen planes on the ground at Giebelstadt airfield just a week before, headed for the airfield again to see if there was anything left. The Mustangs were circling the field at about 5,000ft planning their strafing routes and picking out targets on the ground when Walt Konantz, who was flying Red Three in *Saturday Night*, saw a plane taxiing on the runway. What followed was the first Me 262 to fall to the 55th Fighter Group (the first Me 262 victory had occurred on 28 August 1944 when Ofw Hieronymous 'Ronny' Lauer was shot down by Major Joe Myers and Lt M D Croy of the 78th FG). Konantz was surprised to see him take off, as he says:

I would have thought we had been seen and the tower would have advised him to park the plane and seek shelter. I called out the now airborne plane but no one else saw him. He continued climbing, made a 180-degree turn and came back directly under me headed in the opposite direction. [The Me 262, belonging to I./KG(J)51, was being flown by Uffz Alfred Färber on an acceptance flight following maintenance and repair work.] I did a tight 180 and ended up about 200 yards behind him. At this point, he had built up enough speed that I was no longer closing on him even though I was at full throttle and had made a diving turn behind him. The new K-14 gyroscopic gunsight had been installed in this plane only a week earlier and I had never fired the guns with this new sight before. It worked perfectly and the Me 262 was saturated with nearly forty hits. He made no evasive action whatsoever, possibly the pilot may have been hit. His left engine burst into flames and the Me 262 made a slow, descending spiral and crashed on a railroad track about two miles from the airfield. The plane exploded on impact and probably cut the track.

After downing the jet I made a strafing pass on a parked plane but it was a burned-out hulk from our 6 January strafing and I did not fire. As I went across the field at ten feet and 400 mph, I picked up a single .30 calibre bullet through the cockpit that cut a groove in my leather jacket sleeve and knocked out my radio. Strafed some ammo sheds and exploded a few. There were no other P-51s in sight when I pulled up from my last pass so I started home alone. I searched for any Allied planes headed for England as the weather was bad and without a radio I could not call for a DF steer to my home base. I found a lone P-47, joined up in close formation with him and signalled that my radio was out and I wanted to land with him. I followed him and landed at the 9th AF base at St Trond, Belgium. I spent the night there, had my radio replaced and came back home the next day. When I walked into the barracks, my barracks mates were dividing up my belongings. They had seen the fiery crash of the Me 262, heard nothing more from me on the radio, and when I failed to return that night they figured my stuff no longer had an owner.

187

Walt Konantz's fifty-third mission on 21 January proved uneventful. Then on the twenty-second while leading Red Flight, three crippled B-17s were glad to be escorted by the Mustangs to the Dutch coast on the way back from a raid on Sterkrade, Germany.

A week later, on 29 January, the 55th Fighter Group flew escort for B-17s attacking Kassel. After safely escorting the bombers out to the German border, Acorn White Flight, led by Major Darrell Cramer, turned back into Germany to look for targets of opportunity. Acorn Yellow Flight, led by Lt Roy D Miller, did likewise. Walt Konantz was Acorn Yellow Three in *Saturday Night*. He wrote in his log: 'Two flights (eight P-51s) left the bombers for a fighter sweep on the way out. Our flight ran into three Me 109s at about 5,000ft, 100 miles north-west of Hamburg. I saw them first and led the flight to them.' A flight of five Bf 109s had taken off from Lignitz near Breslau in Silesia to fly to Boyens–Haderslev airfield in Denmark about 400 miles north-west. The flight leader was Fw Horst Petzschler, an experienced combat pilot. No. 2 was Hptm Post, No. 3 Obstlt Waldemar Balasus, No. 4 Oblt Mielke and No. 5 Oblt Mueller. Petzschler had orders to take these student officers, all former Ju 88 bomber pilots, to Denmark to join EJG1, a training wing to check out bomber, transport and even glider pilots, in the Bf 109 to bolster their dwindling pool of fighter pilots. After refuelling in Stendal, the officers pulled rank on Petzschler and all four flew to Hamburg to spend the night with relatives. On 29 January Balasus and two of the others took off from Hamburg at about 1300 hours and flew in the direction of Boyens-Haderslev. Thirty minutes later they came face to face with the 55th FG Mustangs.

Walt Konantz called out three bogies at eleven o'clock level headed north-east. They were about six miles ahead and no one else in the flight could spot them so Konantz assumed the lead and manoeuvred Yellow Flight into a visual stern chase. Konantz wrote in his log:

I picked the leader, who was carrying an external belly tank [Obstlt Waldemar Balasus]. The other two were clean [Roy Miller went after one, Lt Thomas Kiernan the other]. I got a good burst into him, setting his belly tank on fire. He promptly dropped it and continued on, leading me over a small town that was throwing up 20mm flak. We ended up over the town at about fifty feet, circling a brewery smokestack below its top. We were in a hard right turn, pulling three or four Gs when I got a hit on his left aileron, blowing about a third of it off. The sudden loss of lift on that side caused him to violently snap to an inverted position; I left my gun camera

188

running, expecting him to split-ess into the middle of the town but he climbed inverted to a safe altitude and rolled upright. He then headed out into open country flying so low he was pulling up over fences and descending again on the other side. His prop tips were barely clearing the snow-covered ground and his prop wash was blowing up snow behind him like a car on a dusty road. After another good burst of hits, he simply pushed forward on the stick and bellied-in at 280mph. He slid for more than a half mile, coming to rest in a grove of trees with his wings sheared off. When I passed over him, he was climbing out of the cockpit and saluted me as I went by. Lt R Cooper, my wing man, was close behind me and strafed the wreckage, setting it on fire. I then followed Lt Miller and his Me 109 and got a few strikes on it just as it was bellying-in. I strafed it again as the pilot was running about fifty feet away from the plane. I returned and strafed my Me 109 and left it burning good. [The third Bf 109 chased by Kiernan also bellied-in after being this.] Whether or not the pilot escaped the strafing, neither I nor my wing man ever knew.

It was not until forty-nine years later that Walt Konantz found out the answer to this question: Balasus did escape. He survived the war and died in 1989. Horst Petzschler flew 397 combat missions and had twenty-six confirmed victories by the end of the war.

In February 1945 Walt Konantz flew nine more missions to bring his total missions flown to sixty-four. The first of these was on 3 February, his fifty-sixth, when the 55th FG flew escort for B-17s to Berlin. He wrote: 'No fighter opposition but we saw several B-17s go down over the target due to flak. Weather was clear and we could see the bombs plastering Berlin. I also used my relief tube over Berlin.' Ever on the lookout for victory No. 5, on 6 February Walt Konantz escorted B-17s to Bohlen, Germany, and then went on a fighter sweep. He strafed two locomotives and a railway switch house. He added: 'Lots of flak shot at us today. Capt McDowell hit by flak and had to belly-in when his engine quit.' There was more flak on Konantz's fifty-eighth mission: 'I was the lone armed escort for an unarmed photo recon Spitfire to Leipzig. We flew at 35,000ft. I stayed out to the side while he made his photo runs, drawing quite a bit of heavy flak for a single tiny airplane.'

With his tour nearing completion Walt Konantz sought a fifth victory but no enemy fighters came his way. It did not, however, stop him strafing trains, and any other worthwhile targets, at every opportunity. On 14 February, when he led Yellow Flight during an escort for B-17s to Magdeburg, he strafed two locomotives on the way out, and on the nineteenth, during a fighter sweep over Germany when he led Blue Flight, he got five locomotives, two trucks, one horse-drawn wagon ('didn't see the horses until too late', he wrote), and a tractor. The 55th Fighter Group claimed no less than eighty-one locomotives that day. On 21 February Walter Konantz led Acorn Blue Flight: 'We had completed our escort duties with the bombers and headed back into Germany to look for targets of opportunity. Just as our flight of four Mustangs was cruising along at 5,000ft, low enough to see ground targets but high enough to be safe from small-arms fire, I saw a plume of dust on a dirt road a couple of miles away. I turned in that direction to investigate and found a German soldier riding a motorcycle down the road. I positioned my plane for a strafing pass down the road headed in the same direction as the motorcycle. The rider had seen me by this time and had opened his throttle and was tearing down the road at high speed, constantly looking over his shoulder to see where I was. He turned around one more time just as I was coming in range and at the same time came to a right-hand curve in the road. He was still looking back at me when he went straight off the road, through a fence, brush and small trees, then hurtled end over end off a fifty-foot embankment.'

Six days earlier, on 15 February, 2/Lt Dudley M Amoss of the 38th Fighter Squadron scored the 55th Fighter Group's second Me 262 victory when he shot down one flown by Uffz Herman Litzinger of I./KG(J)54, near Obergrasheim (the unit lost two more Me 262s on this day). Amoss wrote: 'I was leading Hellcat Red Flight out from the target on a heading of 245 degrees at 2,000ft when I spotted an Me 262 at two o'clock, 1,000ft on a course of 175 degrees. He was in a shallow turn to port when I came in behind him and started closing. Noticing black smoke, I gave full throttle and started firing between 600 and 800 yards. In a six-second burst I noticed hits on the engines of the blow job, and as he slowed down I pulled in behind again and at about 200 yards gave him a series of short bursts. This time there were strikes all over the E/A and after an explosion he burst into flames. I thought the pilot had been killed and pulled out to the side to watch him crash. Then the pilot was catapulted ten feet straight out the port side and his chute opened almost immediately at about 500ft. The burning plane turned crazily about and crashed with another explosion and burned furiously.'

On 22 February, George Washington's birthday, the 8th launched CLARION, the systematic destruction of the German communications network. More than 6,000 aircraft from seven different commands were airborne this day and they struck at transportation targets throughout western Germany and northern Holland. All targets were selected with the object of preventing troops being transported to the Russian Front, now only a few miles from Berlin. Only five bombers were lost, including one to an Me 262 jet fighter. Walt Konantz saw no enemy fighters and the fighter sweep he flew after escorting B-17s to Dessau also proved uneventful. Then on 23 February he flew his sixty-fourth and final fighter mission, in CL-P *Saturday Night*. He recorded in his log: 'Escorted B-17s to Nürnberg – led Red Flight. After escorting bombers a safe distance out I went back in with my flight, searching desperately for one more enemy aircraft as this was my last mission and I had only four.' (*Saturday Night* was taken over by 2/Lt Harold Konantz, his younger brother, who had just arrived as a replacement pilot. The P-51 earned a Bronze Star for its crew chief S/Sgt James Seibert, by flying over sixty combat missions without a mechanical abort. Harold Konantz left the name on the nose and had only to change the rank and first name on the canopy tail. On 7 April 1945, he was flying his seventh mission when he was hit by gunfire from a B-17 waist gunner fifty miles north-west of Berlin. Harold lost his coolant and the engine caught fire forcing a bale-out. He was a PoW for the rest of the war.)

Walt Konantz was the first pilot in the 55th Fighter Group to down a Me 262 and fifteen more would fall to 55th Fighter Group pilots before the end of hostilities in Europe. Their rivals for the crown of top-scoring jet fighter victories were the 357th Fighter Group and the race to finish top was a close run thing. On 25 February seven Me 262s were downed by the 55th FG and they came from the unfortunate I./KG(J)54 at Giebelstadt. Sixteen Me 262s took off in poor visibility and, led by Kommandeur Obstlt von Riedesel, groped their way through strato-cumulus in search of the enemy formations. Immediately they emerged from the cloud layers they were bounced by Mustangs of the 38th Squadron. Capt Donald M Cummings destroyed two Me 262s. One cartwheeled and burned after attempting to land at Giebelstadt and the other went in from 800ft near Leipheim airfield. 2/Lt John F O'Neil and Capt Frank E Birtciel shared one Me 262 which crashed and exploded on impact shortly after take-off. Capt Donald E Penn blasted an Me 262 just after it took off and the jet's undercarriage came down. Penn blasted it again and it went in and exploded on impact. 2/Lt Donald T Menegay shot down another west of Giebelstadt at 4,000ft and 1/Lt Billy D Clemmons claimed another fifty miles south-east of Mannheim. 1/Lt Millard Anderson, who was heading home after shooting down a Fw 190, claimed another Me 262 (in fact I. and II./KG(J)54 lost six this day). Later that day a further four Me 262s were lost when the airfield was strafed by more American fighters, and two more jets were lost in accidents. The new Kommandeur, Major Hans-Georg Bätcher, arrived to discover that he now commanded just twenty remaining Me 262s.

Fortunately, the German jets and V-weapons had materialised far too late and in too few numbers to alter the outcome of the war. The Allied heavy bombing raids and strafing missions by the US and RAF fighter forces had virtually grounded the Luftwaffe fighter arm and the only units able to operate until final defeat were the jet and rocket-powered fighters. The most successful were the single- and two-seat Me 262s of Oblt Kurt Welter's 10./NJG 11. Many attempts had been made to deal with PFF Mosquito attacks on Berlin but it was only towards the end that the Luftwaffe met with any real success. During the summer of 1944 Welter, then a test pilot at Rechlin, was commissioned to find a solution to the problem. The Bf 109 and Fw 190 had been tried but neither could catch the Mosquito, and even fitting water injection, what the Germans termed 'ice injection', to the 109 was not the answer. Although it increased the speed it also damaged the engines. The jet was considered the answer and Welter was to say whether the Arado 234 or the Me 262 would be more suitable. He flew both and at the same time asked that a two-seat Me 262 fitted with AI be constructed. This only went into operation at the end of March 1945, as the Me 262 B-2a, and had few victories to its credit before the end of the war. Oblt Welter shot down no less than twenty-five Mosquitos at night in the Me 262, with another two Mosquitos in daylight. During ninety-three operational sorties, Kurt Welter claimed sixty-three 'Abschüsse'. He was killed in a car accident in 1949.

Despite fuel and pilot shortages Me 262s put in an appearance just about every day until the end of the war. During March 1945 nearly all enemy fighter attacks on American bombers were carried out by the Jagdverbande. On 2 March, when the bombers were despatched to synthetic oil refineries at Leipzig, Me 262s attacked near Dresden. On 3 March the largest formation of German jets ever seen made attacks on the bomber formations heading for Dresden and oil targets at Ruhland and shot down three bombers. Two Liberators in the 448th BG were lost as a result of the jets' actions, as F/O John W Stanford, co-pilot aboard *Frisco Frisky*, captained by 1/Lt Edward Anderson, wrote:

192

Our P-51 fighter escort had been with us for about an hour sweeping the skies above and around us. Now they seem to be acting most peculiarly – diving, climbing, chasing one another. Suddenly, the top turret, just a few feet behind me, opens fire. Were it not for my seat belt, I would jump about a foot. What are they firing at? I cannot ask because of a problem with my radio. A fighter which I make out to be a P-51 with wing tanks passes through the bomb stream from front to rear, just above us. I reflect on what a foolish thing this is to do – pointing your guns at bombers can be suicidal no matter what your insignia. Ed looks over at me and taps the control column signifying my turn to fly. Our eleven-plane squadron is formed in a seven-plane 'V' inside which and slightly lower, a single 'tail-end Charlie'. At the apex of the three-plane 'V', sometimes called the 'bucket' position, is Egress C-Charlie [*Gung Ho*] commanded by 1/Lt Irving Smarinsky. We are flying on his right wing. Ahead and above, flying on the right wing of the Squadron lead plane is Adel E-Easy, commanded by 2/Lt Jim Guynes.

Now, Guynes's B-24 [*Feuden Rebel*] is dropping slowly down and back forcing us out of position. He pulls back only to slide once again off to the right and down. I watch him, warily, mentally exhorting him to close it up. What I do not know is that the planes I have identified as P-51s with wing tanks are actually Me 262s and, apparently, in one of the passes a 30mm cannon shell has exploded on the flight deck of Guynes's aircraft. Again his B-24 begins dropping back. Again, we are forced to relinquish position but this time the other aircraft does not recover. It slides to the right. Someone on board tries to correct. The plane begins to slide left and down. We watch fascinated as the stricken plane moves in on Smarinsky's 'bucket' slot. Hands tighten on the control column. All in one smooth motion, the left wing of Guynes's aircraft comes down on the right rudder of Smarinsky's B-24. Guynes's plane rolls to the right on to its back. Smarinsky's plane rises up on its tail and over into a loop. As we pull up sharply to get away, Smarinsky's plane falls off to the left and Guynes's aircraft, inverted, drops off to the right. Guynes's B-24 already has its bomb bay doors open as if abandoning the aircraft has already been contemplated. I can see the big 500-pounders nestled inside. Miraculously, none of the other planes in the back of the formation is hit and, hearts pounding, we quickly close ranks again. Although there are eighteen men on the two crews, only five chutes are observed from the fallen aircraft. As I try to concentrate once again on my formation flying, I am aware of the cumbersome flying clothes I am wearing – the flak vest, seat belt, oxygen hose, parachute, headphone cord, microphone cord, the heated suit connection – and wonder what the odds are of getting out of the seat of a spinning plane, through the narrow isle, and down to the bomb bay to get out.

Only the bombardier, 2/Lt Arthur Hoffman, and S/Sgt Gerard J Perry, the engineer, survived from *Gung Ho*. Perry went into the bomb bay to salvo the bombs but not all could be released as he fell unconscious from lack of oxygen or the centrifugal forces of the plane. He only recalled that he was floating in the air with an opened 'chute. *Gung Ho* spun down with *Feuden Rebel* and both aircraft crashed near Gross und Klein Heide, twenty-seven kilometres north of Salzwedel. Only Guynes and Sgt Donald F Schleicher, the tail gunner, who could not remember anything after the explosion and regained consciousness in the air, survived from *Feuden Rebel*. Schleicher pulled the rip cord and then passed out again. When he came to he was draped over a bicycle and several twelve- and thirteen-year-old Hitler Youths were holding guns to his head. They had already rolled up his chute and taken his watch, ring and wallet with $150 in it. Jimmy Guynes, meanwhile, had survived the parachute descent despite shrapnel wounds in his right arm, which was severed almost completely, and his left knee. At Salzwedel hospital, near Magdeburg, Major Freidanck amputated the arm and attended to his left knee. Finally, on 24 March the surgeon had to amputate Guynes's leg but the infection had already spread and five days later he died. In 1946 Iringard Bodenstab, a nurse who attended Guynes, kindly wrote to his wife in Texas informing her of the circumstances of her husband's death.

On 18 March, when a record 1,327 bombers were assembled for yet another large raid on Berlin, thirty-seven Me 262s were sent against the bombers. Six B-17s in the First Air Division were shot down by the jets while in the Third Air Division formation, the 'Bloody Hundredth' lost four bombers from the eleven lost by the Division this day, including one ship which was cleaved in two by Me 262 gunfire. By the end of the month the 8th was to lose thirty bombers to the German twin-engined jets.

The jet menace became such a problem that beginning on 21 March the 8th flew a series of raids on airfields used by the Jagdverbande. The raids also coincided with the build-up for the impending crossing of the Rhine by Allied troops. Capt Birtciel of the 55th FG damaged a Me 262 on 22 March. 2/Lt John W Cunnick, also in the 38th Squadron, went one better when he shot down a Me 262 of III./EJG2 piloted by Fahnenjunker-Oberfeldwebel Helmut Recker near Lechfeld airfield.

194

With the noose tightening around the German neck Oberkommando der Luftwaffe had given the order for Luftflotte Kommando Reich to move its Battle Headquarters to Stapelburg in the Nordharz and to assume control of the Luftwaffe units on the Western Front. The advance of the American 7th Army at the beginning of April 1945 separated Lw Kdo West and Luftflotte Reich. Luftflotte Kommando next moved its Battle HQ to Kassel, then to Rainsfeld (Lübeck). When the British and American armies linked up with the Russian forces southern and northern Germany were separated and the main body of OKL moved to southern Germany. The complete control of the Luftwaffe in the north German area was given over to Lfl Kdo Reich. On the day of the breakthrough by the 2nd British Army from the Lauenburg bridgehead towards Lübeck, the Lw Kdo moved to Missunde, twelve kilometres south-west of Schleswig.

The Luftwaffe though was still very much in evidence. On 4 April when the Liberators went to a jet airfield at Parchim (Wesendorf), twenty-seven kilometres north of Oranienburg, Me 262s successfully intercepted the 20th Wing and singled out B-24s in the 448th lead and high right elements. Captain John M Ray's ship, *Trouble N Mind* in the 713th Squadron, received direct hits from the jets in the cockpit and Nos. 3 and 4 engines. It was abandoned near Kyritz, sixty kilometres west of the target, and all the crew are believed to have baled out before the aircraft entered a spin but three were murdered by hostile civilians. Ray and five other crew were taken prisoner. 1/Lt James J Shafter's B-24 in the 714th Squadron was also shot down by the Me 262s. 2/Lt Harold Major, the co-pilot, baled out but his chute failed to open. Three others went down with the aircraft.

A B-24M in the 714th Squadron, and the third lost overall, was flown by 1/Lt Robert L Mains and 1/Lt John E Riviere. Seven of the crew, who were considered a 'hard luck crew' having baled out twice before (over France in October 1944 and over England in January 1945), were on their twenty-eighth mission (they were scheduled for a seven-day leave starting the next day). T/Sgt Charles E Cupp Jr, the radio operator, who had celebrated his twentieth birthday just two weeks before, recalls what happened after they started the bomb run:

> I dropped down to the generator to open the bomb bay doors. Right after the command to open them I heard over the intercom, 'BANDITS!' I felt the whole ship vibrate (there was no sound) as the .50 machine-guns opened up on the attackers [Me 262s]. Immediately, big balls of fire came

195

in, raking the whole side of the ship. The fuselage split in half at the waist windows and broke away, so there went the two waist gunners [Tony Villari and Harry J Allen] and the tail gunner [Stuart D Van Deventer]. They never had a chance to get out.

I was rolling around and around and had no control over myself. I just couldn't get up. All I could think of was, 'You're done!' The plane went down and down and down. I swear to God it was two hours (we had been at 20,000ft). More like it was two minutes. I expected a big explosion any second. I couldn't see anyone else except the engineer. Frank Merkovich was laying face down, probably killed by the enemy fire.

All of a sudden [the right wing broke off and the weight of the left wing threw the B-24 over on its back] I was upside down looking at clear blue sky. Fortunately, there was a chest chute lying near. I grabbed it, put it on and, looking at the gaping fuselage opening, thought, 'Jeez, give it a real college try.' I tripped, got up again, saw the bomb bay up above, and jumped. If I had been two inches shorter I would not have made it. I managed to grab the lip of the bomb bay or catwalk or whatever and the second I didn't feel any metal against my body I pulled the rip cord. Phew, the chute opened! I was maybe 600 to 800ft from the ground, in the middle of a city [Ludwigslust]. There were pine trees in a parkway and I was heading straight for them. I heard the plane hit the ground and explode as the bombs and fuel blew up. I had not seen any other chutes in the air so I knew that all the crew must be dead [1/Lt Allan L Lake, navigator, 2/Lt George S Alexander, top turret gunner and Sgt Charles H Daman, nose gunner, are those not yet mentioned]. At this stage though all I was concerned about was missing the trees. You worry about the other guys later.

I landed in the street thankfully, but the wind blew me along and I had to pull the shroud lines before I stopped. I took the chute off. A crowd of people gathered. Beneath my coat I had a .45 revolver but the chamber was empty, and anyway, it would have been suicide to pull it out in the middle of Germany. Someone hit me on the side of the face. I hit him back. It was a kid of about sixteen. Then I was jumped on by the crowd. They punched and kicked and it was only when I lay still, face down, that it stopped. There was complete silence. I looked up, right down the barrel of my own .45. A kid of about twelve was pointing it right at my head. Several people grabbed the gun just as two soldiers came up. They took me to a HQ, either Gestapo or SS, and just sat me in an office for an hour while possibly they worked out what to do with me. Then I was marched off out of town about a mile, the two soldiers carrying rifles, walking close behind. I thought the worst. Fortunately, when we came upon an airfield I was taken there and placed in a cell. One of the soldiers, who could speak very good English, asked me where I was from originally. I said, 'Michigan'. He said he used to live in Buffalo! Eventually, I was transported to PoW camp where I spent the last few weeks of the war.

Two other men made prisoner on 4 April were Col Troy Crawford, CO of the 446th Bomb Group, Command Pilot in a 25th BG Mosquito 'Red Tail' monitor aircraft being flown by 1/Lt T B Smith. They converged on the B-24 formation for protection when enemy fighters were reported in the area but the textbook 'pursuit curve' was misinterpreted and he was shot down in mistake for a Me 262. Col Crawford was captured and taken for interrogation near Stendal which he knew was to be the 446th's next target. Crawford was later approached by some Germans who realised that Germany had lost the war. He and forty other Americans finally escaped to the American lines. Crawford eventually arrived back at Flixton on 25 April 1945 and he returned to the States.

By this stage of the war Göring was growing ever more desperate as day after day the Luftwaffe was unable to halt the incessant American air attacks. More than 200 pilots a month had been lost trying to stem the daily armadas, but with no credible results. Perhaps a last desperate stand might yet gain time for Germany?

CHAPTER 10

FIGHTER FINALE

On 7 April 1945, the Luftwaffe day fighter force came up in numbers for the last time in the war to fight the American bomber formations. The main targets of the day for over 1,200 B-17s and B-24s were underground oil storage at Büchen, a munitions factory at Geesthacht near Hamburg and an Army depot at Güstrow. Their opponents were effectively the 'last generation of Luftwaffe fighter pilots' of the war. A small group (some twenty per cent) of pilots, from JG300 and JG400, already had combat experience. Others had served in bomber and reconnaissance units earlier in the war and had recently been converted and trained for the day fighter defence in the Reichsverteidigung. The rest were an estimated 110 young and inexperienced pilots from airfields in central Germany flying Bf 109 G10s, G14s and K4s and had volunteered for Rammjäger duty. Most of them came from the Luftwaffe fighter OTUs – the 'Ergänzungsjagdgeschwader'.

The concept of bringing down a large number of four-engined American bombers by ramming had been conceived by Oberst Hajo Herrmann in September 1944. At age thirty Herrmann was appointed, early in 1944, commander of the 1st Fighter Division and was responsible for the air defence of central Germany, including the Berlin area. Herrmann has gone down in the history of World War Two as the man who initiated many, often radical, new tactical concepts for the Luftwaffe, including the 'Wild Boar' night fighting in 1943.

Herrmann first proposed to Reichsmarschall Göring in September 1944 a plan to inflict a severe blow to the American bomber force by assembling a force of 1,500 Bf 109s, man them with young volunteer fighter pilots and ram the bombers. It would probably cost the lives of at least half of the ramming pilots involved, but he considered this to be much better than having the day fighter force slowly but steadily bled to death, as had been the case since early 1944. Thus, he hoped that the Americans, just like after the disastrous Schweinfurt raid of 17 August 1943, would be forced to interrupt their raids on German cities, and so give the Reich's industry a few weeks', or even months', respite. In that time Germany could build up a strong force of Me 262 jet fighters, and produce enough fuel to restore Luftwaffe air superiority.

At the time Herrmann proposed ramming operations to Göring, the concept could well have brought about a respite from American bombing but Herrmann's plan met with strong opposition from men like Oberst Gollob (General of the Fighter Arm) and Oberst Dahl (Inspector of the Day Fighter Arm), who both objected to the self-sacrificing nature of the concept. However, Göring indicated that he would sanction the formation of the Rammjäger if the scheme gained acceptance from Hitler. In January 1945 the Führer agreed – provided enough pilots volunteered.

Herrmann set about organising the mission. He chose Stendal aerodrome, some hundred kilometres west of Berlin, as the central base for the operation, and Major Otto Köhnke as his direct subordinate for leading the whole undertaking. Köhnke, a highly decorated combat veteran, had been severely injured on operations in September 1942 whilst serving as Gruppenkommandeur of II./KG54. An appeal for the 'Training Course Elbe', as it was codenamed, went out in February 1945 to all Luftwaffe day fighter units and OTUs. However, 'Elbe' was doomed almost from the outset. On 23/24 March the Allies crossed the Rhine and in the east, the Russians were advancing on Berlin, so the whole undertaking could not stall the inevitable defeat of Germany. Moreover, by the end of March, Herrmann could muster only about 150 Bf 109s and between 150 and 250 pilots for ramming, instead of the 1,000 he had originally requested from Luftwaffe reserves. With such a small number of aircraft, the Rammkommando could never hope to strike a crushing blow against the American bomber force. Even so, Herrmann went ahead, possibly against his better judgement.

Some 2,000 volunteers came forward. Uffz Klaus Hahn, a Jagdflieger who had just turned twenty, had completed his fighter pilot training during 1944 and shortly before the call for volunteers for the Training Command Elbe came through, was posted to a Jagdgeschwader in southern Germany. Klaus Hahn stepped forward as one of the first to volunteer for the mission: 'I had experienced the bombing raids on the ground, not only those against important war targets, but also those which were aimed at the major cities and the civilian population that lived there. My idealistic notions on chivalry and fairness in the air war, as I remembered from the books on World War One pilots like Richthofen, Boelke and Immelmann, had been annulled. I had become bitter, and my bitterness had increased from day to day. I contemplated on the raids on the cities of Dresden and Potsdam, and on other cities. I was a fully trained fighter pilot and had but one wish: to fly on operations. The regular fighter units were plagued by a permanent lack of aircraft fuel. Missions in the air defence were flown in ever-decreasing numbers. Yet, as a fighter pilot, I felt that it was my first duty to help in curbing the bombardment raids. I did not enquire after the overall strategic situation at this time. I was a soldier and had to fight for my country, and if need be, fight till my last drop of blood.'

These same thoughts are echoed by Werner Zell, who by February was at Hadersleben in southern Denmark with 4./EJG (Ergänzungsjagdgeschwader) 1 awaiting a posting to an operational unit. He recalls: 'One fine day we had lined up for a roll-call and impatiently awaited things to happen. We were gathered together to listen to an Order of the Day and were told to stand up straight and keep absolutely quiet. In this strictly secret Command affair, our Reichsmarschall was calling up volunteer pilots who were prepared, at the risk of one's own life, to save the Fatherland literally at the last minute; our Fatherland that was surrounded by fanatical enemies who aimed to destroy it. We were given some time to think it over and could then, one by one, have our names put on the list of volunteers in the administration room of the station commander and swear to remain completely silent about it.'

Why did so many volunteers come forward? Fritz Marktscheffel, a Rammkommando Elbe pilot, explains: 'It was the deep-felt love of our Fatherland that decided for us to become Rammjäger. We had been raised in this spirit at school when we were children and we were brought up with this love by our parents. This love towards our Heimat and Fatherland had been deeply rooted into the German people for dozens of years before 1933. One can trace the roots of this spirit and feeling back to the Prussian-German tradition.' Werner Zell continues:

Did anyone stand aside? Did anyone want to be seen as a coward by his comrades? Many of us had not only lost our homes and possessions, but also our parents, sisters, sometimes even our wives and children, in the bombing terror of the Americans and British. One city after another was transformed into rubble and ashes. How many times already had we asked ourselves, 'Where are our fighter aircraft?' Hundreds, at times even over a thousand enemy bombers with almost the same amount of escorting fighters, entered German airspace day after day and brought death and destruction. Perhaps we could really end this horror by our mission. Or were we afraid that we would be transferred to the ground troops because of the lack of aircraft fuel? Moreover, the fate of Dresden and her bestial treatment was blood-fresh in our minds.

Anyway, along with my lively comrade Horst Seidel and some other pilots, I reported for this special mission. At this point I must emphasise that none of us was told what the nature of the mission was. Days of waiting passed. The wildest rumours went round. Some told of new *Vergeltungswaffe* [Revenge] weapons which could turn the tide for us. Others said that we would fly aircraft which were armed with new weapon systems and which would destroy the bomber formations in a radical way, and for this mission one could only use dare-devil, courageous pilots who scorned death. One needn't have made this last remark, as we got to learn what happened to the German fighter force when a few new instructors joined us straight from the operational Wings, and who shared their experiences with us. The Grim Reaper was harvesting freely among the operational Wings. Not only the inexperienced young pilots, who were posted from the OTUs to the front, were killed in action (as they were trained badly) – they were often virtually defenceless victims to a more than twenty times stronger adversary; no, the experienced fighter pilots, who themselves had shot down many adversaries, increasingly fell victim to these superior forces.

This was more the case after the German fighter pilots force had been sharply decimated during December 1944–February 1945 when they had been ordered to fly on absurd missions. Often, 600 to 900 enemy fighter aircraft had flown into Germany to patrol over the aerodromes at low level and destroy any planes that tried to take off or land, or shoot them down in air combat.

Other speculations went around, like flying bombs or rocket-propelled aircraft with many rockets in its belly which had to be fired into the bomber boxes and then explode like loads of shrapnel, and then the aircraft itself break up into several parts and descend to earth again by parachute.

After a seemingly endless wait, we volunteers were ordered to travel to Stendal around 20–23 March. My friend Horst Seidel, who had got to know his fiancée during our training days with JG102 at Flensburg, asked for a short stop at Flensburg to say goodbye to her. He was granted permission to do this. Our journey to Stendal was fraught with all kinds of difficulties. Travelling by day had become impossible, as the American fighter-bombers shot at anything that moved on rails or on the roads. Thus, we were forced to find our way to Stendal by night. Our special passes got us through several times, when we were thoroughly searched by field police who would like to have put us to the side of the road and join the groups of soldiers who were bound for the Eastern Front.

After we had finally and surprisingly made it wearily to Stendal we met some of our former comrades of JG102 there. We were housed in a stone barracks building near the entrance to the airfield, from where we could easily flee into the surrounding woods in case of an emergency, like during an air raid warning for example. We were eager to learn about our task which awaited us but we were told that we had to wait until all the participants in the 'Training Course' had arrived. These soon did, so that in the end around 190 to 200 pilots were gathered. The description of 'Training Course' was soon altered to 'Training Command Elbe' and, finally, was named Sonderkommando (Ramming Command) Elbe. The word 'Elbe' was used as cover for the whole operation.

On arrival at Stendal there awaited a true and already long forgotten 'Cockaigne', which one could describe as a culinary wonderland – at any rate for that particular time – as we were looked after splendidly. There was lots of meat and good quality sausages, the best cheese, excellent wines, French brandy, chocolate and cigarettes. These were all available to us in large quantities to put us in the right frame of mind. This was very necessary, bearing in mind the task ahead. When one morning we had fed ourselves well with real coffee and boiled eggs, margarine and marmalade, we were summoned into a large room. Major Köhnke now revealed the big secret which had surrounded us for some time. 'We should bring down the four-engined bombers with our Me 109 by ramming, without firing a single bullet,' he told us. Complete silence reigned. Some were paralysed with astonishment. Many got a deep fright, but also there was some great enthusiasm. To ensure that the whole thing would not turn into a failure, we were immediately told that we were not expected to sacrifice our lives in this mission but that we would always have a reasonable chance to survive, but only if we considered important facts, which would be discussed during the course of the training. Then everybody was left to reflect on the matter and to discuss it with his comrades.

That evening Horst Seidel finally arrived. I had dozed off a little lying on my bed when he suddenly woke me up. In my joy of meeting him again I didn't notice that he was accompanied by a Leutnant who had also arrived late. I recounted my experiences to Horst and of course also told him about the state of affairs which had been disclosed to us that morning – we had to bring down the bombers by ramming.

At this instant the Leutnant said that he had volunteered for a training course and not for a ramming command. I replied that he had just learned about a matter about which we had been obliged to keep secret and that I now had to act accordingly. Next day he reported to the Administrations room together with my friend Horst and told he could return to his unit without any difficulties.

During the next time our main issue was 'How best to ram a bomber without getting yourself killed?' We often left the airfield at daytime in small groups to gather in the surrounding woods and discuss this item. We also did this because II./JG301 operated from Stendal and, often, Me 262s landed there as well. The Americans had decided to give the Me 262 special treatment and they patrolled over the airfield with strong formations of fighters trying to eliminate them by strafing attacks and carpet bombing. What if they had known what was being cooked up for them at Stendal? Without any doubt, no stone would have been left unturned. In the meantime, we got to know each other better, and amongst the NCOs we addressed each other in the companiable 'Du', as many tried to get over their fears and worries with looser manners. Yet, we felt a common bond and became a strong unit. Among others we met Lt Brökelschen, our old flying instructor from Flensburg, again. We shook hands and remarked, 'Well, you're in the same pack too.' (He rammed a B-17 and survived and I'm glad he did.)

During instruction which now followed increasingly, we were told why the Me 109 had been chosen for the ramming mission. A long and sturdily installed engine; propeller blades of steel, which when they hit something would work like a saw and would not break off immediately, as would happen with the Fw 190-D9; a stable cockpit and a pressurised cabin, as we would approach the enemy from a height of about 11,000 metres [the service ceiling of the Bf 109] in order to avoid the undoubtedly great number of escorting fighter aircraft; the Me 109 could reach this altitude much easier and in an effort to even increase its high level performance, all guns would be removed, apart from one MG 131 with sixty bullets in case of a sudden enemy fighter attack. The models Me 109 G-10 and 14 as well as the K4, which additionally had cabin heating, were placed at our disposal.

In order to demonstrate to us the possibilities of surviving a ramming attack, we were introduced to Feldwebel Willi Maximowitz [who had survived two ramming attacks] of the Sturmgruppe Dahl [IV./JG3], the unit which was equipped with the strongly armoured Focke Wulf 190 A8/R7, and armed with two 30mm cannon, two 20mm cannon (MG 151/20) and a pair of MG 131s with 13mm ammunition. These Sturmgruppen operated in tight formations and approached the bomber boxes with guns blazing

203

and kept firing until very close range. If the target bomber did not go down by this concentration of gunfire, these pilots were obliged to bring the bomber down by ramming. They had signed a written testimony to this end. He had been able to save his life after a ramming attack by baling out. The way in which he told us about the whole procedure made us discuss anew on how best to ram a bomber. Whether to do it from behind, from above, or below, whether the tail unit should be the aiming point, whether the wing roots were a better target, or even whether to do it head-on and aim for the bomber pilot's cockpit – what was the best thing to do, both to ensure bringing down the bomber and saving our own skins?

Questions tumbled over other questions. Should one jettison the cockpit canopy or did it provide better protection for the pilot's head and therefore should remain until after the execution of the ramming punch? One thing was clear: one should never ram in the area of the bomb bay – that would have been curtains for sure. And if possible, one should avoid the engines as in the wings behind the engines were the fuel tanks. Should one remove the 60mm thick armoured glass plate in our backs, which was built into the 'Galland canopy'? And finally, how should one best bale out of the Me 109, if and when one still could? Would it be possible to hit the silk shortly before actually ramming and let the pilotless plane crash into the bomber?

As a means of overcoming our restlessness and divert our attention to other things, we were lectured by the so-called National Socialistic Education Officers. Their task was to turn us into fanatical pilots. One of them, a professor, gifted in oratory, made it clear to us that the enemy camps were divided amongst themselves, but that they had one goal – to destroy Germany for good. If we should lose the war, then there would be no future for us any more he said. The so-called Morgenthau Plan meant that Germany would be eliminated as an industrial nation and turned into agricultural land. Russians would rape the German women and only few men would be made PoW. Germany was in the gravest danger and only a courageous will to fight and a tough determination could still save the Fatherland. Therefore, the time had now come to bring the new wonder weapons into battle and secure victory.

Some of the young pilots were certainly touched by these talks, as a few stated that they resigned from the church, but these remained just special cases – pilots were known to be individualists. At night, we were shown the films that fitted in with this, of which I only clearly recall the heroic defence by Kolberg and the Jew Süss, as the symptom of Judaism.

Yet our minds wandered all the time to the moment when we would inevitably be confronted with the reality, namely our meeting with the bombers. If they were flying in close box formations, then the enormous and deadly firepower of some 250 Browning machine-guns of 13mm or even 20mm cannons, if the so-called gunships flew along, in a formation of thirty-six aircraft would meet us when we would charge in, and this would even make it very hard to get at the bombers at all.

When at last one believed that we were prepared well enough for the mission, we were ordered to wrap up our personal gear and deposit these in the cellar of the barracks building. Later on, when the Americans were approaching, these were blown up, and thus were lost for ever. We also wrote our wills and a last letter to our loved ones at home, but in the chaos of war most of them got lost and never reached their destination, the more so as large parts of Germany had already been occupied by the enemy.

I must once again emphasise here that we, the Elbe men, were not suicide pilots. On the contrary, we had a hunger for life, although some I knew, who had lost their entire families and homes and who saw no use in living any more, often expressed that they were absolutely prepared to sacrifice their lives in a ramming attack. We were anything but kamikaze pilots, which we were often called after the war's end. The survivors, and there are very few of them, know better than that. Still, even today they find little understanding for that, to which they were prepared and also carried out.

On 5 April we were loaded into trucks at night in groups of thirty and another truck followed with our supplies. Sitting on hard wooden benches, the bitter cold made us shiver. We had a few blankets to keep us warm until we reached Delitzsch near Leipzig, our destination. Other Gruppen were at the same time transported to the other dromes at Gardelegen, Mörtitz, Sachau and Solpke. In the late afternoon of 6 April we were even allowed to see the sights of Delitzsch town, probably to prevent anyone separating and possibly betraying the mission. That night after supper, we were informed that we should reckon with the possible execution of our mission the next day, as the weather forecasts were so good that the 'Amis' would undoubtedly take advantage of these conditions and penetrate with a large formation. Of course, everyone had brought his fur-lined boots with him, but everyone was issued with a summer flying suit, which we pilots called a 'bone bag'. In this thing we would fly at heights of over 11,000 metres? We were not convinced about the cabin heating, which could break down. We were not issued with the usual angora underwear or with woollen shawls, apart from the silk shawls which most of us had cut from parachute silk ourselves. This was rather depressing. Were we already completely written off? Anyway, we could expect temperatures of minus forty to fifty degrees Centigrade at these heights. Our electrically heated gloves were scant comfort but should allow us to operate the instruments. As we would climb to such great heights where the sun could almost blind us, we were issued with sunglasses.

After a restless night with little sleep and anxious anticipation of the events which would come, daybreak finally came. It was 7 April, a Saturday and my mother's birthday. For many it would be the last day of their lives. After breakfast we entered the briefing room. A surprise was waiting for us. The tables were lined up in a square and seated in the middle were a number of highly decorated officers in ceremonial dress and with the Knight's Cross around their necks. They should be a shining example to us but later on I did not see any one of them board a kite and lead the way. There were almost no officers anyway who had volunteered for the Elbe command. We were then briefed on the situation: our listening service had established that we should meet a strong formation of bombers and fighter escort penetrating our airspace. They would probably come in over northern Germany. For this reason, the gathering point for the ramming groups would be over Magdeburg. From this departure point we would then proceed to the target. The all-important issue, it was stressed, was to keep a close formation under all circumstances on our way to the bombers.

We slowly left the breakfast room. I handed my 2lb butter case which was almost full, and which I had brought with me from Denmark, to one of the young kitchen maids. I told her that I was sure we would not return to Delitzsch. I think she must have overheard some snippets of the discussion I had had with Horst on our ramming mission, because she suddenly burst into tears. I then gave her the well-meant advice to reach safety before the advancing Russians as one should not expect anything good from them, especially in regard to their treatment of women and young girls.

Horst and I agreed upon flying together, as we were free anyway to decide who would fly with whom in the various flights. Of course, those comrades who had known each other for a long time flew together. We went to the aircraft dispersals. I selected a Me 109 K4 with an auxiliary tank. This held an additional 300 litres of juice, so I would surely have enough fuel for the mission. Unfortunately, the aircraft which was at Horst's disposal was not fitted with an auxiliary tank. While the refuelling personnel topped up aircraft one after the other, we tried to find an auxiliary tank for Horst as well, but to no avail. I noticed that in the canopy of my K4 there was still the armoured glass plate so I immediately ordered it to be removed as I feared that on jettisoning the canopy of my damaged aircraft, it would strike me in the neck. Cigarettes were smoked nervously and we walked around the aircraft and checked if everything was ready.

Uffz Klaus Hahn sat in his Bf 109 at the airfield of Sachau near Gardelegen ready for take-off. He could not keep impossible thoughts from crossing his mind: 'My nerves lay bare. What would the final moments of my life be like? Would death be grievous or would everything be over quickly? Would I be successful or would all the efforts come to nothing? To penetrate a Pulk of B-17s was almost impossible to achieve, and when I also thought about the fighter cover, I could almost not believe in a successful ramming attack. However, foremost in my mind was that I wanted to fight, as long as I was capable to do so, no matter how bad the odds.' Werner Zell continues:

It was getting on for eleven o'clock, when all of a sudden a raised state of readiness was announced over the Tannoy. Immediately after we were ordered to board our aircraft. A final handshake with Horst and I gave my remaining cigarettes to the ground crews while they strapped me in. I plugged in the R/T, fastened the oxygen mask and made sure that it worked OK. Over the R/T I heard marching music, and on inspection, I found out that we could only receive, not transmit. Then silence. One of the ground crews climbed on to the right wing and put the starting handle into the crevice for the fly wheel chain.

Suddenly, a green flare shot up, the signal for the Ramming Command to prepare for take-off. Automatically I closed and locked the canopy, switched on both magnetos, injected some fuel into the suck-up pipe and pulled the control column into my belly. After the ground crews had brought the starter to its highest number of revolutions they gave the signal to start the engine – but then alarm: the engine didn't start! Once again, the groundcrews turned the starter, after having turned the propeller backwards. This time the engine started to cough and the juice, which had leaked on to the auxiliary tank, caught fire, yet the groundcrews immediately put out the fire even before I was out of the cockpit. Now we had to start the whole procedure for the third time. At last the engine started without any further difficulties. I had the engine warming up for a bit before I slowed it down with both magnetos.

Everything seemed to be all right so Horst and I taxied to our take-off position, during which we established that we were probably the last to get airborne. Now I quickly put the flaps at fifteen degrees, checked the trim, a last greeting to the ground crews and I applied full power. The Me 109 accelerated rapidly. The tailplane got off the ground and I made sure that it didn't swing off, by applying opposite rudder. The speed was now high enough. I slowly pulled on the column and I was airborne. I retracted the undercarriage and made sure that it was indeed fully retracted, then I pulled up the flaps and throttled back. A quick glance to the right convinced me that Horst was already in formation with me. I switched on the automatic gunsight, circled the airfield once more, and then, as there were no longer any other machines in sight, set straight off in the direction of Hannover. I did this because Horst had no auxiliary tank and chasing the others in the direction of Magdeburg would have expended too much juice. Besides, we didn't know when and where we would get at the enemy. If I would have been a coward my juice would have been sufficient to reach western Germany and a safe haven.

Now the ground stations reported to us too and gave us a commentary on the state of affairs. Once more, marching music resounded; the 'Horst-Wessel' song, the 'Deutschland' song, and the 'Badenweiler March' rang in my ears. Suddenly, a woman's voice reported and appealed to us, the werewolves of the skies, to think of Dresden and the other cities, and of the dead in the carpet-bombing raids. Save the Fatherland and other such things.

During our lonely flight we were overtaken by one Me 109 which flew past at a height of over 10,000 metres at high speed. This was the only inter-ruption, while we were freezing badly. I don't think that the promise that we would be promoted and awarded a decoration after successfully ramming a bomber came to mind. Also, I don't believe that those who gave their lives during this mission would remain as shining examples in the memory of the Fatherland, by naming streets after them.

Uffz Klaus Hahn, meanwhile, had taken off in his Bf 109 and had already retracted the undercarriage and flaps, when he established that his machine did not reach the speed of the other twenty-nine aircraft that had taken off from Sachau: 'Although the instruments for the engine showed normal readings, I lagged behind ever more, and in the end I was alone. Landing again was out of the question. Under the prevailing circumstances, that would have appeared too much like cowardice. On no account did I want to be a coward, even though the prospect of flying alone now over Germany with the skies pregnant with US aircraft did not exactly fill me with courage. I slowly 'crawled' higher, all the time searching for the cause why my 'Beule' – the nickname for the Bf 109G – was so lame. However, all of a sudden it responded normally and I gained full speed. I never found out what had caused this phenomenon; I suspect that the take-off flaps had not retracted fully.'

Werner Zell had been in the air for some time and was approaching the expected combat area:

We searched the skies restlessly in all directions, especially backwards and downwards. All the time our thoughts circled around this one point: how would this day end for us? Would we survive or would our machines get entangled with the bombers and crash to our deaths, or would we explode in the air together, in a ball of fire? Would we be able to get out of the Me 109 and land by parachute, or would we be so lucky as to be able to belly-land the heavily damaged machine? The reported number of around 1,300 bombers and up to 800 escorting fighters would prepare us a fiery reception at any rate.

There was a flicker in the distance to the north-west, then many more. They flew towards us. There they were, in a scattered formation, and not in the feared close box formation. We saw the escorting fighters flying in front of the formation to ward off any enemy intruders and, what was more clear, our own comrades were approaching from the east, leaving an enormous vapour trail. As we were almost at the same height, I also discovered the tell-tale vapour behind Horst's machine. I immediately lost some height and Horst followed me down. I jettisoned my auxiliary tank after we had overflown Hannover, because a partially filled fuel tank would have been an enormous risk (we really had no kamikaze or suicide thoughts). Now we tucked in really close once more, raised our hand for a final greeting and waggled our wings. This was the sign that we had the Fortresses in a favourable attacking position beneath us. I wanted to have the sun at my back during the attack, hopefully to achieve complete surprise.

I half-rolled my kite on its back and plunged down sideways with increasing speed towards my bomber. Another, which I at first wanted to aim at, I left undisturbed as it had sheered away out of formation and had probably jettisoned its bomb load anyway. It was also trailing a wreath of smoke. Unobserved, or at any rate spotted too late, I approached my target from out of the sun. It flew at a height of some 6,000 metres. No evasive action, no defensive gunfire flashed up. Straight and level it flew its track stately in the skies. About 300 metres from my target I manually turned the propeller blades (they had to have the effect of a circular saw with its sharp teeth spinning round at its highest number of revolutions) to the smallest angle for climbing (in contrast with gliding position), then pushed the throttle through the gate, and with a whining and overturning engine I rushed towards the bomber's right-hand elevator and rudder.

I estimate that my overtaking speed at the moment of hitting the Fortress was at least 200kph. The tail gunner must have spotted the approaching calamity at the last moment as his guns were hanging down and he crossed his hands in front of his face for protection. We collided so violently that my face probably smashed into the gunsight and I immediately lost consciousness. When I regained consciousness I was appalled to find that my Me 109 K4 did not respond to any movement of the control column at all. The glass canopy was smeared with oil and, fearing an engine fire, I pulled out the magneto knob. I couldn't see what my flying altitude was. I could only suspect that I was about to crash. I took one last deep draught from the oxygen mask, and after unfastening the straps I turned the bolt lever of the canopy and thought to myself, 'Well, this will be your first parachute jump.' But then I got a terrible fright. The canopy didn't fly off. It must have got stuck in the collision with the Fortress. With all my strength I now pushed my back against the canopy. It didn't budge. I was terror stricken. I would hit the ground in my machine alive! Once more I exerted all my strength and pushed. Suddenly, there was a rattle of bullets smashing into the left-hand side of my cockpit and into the canopy – the Plexiglas hood splintered and flew off! I was sucked out of the aircraft, hitting the tail with my right shoulder, and my right arm was twisted painfully out of its socket. An enemy fighter had chased me and cut down its defenceless victim. Well, after all, this is what had saved my life. I somersaulted through the air towards the ground until I felt I was going to pass out again. I pulled the ripcord with my left hand and the jerk of the parachute opening rendered me unconscious immediately.

What followed then I can only sum up from the descriptions of other eye witnesses who watched the proceedings. My 'saviour' once more fired a burst at me while I was hanging on my parachute, which was proved by nineteen bullet holes in the silk after I landed. This is proof of what the Americans meant by chivalry towards their downed adversaries in combat. He must have assumed that I had got the worst of it as I was hanging lifeless on my parachute. I don't hold it against him any more as, after all, he was the one who saved my life.

Just when I neared the ground I came to. I saw a pasture with a large watering place for the cattle towards which I was floating, and a farmhouse. Then I was once more overcome with a deep unconsciousness. I didn't feel anything of dropping down on to the ground. I must have lain there for about two hours and as the farmer assumed that I was dead, or was an American, he didn't dare to approach me. My memory came back to me only when I suddenly got to my feet and walked towards the farmer. I unzipped my flying suit, put on my peaked cap and said to him and his wife that I was a German fighter pilot. I handed them my paybook and added that I had multiple injuries before I collapsed once more. They took me into the farmhouse to look after the injuries I had suffered to the right side of the back of my neck, my left forefinger and the bullet wounds in my left upper and lower thigh. They gave me a drink, washed my blood-smeared face and established that so many small veins in my eyes had burst that the whites of my eyes had almost completely disappeared.

In the meantime, the severest air battles raged in the skies. Whining engines and crashing aircraft, wreckages, the population alarmed, so that only late in the day a medic took me to Schwarmstedt, which was two kilometres from the farmhouse. There a lazaret was lodged in a barracks block. My wounds were simply stitched up, without first looking for any shrapnel (this caused me to have a few pieces of shrapnel removed on the operating table some time later). At least three other Elbe men were carried in there too, most of them severely injured also.

Late in the evening a Fähnrich obtained a telephone connection with our Command HQ at Stendal and reported that I had rammed a bomber. I could also speak to Major Köhnke and told him about my successful ramming mission. The Fähnrich then got orders to requisition a vehicle and take me with him to Stendal. I never heard of him again.

My Me 109 had crashed into a barn in the hamlet of Grindau, some 1,500 metres from where I landed. In this barn, which was used by Russian prisoners, around ten men were killed and some others injured. After the ensuing fire had been extinguished, the dead were laid on a ladder truck and taken to Schwarmstedt where they were buried. The remains of the Me 109 are said to have been recovered by a scrap dealer but he could not recover the engine, which stuck in the ground some four to six metres deep.

Two days after our mission, we were taken prisoner by the British but not after our lazaret had been shelled by British artillery. As a sign to my relatives that I was alive, I gave my wristwatch (which had stopped at 1235 hours on 7 April, probably the time of my ramming attack) to a nurse who lived near Metz. My family never received the watch. A few days later the British cleared the lazaret of German soldiers and transported us to Celle. From there, we were loaded into trucks and we travelled past Weeze on the Rhine into Belgium where we were put into PoW Camp 2232. In a labour command in a monastery at Passy near Froyennes I worked as an interpreter for the French-speaking Belgians,

211

the Germans and the British. On 21 January 1946 I was released from captivity.

Uffz Klaus Hahn, meanwhile, had arrived at a height of 10,000 metres over the area east of the Weser and had cruised, waiting for things to happen:

In the north I saw the mouth of the Aller near Verden and in the south was Nienburg. Over the R/T I heard on the wavelength for the Reichsjäger that my comrades were told to go into the attack. I estimated that they had encountered the enemy over Hannover. Suddenly, I spotted four single-engined aircraft, which came straight at me. I thought they could only be friendly aircraft. They flew in typical Schwarm formation and did not carry auxiliary tanks. My initial joy to regain contact with my comrades, however, quickly turned into dismay; these were not my comrades, but P-51 fighters, the dreaded Mustangs. They spread out and there was not the least doubt that 'the dance on the volcano' was about to begin. I did not know what to do next. I was surrounded. I did switch on my single machine gun which was loaded with sixty rounds of ammunition, but that was of no use anyway. I did not stand a chance to get out of this hopeless situation unscathed, apart from immediately abandoning the field and baling out. This thought did not cross my mind in any case, and so it did not take long before I was shot at from the left and behind. The Mustang pilot had aimed well; my left arm fell from the throttle control and splinters from my instrument panel flew into my face. My left upper arm was broken by a bullet and my left hand was badly mangled. The wounds in my face were not severe, but still very painful.

My immediate thoughts were to get out quickly. I intended to do a half roll, and then drop out of the aircraft. My aircraft still responded fully to the movements of the control column with my undamaged right arm. I was already in the inverted position and ready to bale out, when a formation of bombers entered my field of vision, flying a couple of thousand metres below me. At almost the same instant when I spotted the bombers, my injured left arm with the shot-up hand fell down against the cockpit canopy. The spectacle of my hand and the bomber formation must have led to the activation of my remaining inner strengths. It was an emotional reaction, when I spontaneously changed my intention to bale out. I rolled my plane sideways and dived towards the bombers for an attack. On nearing the height on which they flew, I clearly identified them as B-17s. I did not dive straight at my target, but a little from the side. I pulled my machine out of the dive as steeply as I could and charged at the side of the bomber which I could most easily reach. With the high speed that I had built up in the power dive, I approached the bomber very rapidly. Only at this instant, I became aware of the enormous size of the B-17.

What exactly happened during the actual ramming, I cannot tell from my own observations. My last thought was: 'Get out now!' and I must have acted accordingly, since when I regained my senses somewhat I tumbled through the air. I had actually saved my skin by baling out just before the ramming punch. I can't explain how I managed to do so, just like I have no explanation how I managed to get at the bombers at all. I have just one explanation: the Mustang pilots, as well as the gunners at their machine guns, must have thought I was not able to fight any more and carelessly watched how a 'Heini' plunged down to crash. As eye witnesses on the ground later explained to me, my machine was trailing smoke immediately after my combat with the Mustangs. I can't tell any more with absolute certainty, but I seem to recall that the waist gunner of the Boeing which I attacked was not at his post.

My first thought on regaining consciousness was: 'Don't immediately pull the rip cord of the parachute, but free fall to a safe height.' I did not open the parachute until I had reached a height of some 1,000 metres. Undoubtedly, the severe pains that I experienced on the jerk of my parachute opening left me unconscious once more. I did not notice coming down on the ground, but the great pains brought me back to my senses. (As I later learned, both the joints of my hips had twisted out of their sockets.) I kept laying on the ground. Anyway, I could only move very little and only in the severest pain. Yet, I was pleased, perhaps even happy, to have got away alive.

Uffz Hahn was taken to a hospital at Münster-Lager, where his left arm was operated on. It had to be amputated a few weeks later due to a fever. The Fortress that Klaus Hahn rammed was possibly a B-17 of the 487th BG which was observed to be rammed from a four o'clock high position at 1315 hours in position 52° 40' N–09° 50' E, after which the wing of the Bf 109 came off and the fighter exploded. Although damaged in the tail unit, the bomber managed to limp back to base. 'If this would be the case,' Klaus Hahn observes, 'I am glad that the crew of the B-17 that I rammed remained alive. Despite this feeling of joy, a bitter taste is left in my mouth, and that is the bombing raids of German cities and their civil population, at a time when the end of the war was imminent and such a conduct of warfare was not necessary any more. I especially think

213

of the city of Dresden and the many cruelly perished women and children.'

What were the results of the ramming mission on 7 April 1945? Around 130 Bf 109s took off from their airfields around Stendal and Gardelegen. They were escorted by conventional fighter units, probably including Bf 109s of I./JG301 from Salzwedel. Some fifty-nine JG7 Me 262 sorties were also mounted from Kaltenkirchen airfield near Hamburg (Major Erich Rudorffer, one of Germany's leading aces (222 kills), commanded II./Jagdverbande 7, the first true Me 262 squadron composed of famous Luftwaffe pilots), but these did not act as escorting fighters to the Rammkommando Elbe. Yet, not all the ramming pilots reached the American bombers. Many were intercepted and shot down by the American fighter screen. For example, Capt McGraw of the 351st Squadron shot down three Bf 109s in an action-packed ten minutes between 1215 and 1225 hours. The Elbe groups that lay in wait west of Berlin were diverted, and did not meet any B-17s or B-24s. In the end they landed back at their bases due to lack of fuel. At least eight others had technical problems and returned early to their bases.

Even so, around 1300 hours, an estimated twenty-five Bf 109s, and a few Me 262s, managed to break through the American fighter screen, and over the southern Lünenburger Heide, over Nienburg and the Steinhuder Lake, twenty-two bombers were rammed, with another B-17 that was shot down north of Hannover by Lt Hans Nagel at 1300 hours. Nagel then went on to ram a second B-17, which cost him his life. Around 1330 hours a B-17 was rammed by a Bf 109 in the wing, which led to the explosion of the German fighter. The bomber then started to burn and also plunged down. At 1305 hours a 388th BG B-17 was rammed by an unidentified Bf 109 after which the Fortress broke in two north of Lüneburg. Also in this area, a bomber was seen to crash with its right elevator torn off, obviously by ramming. Of the ramming fighter there was no trace. Me 262s of JG7 shot down two more bombers (a B-17 over Parchim and a B-24 at 1234 hours near Bremen) and three escorting fighters. At least seven, but probably more, Elbe men survived their ramming attacks to report their successful mission, although most of them were seriously injured in the process. One of them, Ogfr Heinrich Rossner, was reported to have brought down two B-24s near Visselhövede/Soltau by ramming. He too was injured but managed to bale out.

Altogether, the American bombers and the 830 escorting fighters claimed 104 Luftwaffe fighters shot down, thirteen probables and thirty-two damaged. In fact, Rammkommando Elbe lost thirty-one Bf 109s. Twelve were shot down by Mustangs and Thunderbolts, three by flak, five were lost in crash-landings and another eleven were lost to unknown causes. Eighteen of the Elbe pilots were killed or missing, with seven others wounded. Total German fighter losses on this day were 133 aircraft destroyed. These figures, compared to the total losses of only fourteen B-17s and three B-24s (a 389th BG Liberator was lost when a Me 262 of JG7 collided with it over Lüneburg; another 188 bombers returned damaged), five P-47s and P-51s (one of these Mustangs was shot down by Elbe pilot Ogfr Hugo Harms, after which he himself was shot down and mortally wounded), clearly show that the German fighter pilots stood little chance against the superior Allied forces. The determined onslaught by the Rammkommando Elbe and the Me 262 pilots on 7 April did not stop 1,261 bombers dropping 3,451.2 tons of bombs on sixteen targets in Germany.

At least eight B-17s and B-24s, including five B-17s of the 3rd Air Division, are known to have been lost to Rammkommando Elbe fighters, and another fifteen suffered damage by ramming Bf 109s but were able to regain Allied occupied territory. In at least two instances the rammer succumbed rather than the rammed. A Bf 109 was seen to make a diving attack from eight o'clock and went on to smash its right wing into Fortress 43-38058 of the 490th Bomb Group captained by 1/Lt Carrol Cagle. The impact knocked the waist gunner over, although he was unhurt. The Messerschmitt's wing disintegrated, twisting the fighter down and under the B-17's fuselage, leaving a six-foot gash and mangling the ball turret, before it cartwheeled across the lower surface of the right wing, knocking the supercharger off the inboard engine and part of the propeller from the outer, before finally disintegrating completely. S/Sgt Colby LeNeve, the ball turret gunner, was helped out of his wrecked turret by the other gunners and given first aid. He suffered a broken arm. With two disabled engines the Fortress limped back and was later put down safely on an airfield in liberated territory.

Not only were the number of fighters of Rammkommando Elbe too small to achieve any decisive results, the severe losses sustained on 7 April led directly to the end of the Luftwaffe day fighter arm. In the remaining weeks before the capitulation of Nazi Germany, the Luftwaffe day fighter arm could no longer rise up and fight the bombers in large numbers any more. The desperate 7 April ramming mission remained the Luftwaffe's piston-engined swansong. On 10 April fifty-five Me 262s, the largest number of jets despatched thus far on a single mission, attacked the bomber formations and shot down ten bombers but almost 300 German aircraft were destroyed on the ground. On 14 April the 55th FG claimed its last Me 262 victory of the war and on the same day the 357th FG knocked down four. On 19 April the 357th destroyed six more to finish the top Me 262 'killers' in the 8th AF with seventeen, one ahead of the 55th, who also had total claims for 316½ aircraft destroyed in the air (the 357th had 609½). On 21 April the 56th flew their last mission of the war, with final claims for 674½ aircraft destroyed. On 25 April the 4th FG flew their last mission of the war and gained their 583rd and final victory when a Me 262 was claimed destroyed near Prague.

By now the Allied bombers had all but run out of targets and most of the enemy aircraft that could not take off were destroyed on the ground where they sat, out of fuel and largely abandoned. Some 747 German aircraft were destroyed on 26 April alone. In Italy the Germans surrendered on 29 April and unconditionally surrendered to the Allies on 7 May. On this, the last day of the war, two Me 262s were shot down over Prague by Russian Yaks. VE Day, 8 May 1945, was a splendid affair and would have come sooner if it had not been for the dogged and determined resistance put up by the Jagdflieger and the Nachtjagd.

GLOSSARY

AI	Airborne Interception (radar)
AM	Air Marshal
AVM	Air Vice-Marshal
ASH	AI Mk XV radar
Blip	Radar echo or response
Bogey	Unidentified aircraft
Bordfunker	German wireless/radar operator
CRT	Cathode Ray Tube
'dicke Autos'	'Fat Cars' (B-17s and B-24s)
Düppel	German codename for Window after a town near the Danish border where RAF metal foil strips were first found.
Emil Emil	German codename for AI
F/Lt	Flight Lieutenant
F/O	Flying Officer, Flight Officer in USAAF
F/Sgt	Flight Sergeant
Fähnrich	(Fhr) Flight Sergeant
Feldwebel	(Fw) Sergeant
Flensburg	German device to enable their night fighters to home on to Monica
G/C	Group Captain
Gee	British navigational device
General der Flieger	Air Marshal
Generalleutnant	Air Vice-Marshal
Generalfeldmarschall	Marshal of the Air Force
Generalmajor	Air Commodore
Generaloberst	Air Chief Marshal
H2S	British 10cm navigation radar
Hauptmann	(Hptm) Flight Lieutenant
Helle Nachtjagd	illuminated night fighting
Horrido!	German for 'Tallyho'
IFF	Identification Friend or Foe
Leutnant	(Lt) Pilot Officer
Lichtenstein	German AI
Mahmoud	(British) High-level bomber support sortie
Major	(German) Squadron Leader
Monica	British tail warning radar device
Nachtjagdgeschwader	(NJG) Night fighter Wing
Oberfähnrich	Warrant Officer
Oberfeldwebel	(Ofw) Flight Sergeant
Oberleutnant	(Oblt) Flying Officer

217

Oberst	(Obst) Group Captain
Oberstleutnant	(Obstlt) Wing Commander
Objektnachtjagd	Target Area Night Fighting
Op	Operation
OTU	Operational Training Unit
P/O	Pilot Officer
Pauke! Pauke!	'Kettledrum! Kettledrum!' ('Going into attack!')
R/T	Radio Telephony
Rhubarb	British; low-level daylight fighter sweep
S/L	Squadron Leader
Schräge Musik	'Slanting Music'; night fighters' guns firing upwards
Serrate	British equipment designed to home in on Lichtenstein AI.
St.Kpt.	Staffelkapitän (officer in command of a Staffel)
Unteroffizier	(Uffz) Corporal
Viermot	Four-engined bomber
W/C	Wing Commander
W/O	Warrant Officer
Wilde Sau	Use by Germans of single-engined night fighters over the RAF's target, relying on freelance interceptions from a running commentary aided by the lights from fires and from searchlights ('Wild Boar')
Zahme Sau	German single- and twin-engined fighters fed into the bomber stream as soon as its track was properly established on the way to or from the target ('Tame Boar')
Zweimot	Twin-engined aircraft
Zerstörergeschwader	Bf 110 unit roughly equivalent to four RAF squadrons (Geschwader consisted of between 100 and 120 aircraft; each Geschwader had a Geschwader Stab and three or four Gruppen, with 25 to 35 aircraft each; each Gruppe had three Staffeln of some ten aircraft each)

BIBLIOGRAPHY

Manfred Bochne, *JG7 Die Chronik eines Me 262 – Geschwaders 1944–45* (Stuttgart 1983)

Martin W Bowman, *Fields of Little America* (PSL 1977); *Castles in the Air* (PSL 1984); *Wellington, the Geodetic Giant* (Airlife 1989).

Charles L Brown, *The 13th Minute Gap* (unpublished).

Donald L Caldwell, *JG26, Top Guns of the Luftwaffe* (Orion Books, New York, 1991)

John Foreman & S E Harvey, *The Messerschmitt 262 Combat Diary* (ARP 1990)

Norman Franks, *Forever Strong: The Story of 75 Squadron RNZAF 1916–1990* (Random Century 1991)

Roger A Freeman, *The Mighty Eighth War Diary* (Macdonald); *The Mighty Eighth* (Macdonald 1970)

Eric Mombeek, *Defending the Reich – The History of Jagdgeschwader 1 'Oesau'* (JAC Publications 1992)

Achille Rely, *Bommen op Mortsel, Mission No. 50, luchtaanval op de ERLA-fabrieken 5 April 1943* (Antwerpen 1988)

Jerry Scutts, *JG54, Jagdgeschwader 54 Grünherz, Aces of the Eastern Front* (Airlife 1992)

Robert H Sherwood, *Certified Brave* (unpublished)

Tony Wood & Bill Gunston, *Hitler's Luftwaffe* (Salamander Books 1977)

Drs. Theo Boiten. *The Luftwaffe Nachtjagd, 1933–1945. History of a strategic failure* (unpublished university graduate thesis, Groningen 1992).

Walther Dahl, *Rammjäger. Das letzte Aufgebot* (Heusenstamm 1973).

Jan Derix, *Vliegveld Venlo. Met een kroniek van de luchtoorlog in Zuid-Nederland 1941–1944*, Vols. I & II (Horst 1990).

Wolfgang Dierich, *Kampfgeschwader 'Edelweiss'. The history of a German bomber unit 1939–1945* (London 1975).

Wolfgang Dierich. *Die Verbände der Luftwaffe 1935–1945. Gliederungen und Kurzchroniken – eine Dokumentation* (Stuttgart 1976).

Werner Girbig. *Start im Morgengrauen. Eine Chronik vom Untergang der deutschen Jagdwaffe im Westen 1944/1945* (Stuttgart 1973).

Werner Held & Holger Nauroth. *Die deutsche Nachtjagd. Bildchronik der deutschen Nachtjäger bis 1945* (Stuttgart 1982).

Hajo Herrmann. *Bewegtes Leben. Kampf und Jagdflieger 1935–1945* (Stuttgart 1984).

Das Jägerblatt, Offizielles Organ der Gemeinschaft der Jagdflieger.

Ab A. Jansen, *Wespennest Leeuwarden*. Vol. II (Baarn 1979).

Ab A. Jansen, *Sporen aan de Hemel*, Vols I–III (Baarn 1979–1981).

Drs. W.H. Lutgert and Drs. R. de Winter, 'Nederland en de Duitse Nachtjacht. Van jager tot prooi', in *Militaire Spectator* 1994/12 & 1995/1.

Martin Middlebrook and Chris Everitt, *The Bomber Command War Diaries. An operational reference book, 1939–1945* (Harmondsworth 1985).

Ernst Obermaier, *Die Ritterkreuzträger der Luftwaffe 1939–1945. Band I Jagdflieger* (Mainz 1989).

Alfred Price, *Instruments of Darkness. The History of Electronic Warfare* (London 1987).

Alfred Price, *Luftschlacht über Deutschland. Angriff und Verteidigung* (Stuttgart 1987).

Alfred Price, *The Last Year of the Luftwaffe*.

Josef Priller, *J.G.26, Geschichte eines Jagdgeschwaders. Das J.G.26 (Schlageter) 1937–1945* (Stuttgart 1980).

Ron Pütz, *Duel in de wolken. De luchtoorlog in de gevarendriehoek Roermond-Luik-Aken* (Amsterdam 1994).

Sybille Schneider, *Fliegerhorst Upjever – Luftwaffe in Friesland – Versuch einer Dokumentation 1936–1986* (München 1987).

Werner Zell, *Erlebnisbericht bei der Luftwaffe* (unpublished).

INDEX

221

10/98